SUDAN ARCHAEOLOGICAL RESEARCH SOCIETY
PUBLICATION NUMBER 11

Meinarti IV and V

The Church and the Cemetery

The History of Meinarti
An Interpretive Overview

William Y. Adams

BAR International Series 1178
2003

Published in 2019 by
BAR Publishing, Oxford

BAR International Series 1178

Sudan Archaeological Research Society 11
Meinarti IV and V

ISBN 9781841715452 paperback
ISBN 9781407325842 e-book

DOI https://doi.org/10.30861/9781841715452

A catalogue record for this book is available from the British Library

This book is available at www.barpublishing.com

BAR Publishing is the trading name of British Archaeological Reports (Oxford) Ltd.
British Archaeological Reports was first incorporated in 1974 to publish the BAR
Series, International and British. In 1992 Hadrian Books Ltd became part of the BAR
group. This volume was originally published by Archaeopress in conjunction with
British Archaeological Reports (Oxford) Ltd / Hadrian Books Ltd, the Series principal
publisher, in 2003. This present volume is published by BAR Publishing, 2019.

BAR

PUBLISHING

BAR titles are available from:

BAR Publishing
122 Banbury Rd, Oxford, OX2 7BP, UK
EMAIL   info@barpublishing.com
PHONE   +44 (0)1865 310431
FAX   +44 (0)1865 316916
www.barpublishing.com

CONTENTS

MEINARTI IV

MEINARTI V

Arabic summary of *Meinarti IV* **and** *V*

LIST OF TABLES

LIST OF FIGURES

Please view figures 2, 3, 17, & 19 at this link:
https://doi.org/10.30861/9781841715452_original

LIST OF PLATES

Colour plates

Black and white plates

MEINARTI IV

The Church and the Cemetery

INTRODUCTION

This is the fourth and final volume, presenting the results of excavations carried out at the Nubian site of Meinarti in 1963 and 1964. Previous volumes dealt with the pre-Christian remains (*Meinarti I;* Adams 2000), the Early and Classic Christian remains (*Meinarti II;* Adams 2001), and the Late and Terminal Christian remains (*Meinarti III;* Adams 2002). It remains here to consider the church and the cemetery - two features of the site whose use continued through most of the Christian period. Both were described briefly in earlier volumes, in relation to specific occupation levels, but they will be more comprehensively dealt with here.

The site

The site of Meinarti, and the circumstances of its excavation, were described in very full detail in *Meinarti I,* and only a brief synopsis will be given here. To recapitulate briefly, Meinarti before its inundation was a low-lying alluvial island situated just at the foot of the Second Nile Cataract, about 10km to the south of the town of Wadi Halfa (Figure 1). The archaeological site of Meinarti (designated as Site 6-K-3 in Antiquities Service records[1]) was located at the southern or upstream end of the island. Before excavation is was a *kom* (mound) measuring 175m from north to south and 95m from east to west, with a maximum height of 12.5m above the surrounding floodplain. The mound had been sculptured to its modern shape by two endlessly repeating taphonomic processes: the buildup of windblown sand in the middle of the site, and the cutting away of the edges by flooding. Thus, remains in the middle of the mound were usually deeply buried and well preserved, while those at the outer edges had in every case been partially carried away. It is evident therefore that none of the published plans (including Figures 2-6 and 9-14 in this volume) show the full extent of what formerly existed; they show only what was left for the archaeologist to find.

The southern and higher half of the Meinarti mound was selected for excavation, and this portion was entirely stripped, level by level, down to sterile subsoil. The remains encountered were mostly those of a densely nucleated peasant village, or rather a succession of villages built one on top of another. At most levels, individual rooms were clustered into large, irregular room blocks which were designated as "houses." Here and there, houses were separated from each other by narrow, winding streets and by small plazas. There were also, at most levels, a few non-residential buildings: administrative and commercial buildings in the Meroitic and Ballaña periods, and a succession of churches during the Christian period. Virtually all construction, at every level, was of mud brick.

The excavations at Meinarti, sponsored by the Sudan Government Antiquities Service[2] with assistance from UNESCO, were carried out in two seasons, in the spring of 1963 and from the fall of 1963 until the summer of 1964.[3] The excavations were conducted almost entirely by myself, with occasional assistance from others as noted in later paragraphs. Whatever deficiencies may be encountered in this report are the sole responsibility of the present author.

Levels, phases, and subphases

Upon excavation, the mound at Meinarti was found to contain eighteen well defined stratigraphic levels, extending in time from the Late Meroitic to the early Post-Christian periods, or from perhaps A.D. 200 to 1600 (Figure 3). It became clear, after analysis of the findings, that the successive levels represented six major phases of occupation, each of which had begun with a general program of building or rebuilding, and ended, in most cases, with a temporary abandonment of the site. Each phase was represented by the remains of two, three, or four successive levels. Phases have been given the numbers from 1 to 7, in chronological rather than in stratigraphic order (that is, from the bottom up).

Within each phase there were recognizable subphases, each differentiated from its predecessor by minor architectural modifications, and by a buildup of floor deposits. Each subphase corresponds to one stratigraphic level, as represented in the plans and profiles. Subphases are designated by letters following the phase number.

The relationship between stratigraphic levels, phases, and subphases is shown in Table 1.

Occupation of the Meinarti Church extended through the whole of Phases 3, 4, and 5. All of the graves in the cemetery that could be accurately dated belonged to Phases 4 and 5, but it is probable that many graves without superstructures should be assigned to Phase 6. Questions of chronology will be much more fully discussed in a later section.

Building designations

Throughout the excavations, buildings were given identifying numbers (in all cases Roman numerals) at the time of their discovery. Thus, the latest and uppermost buildings have the lowest numbers, since they were the first encountered in excavation, and the earliest buildings have the highest numbers. The three successive phases of the Meinarti Church were designated, in chronological order, as Church XXXVIII, Church XXXVI, and Church VI.

---

[1] For the system of site numbering see Adams 1961, 8.

[2] Now called the National Corporation for Antiquities and Museums.

[3] The dates were from 10 February to 2 May 1963, and from 10 September 1963 to 11 June 1964.

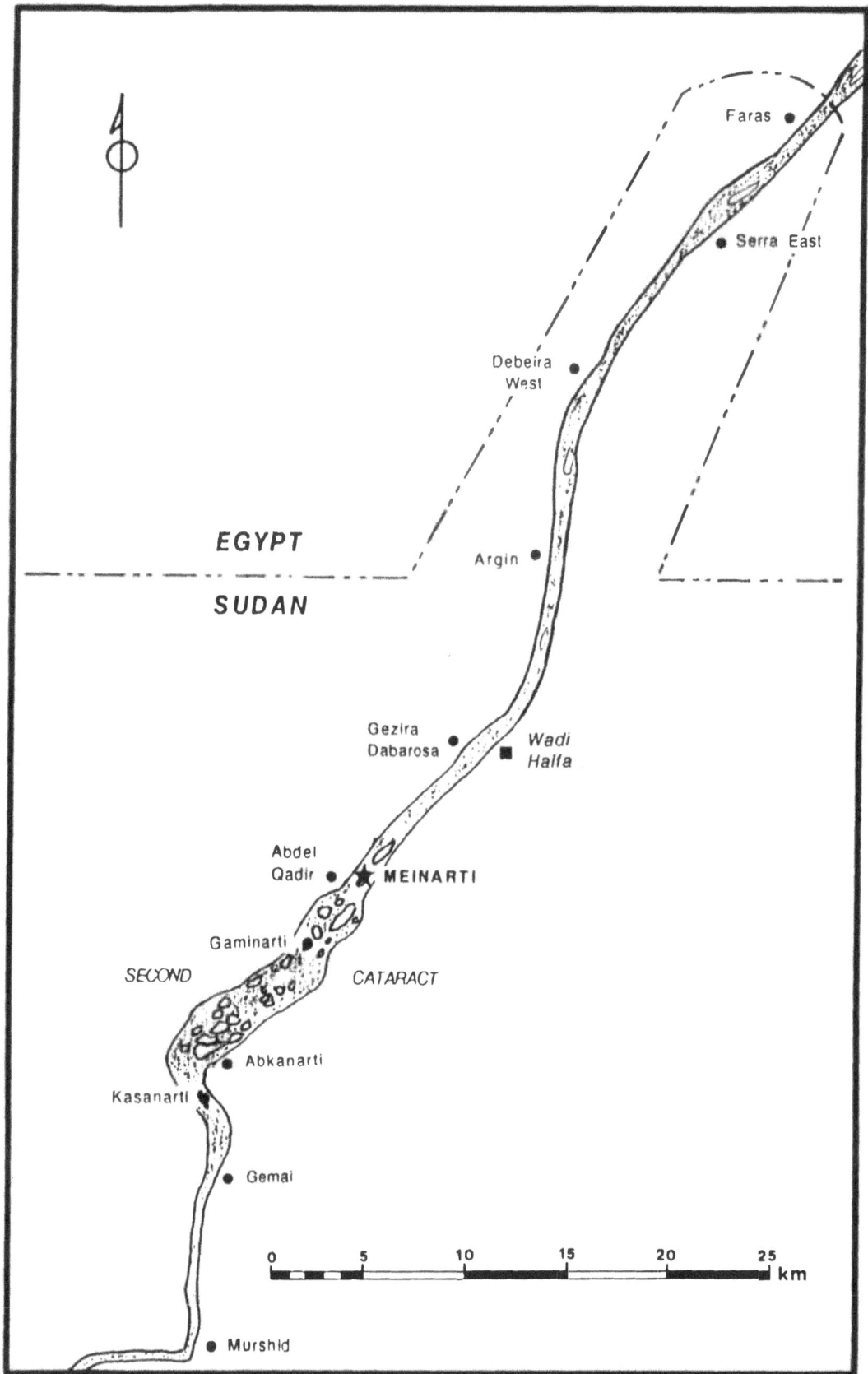

Figure 1. Map of Nubia showing the location of Meinarti.

The excavations

The excavations at Meinarti were carried out under what can only be described as emergency conditions. At the time when the site was relinquished by the Egypt Explo-

ration Society,[4] and became the responsibility of the Sudan Antiquities Service, only about 18 months remained before the waters of Lake Nubia were scheduled to begin

[4] For the circumstances see *Meinarti I*, xi.

2

TABLE 1. CHRONOLOGY OF MEINARTI PHASES AND LEVELS

Phase	Strat. level	Historic period[1]	Est. dates, A.D.[2]
7	1	Modern	1886-1898
Abandonment of the medieval community			*1600*
6b	2	Post-Christian	1500-1600
6a	3	Terminal Christian	1400-1500
Occupation by Beni Kanz and Beni Ikrima, + hiatus 1365-1400			
5c	4	Late Christian 2	1300-1365
5b	5	Late Christian 1	1265-1300
5a	6	Late Christian 1	1200-1265
Invasion and destruction by Shams ed-Dawla			*1172-1174*
4c	7	Late Christian 1	1100-1172
4b	8	Classic Christian 2	1050-1100
4a	9	Classic Christian 2	1020-1050
Hiatus followed by total rebuilding			*1000-1020*
3d	11a*	Classic Christian 1b	960-1000
3c	11b	Classic Christian 1a	850-960
3b	12	Early Christian 2	750-850
3a	13	Early Christian 1	660-750
Arab invasion; major flood damage and rebuilding			*650-660*
2c	14	Transitional	575-650
2b	15a	Late Ballaña	500-575
2a	15b	Late Ballaña	475-500
Major hiatus followed by rebuilding			*425-475*
1c	16	Early Ballaña	400-425
1b	17	Late Meroitic	350-400
1a	18	Late Meroitic	200-350

[1] According to the system of Christian Nubian phase designations first designated by the present author in Adams 1964b, 243-6.

[2] Dating based mainly on pottery finds. For the system see Adams 1986, 601-33. The dates given here have been revised more than once, and do not always correspond those appearing in the preliminary excavation reports.

* There is no Level 10, as this number was not assigned.

covering it. For that reason I began work immediately, in February of 1963, with a crew of 150 laborers, and after two weeks their number was increased to 200. During all but the last weeks of the nine-month second season a crew of 250 was employed. Throughout that time the work of excavation supervision, mapping, photography, and all other aspects of recording was carried on very largely by myself, although I had occasional help from my UNESCO colleague Anthony Mills and from colleagues loaned by foreign missions.[5]

My objective from the beginning was to try and work all the way through the mound from top to bottom, stripping it level by level. In terms of what was then known and not known about medieval Nubian history, I considered that the dynamic of growth and decay from period to period, rather than detailed information about any one period, was the most important story that Meinarti had to tell. The excavations however were confined to one-half of the mound because it was evident from the beginning that no larger area could be fully investigated in the time available.

Under the circumstances, there had to be many compromises and many departures from preferred archaeological practice, mostly due to the fact that there was usually no one but myself to do both excavation supervision and recording. Some of the consequences of that limitation will be evident to readers of this and the companion

volumes. Artifact and sherd locations are not as precisely recorded as they should be, and certain other records are less complete and less detailed than I could wish. The only justification I can offer is that the excavations really did reach the bottom of the mound (Level 18), just weeks before the lake waters got there.

Excavation of the church

The existence of the Meinarti Church was discovered early in the first excavation season, since small bits of its uppermost walls were still projecting above the ground surface. However, trial excavations revealed at once that there were remnants of painting on the interior walls, and our overriding concern was thereafter to try and conserve these. Since no conservator was immediately available, excavation of the church was deferred until the second season. Arrangements were made for Mr. Jozef Gazy, of the Polish Mission at Faras, to come to Meinarti at the beginning of the second season, and to work on the conservation of the Meinarti paintings until such time as the work at Faras should be resumed. It was, then, thanks to the generosity of the Polish Mission and its Director, Professor Kazimierz Michałowski, and to the diligence of Mr. Gazy, that the Meinarti paintings can be described in this volume, and some of them can also be seen in the National Museum of Antiquities in Khartoum.

Mr. Gazy's work was completed in the first weeks of the second excavation season. Before the paintings were actually removed from the walls, facsimile copies and also

[5] For detailed acknowledgments see *ibid.*, Preface xii-xiv.

3

miniature copies were made by Sayyed Abdel Rahim Haj el-Amin. The illustrations in this volume (Plate I) are made from his copies.

After completion of the painting conservation, excavations in the church continued intermittently during several additional weeks, until the earliest remains were uncovered.

Excavation of the cemetery

The existence of the Meinarti cemetery did not become apparent until the second excavation season, because no grave superstructures were preserved at or near the pre-excavation ground surface. Its existence was soon discovered, however, when we began removing sand deposit from around the outside of the church. The first burials encountered (i.e. the last made) were without superstructures and were in soft windblown sand fill, in which the outlines of grave shafts could not be recognized. We soon noted however that there were burials at various depths, and that some of them had been cut into the tops of older tomb structures. The cemetery, in fact, exhibited a nearly unique feature of vertical stratification, and this necessitated a departure from usual excavation procedures. The methodology adopted will be more fully explained in the chapter on the Cemetery.

While the clearing and recording of the tomb superstructures was done by me, the cleaning and recording of most of the actual burials was done by my physical anthropologist colleagues from the University of Colorado, Messrs. George Armelagos, George Ewing, and David Greene. The biological and anthropometric information presented in this volume has been provided entirely by them, and is gratefully acknowledged.

The records

The documentation from Meinarti, on which this and the companion volumes are based, consists of field notes, plans, cross-sections, site photographs, artifact cards and drawings, artifact photographs, and sherd tallies. The artifacts themselves are in the National Museum in Khartoum, and have not been accessible to me during the writing of this report.

Field notes

The quantity and quality of field notes is highly variable from building to building, and there are no notes at all on a few structures. The completeness of notes was determined very largely by the time available to write them, and this in turn was governed by the scope of the operations. The notes are therefore best for the uppermost levels (essentially Levels 1-4), before the crew had been enlarged from its original complement of 150, and for the lowermost levels (Levels 16-18), after the work force had been reduced from 250 to 100 men. In general however the notes on the churches are very complete; those for the cemetery are somewhat less so.

Plans

The 18 architectural plans, one for each level, are the most complete and most reliable part of the Meinarti record,

reflecting my belief in the special importance of architectural remains. Every detail of architecture that was uncovered was recorded on one or another of the plans (Figures 2, 4-6, and 9-14 in this volume).

Cross-sections

These, as far as they go, are also detailed and complete, though it could be argued that there are not enough of them. From beginning to end of the dig I maintained one north-south cross-section (B-B') and five east-west sections (F-F', G-G', J-J', K-K', and L-L'). Two additional north-south sections (A-A' and C-C') were maintained only in the second season, from Level 7 downward. Additional sections were recorded through specific buildings: Section M-M' through the "Castle-House" at Level 3, Sections D-D' and E-E' through the Church, at Levels 4-13, and Sections N-N' and P-P' through some of the Meroitic buildings at Level 18. The various cross-sections that are relevant to the present volume are shown in Figure 3, and all of the section lines are shown on the site plans (Figures 2, 4-6 and 9-14).

Site photographs

Site photographs represent the least time-consuming way of recording archaeological data, and therefore I relied on them very heavily. The site photographic record is very complete, encompassing more than 3000 individual photos. There are photos of nearly every house, of many interior features, and of most tomb superstructures and most burials.

Dates and dating

The dating of phases, levels, and buildings

There are only three or four securely fixed points in the Meinarti "calendar." There was a single dated tombstone *in situ*, and there were certain architectural remains that can be connected with known and dated historical events. Otherwise, the dating of levels and their associated remains can be based only on the inferential evidence of stratigraphy and of pottery. Stratigraphy provides a basis only for relative dating, in that the duration of phases can be estimated to a degree from the amount of architectural change that took place, and the extent of sand and refuse buildup over the floors. Potsherd counts from each level provide the only basis for absolute dating, according to the system of frequency seriation (Index Clusters) that was developed at Qasr Ibrim (see Adams 1986, 601-33).

Under the circumstances, it goes without saying that all the dates given in this volume are approximations, and subject to revision if and when certain pottery types are more securely dated.

The dating of the Meinarti church and its interior features is especially problematical, for two reasons. First, the church floors, at all levels, were virtually devoid of ceramic refuse that might have provided a basis for dating. Second, the outside ground surfaces, which could be dated on the basis of ceramic refuse, could not simply be followed through the doorways and into the church (as they could in many secular buildings), because the church doors always had raised thresholds. I think it is a reasonable supposition that the original building of the church at Phase 3, the rebuilding at Phase 4, and the major modifications at Phase 5, all took place at the beginning of those periods, concurrently with major rebuildings throughout the rest of the site. On the other hand there is no good way of calculating the date for the various interior modifications that took place during each subphase. I have assigned them to subphases largely on the basis of interior stratigraphy, but it should not be supposed that the changes identified with any particular subphase always took place at its beginning, or that they all took place at the same time.

The dating of graves and superstructures in the cemetery presents problems of another kind, arising from the somewhat unorthodox excavation methodology that was employed. This will be further discussed in the chapter on the cemetery.

The finds

Artifactual finds were registered and numbered in the order of discovery, the number in each case being preceded by the site number, 6-K-3. Wherever specific artifacts are mentioned in this volume, registration numbers are usually given in parentheses, but without the 6-K-3 prefix. All but a small handful of the finds are now in the National Museum in Khartoum, and National Museum accession numbers are given in the Appendix at the end of the volume.

The present text

In writing the Meinarti reports, I have proceeded on the assumption that archaeological reports are primarily works of reference: they are much more often "used" than "read" in the conventional sense. With that in mind, I have sought to make the volumes as user-friendly as possible, by making each section self-contained. As a result, readers will find a good deal of repetition between one chapter and another, and between this and the preceding volumes.

Acknowledgments

The many kinds of assistance that I received from colleagues and friends in the course of the Meinarti dig are fully acknowledged in the Preface to *Meinarti I*. With reference to the present volume, special debts must be acknowledged to the late Mr. Jozef Gazy, who conserved many of the mural paintings in the Meinarti church and in Building III, and to the artist Abdel Rahim Hag el-Amin, who made both full-size and miniature copies of the same paintings (shown in Plate I). All other figures as well as all photographs are by the author.

I am heavily indebted to my physical anthropologist colleagues, George Armelagos, George Ewing, and David Greene, for their collaboration in the excavation of the Meinarti cemetery. They not only relieved me of most of the burden of excavation supervision, but also recorded the basic data on age and sex for each burial, that are presented in this volume.

I have needed the help of many persons for translation and interpretation of textual finds in Greek, Coptic, Old Nubian, and Arabic. The late Mr. A. F. Shore provided translations of the Greek inscriptions found in Room 50 of Building II-III, and of an *ostrakon*. Professor G. Michael Browne of the University of Illinois was, as always, an enormous help in the identification and translation both of mural inscriptions and of mortuary texts. Professors Jacques van der Vliet of the University of Leiden and Adam Łajtar of the University of Warsaw were kind enough to provide me with so-far-unpublished translations of several tombstone texts. My much-lamented colleague Negm el-Din Mohammed Sherif provided the original translations of some of the Islamic tombstone texts, which were published in *Kush,* vol. XII (Sherif 1964). The late Ray Winfield Smith provided translations of some fragmentary Islamic tombstone texts.

Finally, my thanks must go once again to Derek Welsby for his painstaking labors as editor.

THE CHURCH

Although the Christianization of Nubia was apparently complete before the end of the sixth century,[1] there is no evidence that a church was built at Meinarti until the middle of the following century, at the beginning of Phase 3. Only one church was encountered in the course of the excavations, although other Nubian communities of equal size had two, three, or even four churches (see Adams 1977, 478). However, the possibility of a second Meinarti church in the northern, unexcavated part of the mound cannot be entirely ruled out. There was also, during Phase 5, a rather mysterious building (Building VIII) that was decorated like a church, but did not have some of the most basic architectural characteristics of a church (see *Meinarti III*, 28-30).

The term "church," in the singular, is here used only in an institutional sense. Architecturally there was a succession of three church buildings, all erected on the same site (cf. Figure 3). They were designated, during excavation, as Churches XXXVIII (the earliest), XXXVI (the second), and VI (the latest). Collectively, they endured throughout most of the Christian period; that is, for at least seven centuries.

The churches stood on the eastern slope of the Meinarti mound, well below its summit and at the outer limit of the village (Figure 2). The area chosen may have been occupied by houses in the early Ballaña period, but in the immediate pre-Christian period it had served as a refuse dump. At all times, the churches were separated from the remainder of the village by a street or passage. Only the second church (Church XXXVI) was directly adjoined by a non-ecclesiastical building, and then only for a brief period. The third church throughout its history was adjoined on the east and south, and to a small extent also on the north, by the village cemetery.

Church XXXVIII: the first church

Subphase 3a

The first Meinarti Church (Figure 4; Plate 1) was probably built around A.D. 660, and was razed about a century later.

Preservation

Church XXXVIII was almost wholly dismantled at the end of Subphase 3a, and was overbuilt by Church XXXVI. Because it had had a sloping floor, however, it was more completely razed at the western end than at the east. To provide a level footing for the new church, the most easterly walls of the older one were left standing to a uniform height of 30 to 40cm above the floor level, while the most westerly walls were dismantled all the way to floor level. As a result, the original plan of Church XXXVIII was

most clearly preserved at the east end, where the stumps of the original walls remained *in situ*. In the middle of the church, locations of the western nave pilasters were indicated only by foundations and by interruptions in the cobblestone floor pavement, and parts of the western walls were missing altogether. As a result, interior features in the west end of the building were difficult to reconstruct.

The foundation platform

To compensate for the sloping ground surface on the east side of the mound, the first Meinarti church was erected on a kind of foundation platform, which at the east end stood a meter above the level of the surrounding ground (cf. Figure 3, Section H-H'). The platform was built up of mud and sand fill, enclosed within stout masonry walls. Curiously enough, the platform seems to have been designed from the beginning to accommodate a regularly rectangular building, although the first church actually built on it was far from regular in shape (see below). Because of this anomaly, a part of the platform extended eastward beyond the east wall of the church itself, as shown in Figure 4. On the north and south sides however the platform retaining walls were simply the foundation walls of the church.

Construction

Church XXXVIII was constructed throughout of mud bricks, having average dimensions of 36 x 18 x 7cm; the typical size of Early Christian bricks in Nubia. The north wall, up to a height of 50 to 60cm, rested on a foundation of large sandstone blocks, some of which appeared to have been reused from an earlier building. However, none bore any traces of decoration. All the other walls rested on foundations of horizontal brick. Because of the sloping ground at the site, the easternmost foundations were at a level almost a meter below those at the west end of the building. After the wall foundations had been laid, the area within them was filled with sand and mud to create a more nearly level floor. It was not however completely level; there was a slight but uniform downward slope from west to east, so that the floor at the east end of the church was about 40cm below that at the west end (cf. especially Figure 3, Section H-H').

The east and west end walls in Church XXXVIII, and all of the interior walls parallel to them, were 40cm thick, while the north and south outside walls, and interior walls parallel to them, were 60cm thick.[2] This differential was probably due to the fact that the north and south walls, and interior piers, had to bear with weight of brick vaulted ceilings. It was noteworthy, and surprising, that the east

---

[1] For the conversion of the Nubians see Adams 1977, 438-45.

[2] For convenience, walls having the thickness of one header brick or two stretcher bricks are described as 40-cm walls; walls having the thickness of one header and one stretcher brick are described as 60-cm walls.

7

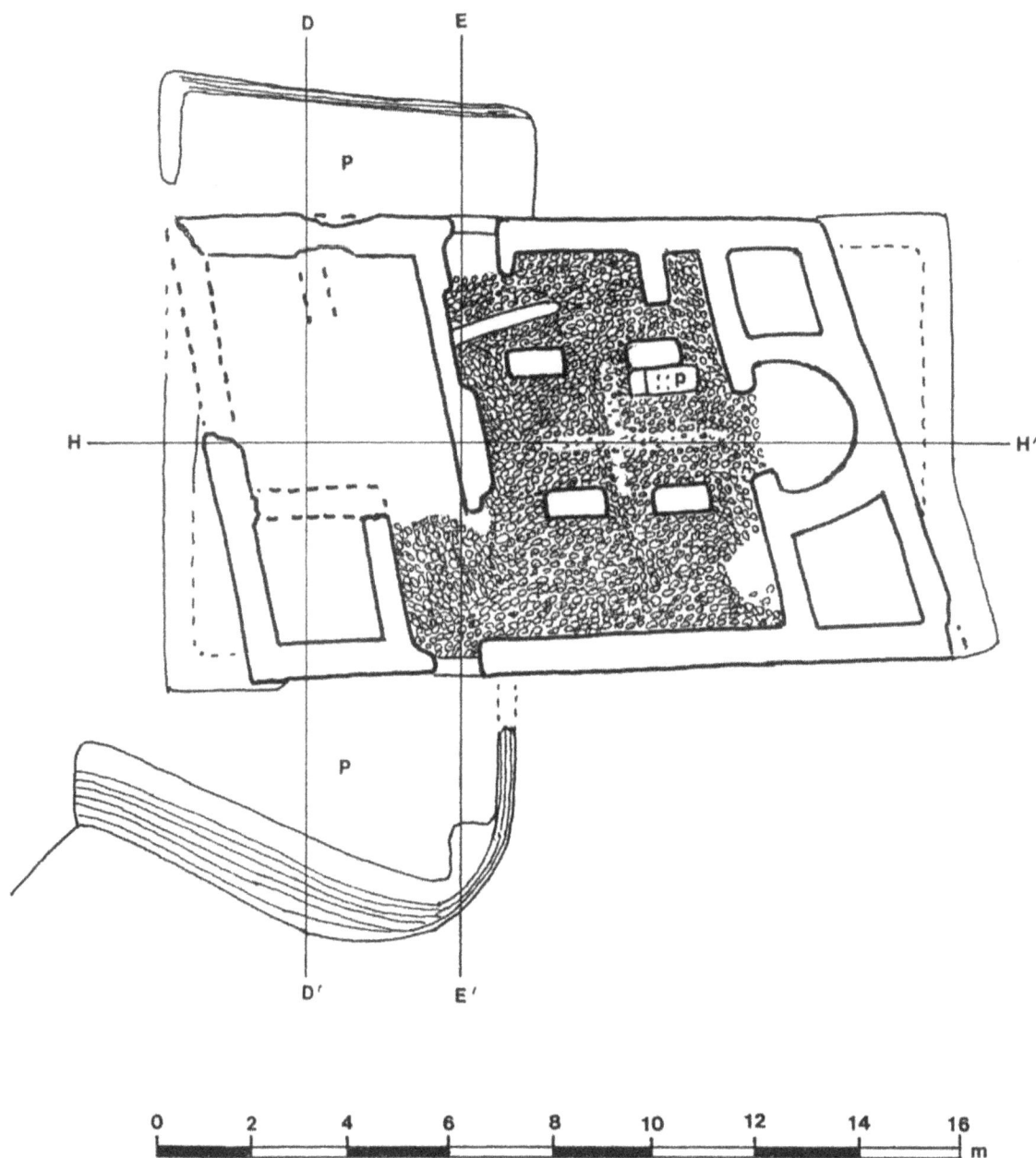

Figure 4. Plan of Church XXXVIII, at Subphase 3a. **P**=platform; **p**=pulpit; **D-D'**, **E-E'**, and **H-H'** are cross-section lines; see Figure 3.

and west outside walls were not firmly bonded to the north and south walls.

Traces of whitewash were found both on the interior and on the exterior of Church XXXVIII. Within the nave, the remains of three successive coats could be made out.

The plan

The most immediately striking feature of the original Meinarti church was its skewed plan. The angle formed by the juncture between end walls and side walls deviated from a true right angle by almost 20°, and this skewing was repeated in the arrangement of interior walls and piers also. The deviance however was more extreme in the east wall than in any of the interior walls, with the result that the southeast corner room was considerably larger than the counterpart room on the northeast; this feature can be seen clearly on the plan (Figure 4).

Apart from its skewed outline, the eastern portion of Church XXXVIII exhibited the typical basilican plan of early Nubian churches, elsewhere designated by me as Type 2b (Adams 1965, 108-10). Distinguishing features of this type are essentially negative: the absence of an eastern passage behind the apse, the absence of a tribune (stepped choir seats) in the apse, the lack of direct communication between the eastern corner rooms and the apse, and the absence of a *higab* or ikonostasis, separating the sanctuary from the body of the church. On the other hand the plan at the western end of Church XXXVIII, to the extent that it could be reconstructed from the scanty remains, appears anomalous; it does not correspond to any of the familiar Nubian church types.

Although the exterior doorways were, as usual, in the north and south walls, their placement does not appear to have been symmetrical. The north doorway was at a

8

distance of 7m from the northeast church corner, while the south doorway was almost 10m from the southeast corner. Both doorways had brick thresholds raised somewhat above the level of the floor.

The apse. At its eastern end, Church XXXVIII had a simple and rather short half-round apse, encased as usual within a solid block of masonry (Plates 1b and 1c). It is noteworthy however that the enclosing masonry in this case did not form a regularly rectangular block, as in other Nubian churches. The shape was more nearly rhomboidal, as can be seen in the plan (Figure 4). As a result, the adjoining corner rooms to the north and south were quite irregular in shape. The floor of the apse was very slightly higher than that of the adjoining nave, and it was paved with mud bricks set on edge rather than with cobblestones. The presence of whitewash on the interior walls, extending down to floor level, showed that there had never been a tribune (choir seats) installed in the apse. Interruptions on the floor paving, just where the apse joined the nave, suggested that there may have been a "triumphal arch" at this point – a common feature in early Nubian churches (Adams 1965, 99). However, no actual remnants of such a feature were found.

The eastern corner rooms. Flanking the apse on either side were the usual small corner rooms, which had no direct connection to the apse (cf. Plates 1b and 1c). These rooms in other Nubian churches have often been designated as the sacristy (on the north) and the baptistry, though there is rarely any direct evidence as to their function (Adams 1965, 93-4). Because of the differential orientation of their east and west walls, the corner rooms in Church XXXVIII were quite unequal in size, as can be seen in Figure 4. In a normal church plan these two rooms should have opened respectively onto the north and south aisles, but no doorways could actually be discerned in the preserved portions of the walls at Meinarti. It can only be assumed that the doorways had high thresholds, at a level above that to which the walls were preserved. Both rooms, like the apse between them, were floored with bricks laid on edge. There was no passage to the east of the apse, connecting the two corner rooms.

The nave. To the west of the apse, the central portion of the church consisted of a nave, flanked on the north and south by long masonry piers. There were two such piers on each side of the nave, each 1.2m long and 60cm wide. Most probably they were supports for arcading, separating the nave from the aisles. The stumps of the two eastern piers were preserved in situ, while the locations of the western two were indicated only by interruptions in the floor pavement, and subfloor foundation bricks (cf. especially Plate 1b).

The nave was terminated at its western end by a stout transverse pier, originally about 2.4m long and 60cm thick, which separated the nave from the adjoining room or rooms to the west (seen in the foreground in Plate 1b). At a later date the pier was extended northward by thinner masonry, extending all the way to the north church wall, so that it closed off the west end of the north aisle as well as of the nave. It also appears to have been extended southward for a short distance, but not as far as the south church

wall. No part of the southern extension was actually preserved; its former presence was indicated by an interruption in the cobblestone floor pavement (see below).

A mud brick pulpit, 50cm wide and 1.5m long, had stood at the usual position near the northeastern corner of the nave, adjoining the nave pier. The top was denuded, but the lowermost ascending step was preserved at the west end. Its tread was 40cm above the adjoining floor. There was one coat of whitewash on the sides of the pulpit, but there were also two coats on the pier wall behind it, which can only have been applied before the pulpit was installed. The pulpit was therefore not an original feature but a later addition to the church. On the other hand the cobblestone pavement (see below) did not extend under the pulpit, and must therefore have been added later still.

The aisles. Near the east end of the north aisle, a section of stout wall ran across from the north wall most of the way to the pier opposite, in effect screening off a small eastern room, which I have elsewhere called a vestibule (Adams 1965, 97). This feature was common in those Nubian churches in which there was no direct communication between the sacristy (northeast corner room) and the sanctuary. Presumably it was meant to provide a screened passage through which clergy could proceed from the sacristy to the sanctuary, without passing through the "open" portion of the church.

The north church doorway was located at the west end of the north aisle. On the interior, it was flanked on either side by stout buttresses which were original features of construction. At a later date, apparently, the more westerly buttress was extended southward by a thin masonry wall until it joined the pier at the west end of the nave, thus closing off the western end of the north aisle. Prior to this addition the north aisle may have extended somewhat further to the west, as did the south aisle.

Within the western end of the north aisle, at a point opposite the doorway, there was a short section of curving wing wall, of thin masonry, extending eastward from the west wall. Probably it was meant as a deflector, to prevent wind from blowing directly into the church interior through the north doorway.

The south aisle was entirely without features. There was no small room partitioned off at its eastern end, as in the north aisle, and it was not closed off by a thin wall at its western end. As a result it extended westward considerably further than did the north aisle, terminating at the east wall of what was apparently a southwest corner room. The south church door was at the west end of the south aisle, but it was not adjoined by buttresses as was the north door. The absence of buttresses, rebates, or jambs leaves a question as to whether there was ever any closure of this door.

The "mosaic" floor. Although Church XXXVIII was unusual in a number of respects, its most distinctive interior feature was its "mosaic" floor. The entire floor area within the nave and in both aisles had a continuous paving of rounded, waterworn river cobbles, set in a mortar of mud. Individual stones varied considerably in size and shape; most were a bit larger than the size of a grapefruit (Plates 1c and 1d). Nearly all the cobbles were of a fine, granular stone of reddish-brown color, but in the center of the nave these had been replaced by cobbles of white quartzite so as to form a cross design in the pavement. The center of the cross was just in the center of the nave, with the long member extending eastward toward the apse (Plate 1c). As the plate shows, the cross design was not fully preserved; some of the original white stones had been replaced at a later date with red-brown ones, destroying the symmetry of the design.

The cobblestone pavement did not extent into the apse or the two eastern corner rooms, all of which were floored with mud bricks set on edge. If any part of the pavement had extended into the western part of the church, it was entirely destroyed by the leveling operation when the church was rebuilt at Subphase 3b.

That the "mosaic" floor was not an original feature but a later addition was shown by the fact that it did not extend under the pulpit in the nave, which itself was a later addition.

The western rooms. For the reasons discussed earlier, the western end of Church XXXVIII was poorly preserved, and the surviving remains are not easy to interpret. They do not correspond exactly to any of the familiar Nubian church plans (Adams 1965, fig. 4). The western portion of the church, comprising about one-third of its total area, was largely separated from the remainder by a cross-wall closing off the western ends of both the nave and the north aisle (Plate 1b, foreground). As a result, the only communication between the eastern and western portions was via the south aisle, which was not completely closed off like its counterpart to the north.

A cross-wall of the type described here, in the very earliest Nubian churches, would have served to partition off a narthex at the western end of the building.[3] However, churches having a narthex were usually entered through a wide doorway in the middle of the west wall, and there were usually symmetrically placed doorways communicating between the narthex and the remainder of the church; features that were apparently lacking in Church XXXVIII. Moreover, the partitioned area at Meinarti was much larger than the usual church narthex. In addition, there were definite traces of a square room in the southwest corner of the building, although only its east wall was preserved (Plate 1a, lower right). There were slight indications of a possible corner room in the northwest corner as well.

There were no surviving traces of flooring in the western rooms. Judging from the level of the surviving wall foundations, however, it appears that the floor levels in these rooms must have been somewhat higher than those in the rest of the church. There were no remnants of whitewash on the western walls.

Interior features

The only interior feature preserved in Church XXXVIII was the pulpit adjoining the northeast nave pier. No trace of an altar was found, but it seems probable that the altar would have been located directly within the apse, as in other early Nubian churches (Adams 1965, 98). If located

[3] In churches of Type 1a; see Adams 1965, 103-5.

within the nave, it would have partially obscured the "mosaic" cross design in the floor. There was no evidence that the church had ever been equipped with a *higab* or ikonostasis, which if present would also have obscured a part of the mosaic floor design.

The approach ramps

The north and south walls of Church XXXVIII were adjoined, at their western ends, by low platforms that extended eastward as far as the doorways. These were clearly meant to provide a level access to the two church doors, whose thresholds would otherwise have been well above the sloping ground surface outside. Both platforms were created by using, as retaining walls, the tops of old house walls from Phase 2 (Buildings XLIV and XLV). As a result of this opportunistic reusage, the shapes of the two platforms were somewhat irregular, and their outer walls did not exactly parallel those of the church. The northern platform was more or less rectangular, while that on the south had a kind of half-oval shape (cf. Figure 4). There were traces suggesting the presence of steps ascending from ground level to the top of the southern platform, at its high eastern end.

Behind their masonry retaining walls, the platforms were solidly filled with mud and rubble to create the ramp surfaces. The outer faces of the two platforms were revetted with large stones leaned against them at an angle, and set in thick mud mortar, giving them a considerably battered profile.

Finds in Church XXXVIII

Given the extremely poor preservation of Church XXXVIII, it is not surprising that object finds were few. Only one vessel, an undecorated white bowl of Early Christian Ware W2 (829), was found within the church; it was crushed on the floor of the southeast corner room. A similar bowl (827) was found on the surface of the north exterior ramp. Both had probably been used as votive lamps. A portion of a ceramic incense stand (854, shown in Plate 6a), found in the fill of the church, was almost certainly of X-Group origin, but may have been retained for use as part of the church furniture.[4] A small scrap of sheet bronze (858), of unknown use, was found in the fill under the floor. The finds are listed in Table 2, which also lists the amphorae found in the cache just outside the building (see below).

The amphora cache

Just to the west of Church XXXVIII, in the narrow street separating it from Building XXXI, a hole 1.6m long, 1m wide, and 60cm deep had been dug. It was found to contain no fewer than 25 empty wine amphorae of Early Christian types, which had been very carefully laid on their sides (Plates 1e and 1f). Two of the uppermost vessels were of the Theban Ware U4 (1107), while all the others were of Aswan Ware U2 (1046).[5] All the amphorae were appar-

[4] It was reported and illustrated previously in *Meinarti II*, 89, pls 20a-b.

[5] All of the amphorae were collectively registered under the two numbers 1046 and 1106.

ently intact when buried, though several of the uppermost ones had subsequently been cracked from the pressure of overburden. The amphora cache could be assigned with confidence to Subphase 3a, because at Subphase 3b, when the church was rebuilt, the hole and its contents were covered by a platform built along the west church wall (cf. Figure 5). Why these vessels were so carefully preserved is something of a mystery, since it is clear, from the evidence of thousands of discarded and broken vessels, that amphorae were not normally returnable. In any case, the location of the cache suggests some connection with the church.

Summary and comparisons of Church XXXVIII

Church XXXVIII was one of at least four very early Nubian churches that were built on a highly skewed plan. The other examples were all in the Faras area: the earliest cathedral at Faras West (Michałowski and Gerster 1967, 48), the South Desert Church at Faras West (Mileham 1910, pl. 17), and the North Church at Faras East (*ibid.*, pl. 23). In none of these other cases however was the angle of skew quite so extreme as at Meinarti. The earliest cathedral at Faras, like the Meinarti church, was soon dismantled and replaced by a more conventional structure, while the other two churches survived in their original condition. The skewed construction was certainly not the result of architectural incompetence, and the possibility therefore exists that it had some iconic significance, though what that could have been cannot now be guessed.

The features in the eastern part of Church XXXVIII were generally similar to those in other Nubian churches of Type 2b (the "Buhen type"), which I have tentatively dated between A.D. 650 and 800 (Adams 1965, 110). They included the absence of an eastern passage, the lack of direct communication between the eastern corner rooms and the apse, and the absence of a tribune within the apse. All of these are hallmarks of the early Nubian churches in general. However, the anomalous features at the western end of Church XXXVIII do not bear comparison to any other known Nubian church.

Church XXXVIII was almost wholly dismantled, and overbuilt by Church XXXVI, at the end of Subphase 3a, after just about a century of occupation. Although there is a possibility that the original building had been heavily damaged by floods, which were common during Phase 3, it seems just as probable that the villagers simply wished to eliminate the skewed plan.

Church XXXVI: the second church

Subphase 3b

The second Meinarti church (Figure 5; Plate 2) was erected directly on the site of dismantled Church XXXVIII, apparently at or near the beginning of Subphase 3b. The long side walls, at the north and south, were built directly on the stumps of the earlier walls, but the end walls were realigned to give the building a regularly rectangular outline. The interior walls were also realigned, although the basic interior dimensions of the church remained unchanged.

The floor in the new building was made level, eliminating the downward slope that had been present in the original church. As a result, the new floor at the east end of Church XXXVI was at a level over 40cm higher than that of its predecessor, while at the west end of the building the new floor was at the same level as the original.

Preservation

Church XXXVI, like the rest of the Meinarti village, seems to have been heavily damaged by flood waters during and at the end of Phase 3. As a result, it was fully rebuilt for a second time at the beginning of Phase 4, as Church VI. The upper parts of the Church XXXVI walls, to the extent that they were still standing, were once again partially razed in the process of rebuilding. In consequence, the walls of Church XXXVI were mostly preserved only to a height of about 25-40cm (cf. Plates 2a and 2b). Except at the extreme east end of the building, however, all of them had survived to a sufficient height so that the original floor plan of the church could be fully made out.

The foundation platform

At its eastern end, Church XXXVI stood even higher above the surrounding ground surface than had its predecessor, because it was built on top not only of the original foundation platform, but also on the surviving wall stumps of Church XXXVIII (see Figure 3, Section H-H'). As a result, the east end of the building was no less than 1.6m above the neighboring ground surface, while at the west end, the base of the outside wall was more or less at the natural ground level.

The original foundation platform had not extended to the north or south of the church walls, but the newly built church was adjoined by wide, elevated platforms on both the north and south sides, and by a small platform on the west as well. These features will be separately described in later paragraphs.

Construction

Church XXXVI, like its predecessor, was built entirely of mud bricks, having average dimensions of 36 x 18 x 7cm. The walls throughout the building were now 60cm thick, except for four central piers which were 1m thick. The presence of these four symmetrically placed, L-shaped elements in the middle of the building suggests the possibility of a central cupola, though this is not a certainty. All other roofs were most probably vaulted, although this too could not be definitely confirmed from the denuded remains.[6]

No trace remained of the original "mosaic" floor of Church XXXVIII, which was buried under the newly laid floor of Church XXXVI. In the new building, the floor in the apse and the adjoining portion of the nave was of horizontally laid brick paving, while the floors in other rooms were of hard packed mud.

The interior of Church XXXVI was whitewashed throughout, and there were a few traces of whitewash on the outside walls as well. On the surviving walls no splashes

---

[6] Many early Nubian churches had flat roofs, but these usually rested on columns. See Adams 1965, 91.

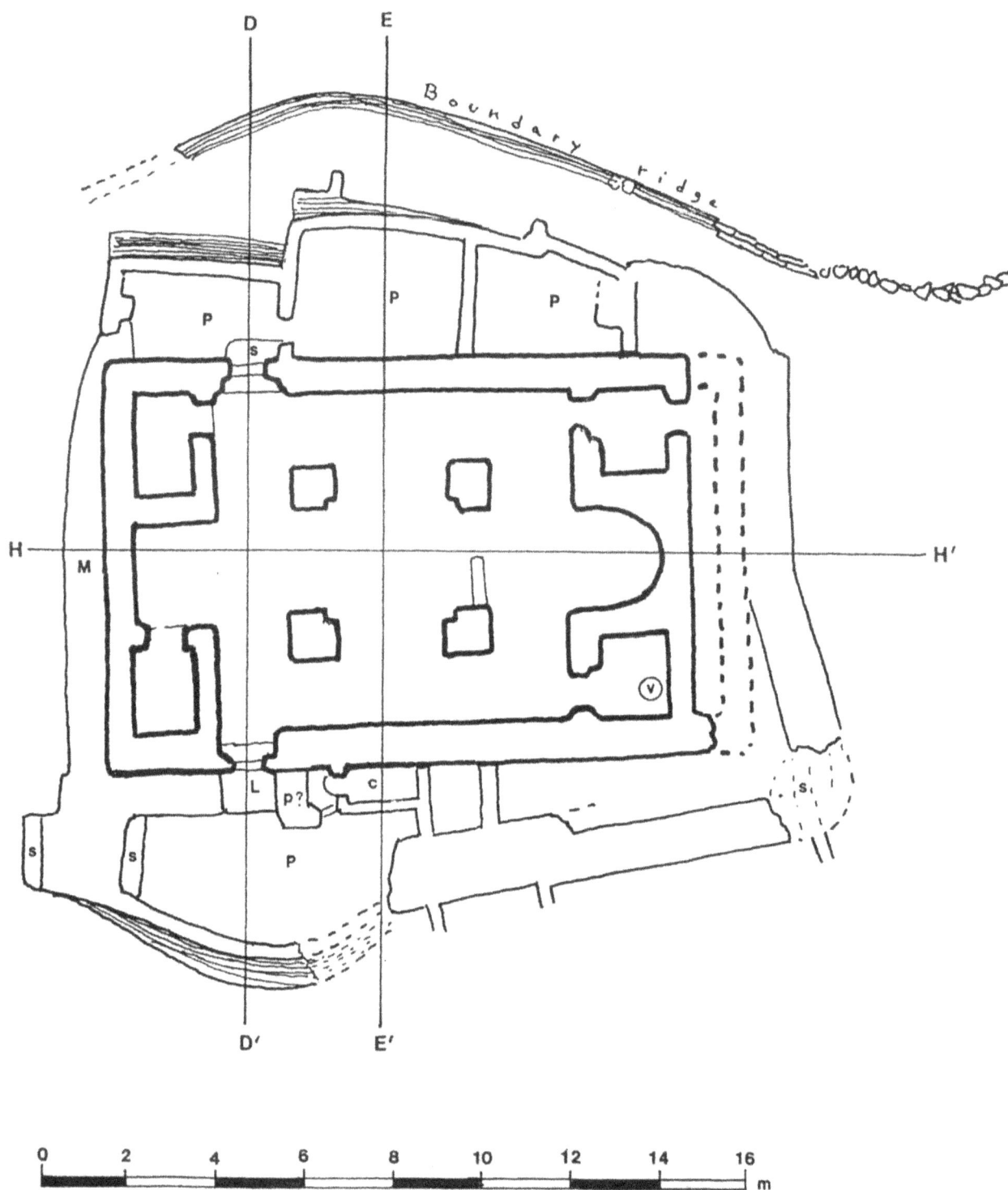

Figure 5. Plan of Church XXXVI as first built, at Subphase 3b. c=crypt; L=landing; M=external mastaba; P= platform; p=pulpit; s=steps; v=buried pottery vessel. **D-D', E-E',** and **H-H'** are cross-section lines; see Figure 3.

of colored paint were observed, which if present might have suggested the presence of murals on the upper walls.

The plan

Church XXXVI was in nearly all respects a typical example of early Nubian church Type 2b (see Adams 1965, 108-10). The eastern end comprised an apse, without tribune, encased within a heavy rectangular shell of masonry. It was flanked on the north and south by small corner rooms that did not directly communicate with it. The cen-

tral part of the church consisted of a nave, separated from the adjoining aisles by arcading which rested on stout masonry piers. At the west end there were two small corner rooms, flanking the western end of the nave. Entry to the church was through symmetrically placed doorways in the north and south walls, at the extreme western ends of the north and south aisles.

Church XXXVI may nevertheless have departed from the usual Type 2b plan in one important respect: there may have been a narrow passage at the eastern end of the building, running behind the apse and connecting the corner rooms. This feature was characteristic of Classic Christian Nubian churches (Types 3b and 3c), but not of most earlier ones (Adams 1965, 125-5). Whether it was actually present in Church XXXVI could not be determined with certainty, due to very poor preservation at the eastern end of the building. It was however suggested by two factors. First, there was definitely a door in the east wall of the northeast corner room (often called the sacristy), which must have opened either into a passage or to the outside of the church. The latter possibility seems unlikely, since only one other Nubian church (a very late one) is known to have had an external doorway at this point.[7] Second, the southern church wall extended eastward a short distance beyond the point where the church corner should have been, had there been no eastern passage, as can be seen in Figure 5. On the other hand there was no evidence of a door in the east wall of the southeast corner room, which would have communicated with the passage.

The entryways. The church doorways were at their usual loci in the north and south walls, at the west ends of the north and south aisles. Both doors were fitted with raised, cut stone thresholds of sandstone. In each case, there was an extra step up from the outside ground surface to the level of the threshold, and an extra step down from the threshold to the interior floor of the church (cf. Figures 3 and 5).

The apse. The apse in Church XXXVI was slightly narrower, in relation to its depth, than was its predecessor, and it was encased within a heavier mass of masonry forming a regular rectangle. Whitewash extending down to floor level showed that there had been no tribune in the apse as originally built, although one was added at Subphase 3c (cf. Plate 2c, which shows the apse before installation of the tribune). The apse was floored with brick flagging, but there was no surviving trace of an altar. Fragments of small sandstone columns, found in the fill of the church, may have belonged to a triumphal arch, standing at the juncture between the apse and the nave. The apse was most probably covered by a semi-dome, as was usual in Nubian church architecture.

The eastern corner rooms. These two small rooms, which in the new plan were equal in size, were entered through rebated doorways from the adjoining north and south aisles. The thresholds were not raised, but the presence of pivot stones set into the floor showed that both rooms had been fitted with closing doors, which opened inward. As previously noted, a small doorway in the eastern wall of the northeast corner room opened either into an eastern passage, or to the outside of the church.

In the southeast corner room a large cylindrical basin of coarse pottery (Ware U5) was sunk into the floor near the southeast room corner. Since the southeast corner rooms in several other Nubian churches have been identified as baptistries (Adams 1965, 97), it seems very possible that this was the function of the basin in Church XXXVI. The

rim of the basin, which was broken away at the top, extended for about 35cm above the level of the original church floor; in fact, it extended above the level of several overlying floors that were put in at later times. For that reason, it could not be determined with certainty if the basin was an original feature, dating from Subphase 3b, or was sunk into the floor in the course of a later refurbishing.

The nave. The nave in Church XXXVI extended from the apse westward for the full length of the building. Along most of its length it was flanked by the north and south aisles, from which it was separated only by pairs of stout, L-shaped masonry piers, two each on the north and on the south. The symmetrical placement as well as the shape of these constructions suggests that the space between each pair of piers was spanned by an arch, and that collectively they supported a central cupola.

The southeastern nave pier was adjoined on its north side by a short section of 20-cm wall, which ran half-way across the width of the nave (visible in Plate 2c). This appeared to be the remnant of the typical *higab* (*ikonostasis*), which in classic Nubian churches screened off the sanctuary area (*haikal*) from the remainder of the nave. If it was, then there should have been a similar wing wall adjoining the northeast pier, leaving only a narrow opening between the two. However, no remnant of the northerly section of the wall was found.

The floor within the sanctuary area – that is, at the eastern end of the nave – was flagged with brick, like the adjoining apse, while the remainder of the nave had a mud floor. A wide doorway in the south wall of the nave, at its far western end, opened into the southwest corner room, but there was no matching door opening into the northwest corner room.

The aisles. In the original design of Church XXXVI, the north and south aisles were featureless. There was no vestibule (screened off area) at the east end of the north aisle, as in Church XXXVIII. A doorway in the west wall of the north aisle opened into the northwest corner room.

The western corner rooms. The west end of Church XXXVI was occupied, as usual in Nubia, by two small corner rooms of equal size, but their entryways were not symmetrically placed. The northwest corner room was entered from the north aisle, while the southwest corner room was entered from the west end of the nave. The floor level in both corner rooms was one step higher than that in the remainder of the church. There were no surviving traces of a stairway in either of the western rooms, although this feature was usual in other Nubian churches of the same age (Adams 1965, 110).

Interior features

The surviving portion of *higab* wall, if such it was, and the putative baptismal basin in the southeast corner room were the only interior features preserved in Church XXXVI, as originally built. There was no trace of either an altar or a pulpit, although the former at least must surely have been present. It could have been either within the apse, as was common in the earliest Nubian churches, or in the adjoining eastern part of the nave. There was also

---

[7] The church at Site 21-S-2, Kulubnarti; see Adams 1994b, 150-51.

no screen wall running across the east end of the north aisle, and no trace of a staircase in either of the western corner rooms.

Exterior features

The original Meinarti church (Church XXXVIII) had been adjoined on the north and south by built-up ramps, extending from the west end of the building as far as the church doors. They provided a level access to doorways, which otherwise would have been considerably above ground level. The original ramps remained *in situ* when Church XXXVI was overbuilt, but they were now extended eastward along the full length of the building, until at the east end they merged with the original platform on which both Church XXXVIII and Church XXXVI were built. There was in addition a narrow and very low mastaba running the full length of the west wall. As a result, Church XXXVI was adjoined on all four sides by elevated platforms or terraces, which at the west end were only a few centimeters higher than ground level, while at the east end their surfaces were over 1.5m above the level of the adjoining ground. All of the platforms, except at the west, were quite irregular in shape, and some of their features are difficult to interpret.

The western platform. The western platform adjoining Church XXXVI was the only one constructed in its entirety after the new church was built. It was in reality only a narrow and rather low mastaba of hard packed mud, about 30cm high, which ran along the full length of the western church wall. It was about 1m wide along most of its length, but toward the northern end it tapered inward to a width of only 65cm. At the northern end there was a narrow doorway giving access to the newly built antechamber adjoining the northern church door (see below). At the southern end, the western platform merged into the platform adjoining the south side of the church.

The northern platform. The western portion of the north platform was the surviving, original approach ramp to Church XXXVIII, and was about 2m wide. The newly added extension to the east was somewhat wider, although it tapered in width from west to east, as can be seen in the plan (Figure 5). Both portions were built up of hard packed mud, within brick retaining walls; they can be seen in Plates 2a and 3c.

The western portion of the north platform (i.e. the portion surviving from Church XXXVIII) was now bordered by a 40-cm wall, suggesting that this had become an enclosed antechamber, adjoining the north church door. A narrow doorway at its western end, adjoined by a buttress, gave access to the antechamber from the western church platform, while a doorway in the eastern wall opened onto the adjoining, eastern portion of the platform. In the south wall, a low step adjoined the outer side of the north church doorway.

The newly built eastern portion of the north platform had only a thin, 20-cm wall, something like a parapet wall, running along its outer edge, perhaps as a safety feature. About halfway along the length of the eastern portion, a low retaining wall ran across it, separating a higher floor level on the west from a lower one on the east. At the eastern end of the platform there was another step down, to the level of the adjoining eastern platform. There may have been a cross-wall and a doorway at this point, but this could not be established with certainly because of very poor preservation.

The southern platform. The southern platform was also, at its western end, the survival of the old ramp leading to the south door of Church XXXVIII. This portion retained its half-oval shape from earlier times, and was supported as before by a sloping wall of mud brick. The surface was at the same level as before, but it was now bordered by a thin and probably low brick parapet wall along its outer edge. Adjoining the western end, there were two steps up from the outside ground surface to the top of the parapet wall, and then two steps down to the platform surface within. From this surface there was a small step up, to a landing just outside the south church doorway, and a second step up to the door threshold itself.

The original, western portion of the south platform was extended eastward by the building of a massive brick retaining wall, which as preserved was no less than 1.4m thick at its western end, and 1m thick at its eastern end. The lesser thickness of the eastern end may however be due to the later intrusion of graves in this area. Why such a heavy wall was thought necessary is unclear, nor is it clear why the wall was not built exactly parallel to the south wall of the church. When first discovered I thought it must be the remnant of some older building underlying the church, but it definitely was not; it was built unmistakably at Subphase 3b, and was unmistakably a retaining wall. This was demonstrated by the fact that its northern face was uneven and unfinished, since it served only to retain the mud fill forming the south church platform. The thick retaining wall served also as the north wall of adjoining Building XXXVII, but it was built prior to the construction of the house, all of whose other walls were 20-cm walls.

Two thin cross-walls, 1.2m apart, ran across between the inner face of the retaining wall and the southern church foundations, enclosing between them a square, sunken chamber within the south platform (see Figure 5). Perhaps this was meant to serve as a crypt, like the adjoining small chamber to the west of it (described below), but it had no discernible floor. In any case it did not remain in use as a crypt, for when found it was solidly filled with the same dense mud packing as was the remainder of the south church platform.

There were suggestions of a stairway ascending to the southern platform at its eastern end, from the ground surface more than 1.5m below. This could not be determined with certainty, however, due to destruction caused by the later intrusion of graves.

Exterior pulpit? On the southern platform, just to the east of the south church doorway, the church wall was adjoined by a solid mass of brick masonry 80cm wide, and projecting 1.2m outward from the church. (It is partially visible at the left in Plate 2d.) It was preserved to a height of 40cm, but may originally have been higher; the upper part might have been dismantled, along with the adjoining wall, when the church was rebuilt at Phase 4.

The whole structure was whitewashed, except for the top. It is surmised that this might have been an exterior pulpit from which a lesson could be read to persons outside the church – a feature sometimes found in Ethiopian churches today.

Crypt. Just to the east of the feature described above, alongside the south church wall, a small vaulted crypt was sunk into the mud and rubble fill of the south church platform (Plate 2d). It was 1.8m long and 75cm wide, with a maximum interior height of 75cm. The floor of the crypt was 75cm below the level of the surrounding platform, while the top of the vault projected 40cm above it. The projecting top of the vault was encased within a rectangular mass or masonry, which thus formed a kind of mastaba adjoining the south church wall (see Figure 3, Section E-E', and Plate 2e). The vault interior was reached by means of a small square *dromos*, with two descending steps, at its western end (visible in the foreground in Plate 2d).

The crypt was fully intact when found, and the doorway from the *dromos* to the crypt interior was sealed with a large stone slab, mortared into place. It is possible that the crypt was designed originally as a burial chamber, since it had approximately the correct dimensions, and the correct orientation. It is noteworthy that the church at Sahaba (Site 100) had a subterranean, vaulted crypt in this same location, that was definitely used as a burial chamber (Gardberg 1970, 34 and fig. 6).[8] However, the crypt at Meinarti was never used as such. The interior contained instead a single empty amphora, of Aswan Ware U2 (856), shown in Plate 2d.

The eastern platform. The eastern platform, whose upper surface was over 1.5m above the neighboring ground surface, was relatively narrow. If the church did indeed include an eastern passage, as I have surmised, then the width of the adjoining platform, at the middle, would have been only 1.3m. The platform however was irregularly shaped, since it was built up from two separate components. The southern half was formed by building up and reinforcing the still-standing foundations of Church XXXVIII, and using them as a retaining wall for the platform fill within. Since the alignment of this wall was not parallel to that of the newly built church, the southern half of the eastern platform became progressively wider toward the south, where it reached a width of 2m. The northern half however was bordered by a newly built retaining wall which paralleled the church wall, and was uniformly about 1.3m wide. The top of the eastern platform was featureless.

The "border ridge." The curving exterior wall of the northern church platform was roughly paralleled, at a point about 3m further north, by a low ridge formed partly of molded mud, partly of sections of ceramic pipe, and partly of small upright stones (cf. Figure 5 and Plate 2f). The average height all along was about 20cm. The ridge was broken away at both ends; the preserved portion had a length of about 30m. The western half, situated directly

to the north of the church, was formed largely of molded mud, although a couple of upright stones were set into the top at one point.

From a point more or less opposite the northeast corner of the church, the ridge began a gradual reverse curvature toward the north, as shown on the plan. Adjoining the mud section, a short middle section of the ridge was formed by broken sections of ceramic pipe laid end-to-end. Beyond this, the more easterly portion was formed entirely of small stones laid in a line. The only purpose that can be suggested for this feature is as a kind of demarcation for the consecrated ground adjoining the church, and for a cemetery that may have adjoined on the east (although no graves datable to Phase 3 were actually found). However, no similar demarcation feature was found on any of the other sides of the church.

Adjoining Building XXXVII. The massive retaining wall enclosing the south church platform served also as the north wall of Building XXXVII (Figure 5). This was a large, regularly square building, constructed entirely with 20-cm walls except for the stout wall at the north. The interior arrangement comprised a single suite of nine interconnected rooms, entered through a doorway at the south side. Although it directly adjoined the church, the house stood well apart from all of the other buildings of Subphase 3b, most of which formed a single contiguous cluster (see *Meinarti II*, fig. 8). This setting suggests some kind of functional connection with the church; particularly since Nubian churches were rarely adjoined directly by secular buildings (cf. Adams 1965, 90). Possibly, Building XXXVII was a parsonage. Whatever its function, it was completely dismantled at the end of Subphase 3b, and the area it had occupied later became part of the cemetery.

Subphases 3c and 3d

During Subphase 3c (Figure 6), at or sometime after A.D. 850, the interior of Church XXXVI underwent a series of modifications. First, the floor level throughout the building was raised by about 40cm (cf. Figure 3). The new floor was entirely of hard packed mud, with no areas of brick flagging. Then, a series of interior features were added, the effect of which was to convert the building from a Church of Type 2b to one of Type 3b (cf. Adams 1965, 114-116). Similar conversions were made in many Nubian churches at about this time (*ibid.*, 110-111); almost certainly they reflect a change in the basic nature of the holy service (*ibid.*, 121).

It seems most probable that these changes were made at the time of Subphase 3c, when there were a good many other modifications in the Meinarti village (see *Meinarti II*, 18-19). There were no changes in the building that could be attributed specifically to Subphase 3d, which was a time almost wholly of deterioration.

The plan

The new additions to Church XXXVI included the installation of a tribune in the apse, the screening off of the sanctuary area (now at the east end of the nave) both from

[8] However, it was attributed by the excavator to a late period in the history of the church; see Gardberg 1970, fig. 6.

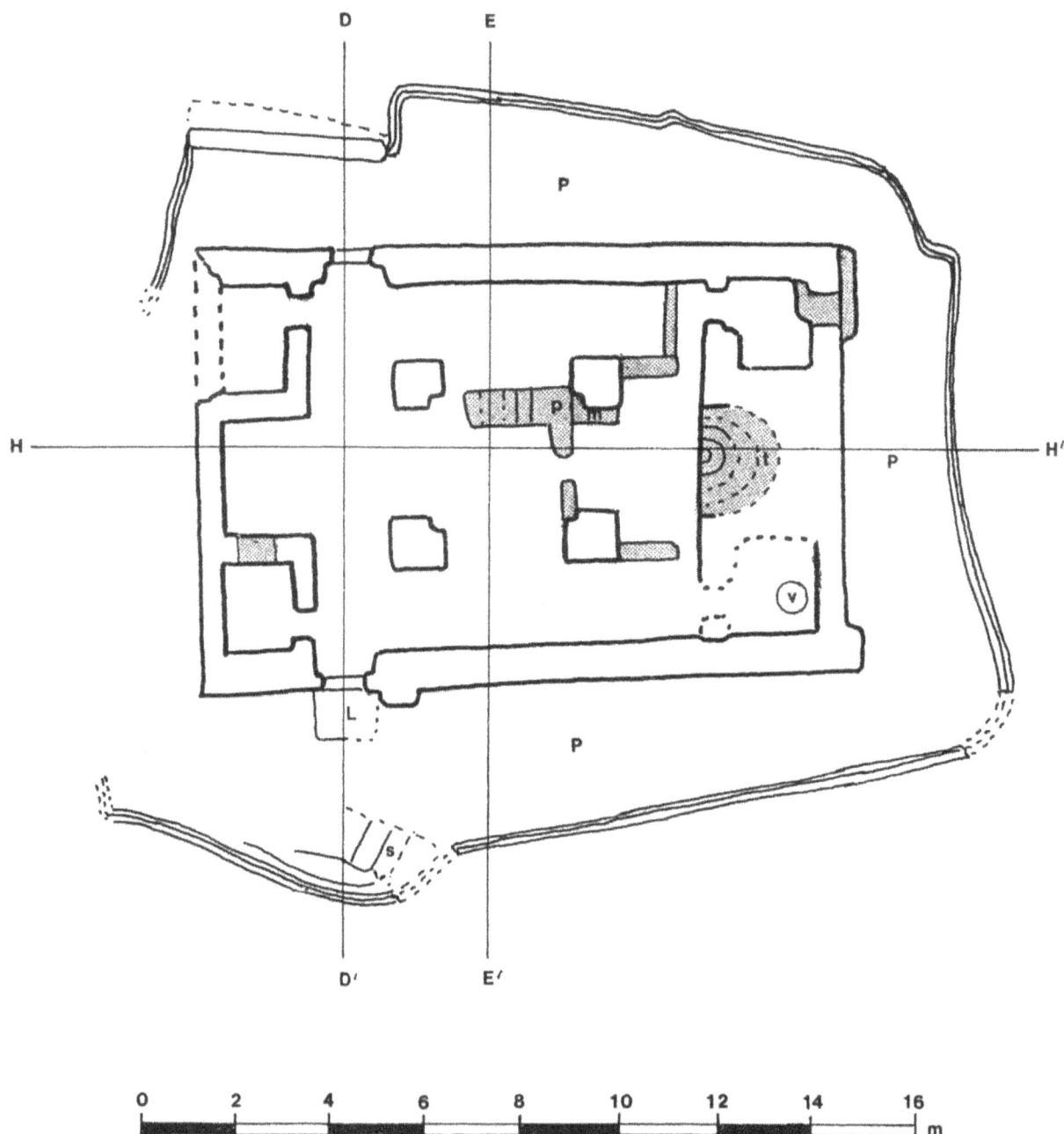

Figure 6. Plan of Church XXXVI, at Subphases 3c and 3d. Shading identifies newly added features at Subphase 3c.
m=internal mastaba; **L**=landing; **P**=platform; **p**=pulpit; **s**=steps; **t**=tribune; **v**=buried pottery vessel. **D-D'**, **E-E'**, and **H-H'** are cross-section lines; see Figure 3.

the remainder of the nave and from the north and south aisles, the construction of a partition wall across the north aisle, and the installation of a pulpit adjoining the northeast nave pier. In addition, the former doorway through the east wall of the sacristy (the northeast corner room) was very solidly blocked. A small addition was even made to the masonry at the exterior of the building, hiding the site of the door blockage. It is certain therefore that from this time onward there was no eastern passage, behind the apse, if indeed there ever was one earlier. Finally, there is a possibility that stairs were installed in the southwest corner room, a feature that was usual in Nubian churches.

The apse. The apse was now entirely filled by a tribune (stepped choir seats), of which the two lowermost were

fully preserved, while only remnants of the upper steps survived, at the north side (Plate 4c). Individual steps were 20cm wide and 20cm high.

The eastern corner rooms. There was no apparent change in these two rooms, apart from the raising of the floor level and the blockage of the eastern doorway in the northeast room. In the southeast room, the ceramic basin that had been (most probably) installed at Subphase 3b continued to project above the newly raised floor level, and therefore presumably remained in use.

The *hiakal*. In traditional Coptic churches, a sanctuary area (called the *haikal*) containing the altar is clearly screened off at the eastern end of the nave. Within, portions of the holy service are performed in secret, out of

16

sight of the congregation. Architectural evidence suggests that this was not true in the earliest Nubian churches, which perhaps were not yet definitely affiliated with Alexandria (cf. Adams 1965, 121). The screening off of the *haikal* however became universal in Nubian churches after the ninth century.

As indicated earlier, there was some suggestion of a *haikal* screen in Church XXXVI as originally built. In the Subphase 3c church however the evidence was much more conclusive; the *haikal* was screened off, both from the nave and from the adjoining north and south aisles, by the construction of 20-cm wing walls extending outward from the eastern nave piers. The wall (called *higab*) separating the *haikal* from the nave ran across from the northeast to the southeast nave pier, leaving a very narrow doorway with a raised threshold in the center. This was not built directly on the remnant of the *higab* that had existed at Subphase 3b; it was situated somewhat further to the east. Additional 20-cm walls were extended eastward from the two eastern nave piers, separating the *haikal* from the aisles to the north and south; there was a narrow doorway at the eastern end of each. In addition, a thin partition was run across the east end of the north aisle, creating a closed passage through which the clergy could pass on their way from the sacristy (northeast corner room) to the *haikal*.

Within the *haikal*, there was a small and very low mastaba adjoining the south side of the northeast nave pier. There was no surviving trace of an altar, although one almost certainly had stood here.

The nave. Just to the west of the *haikal*, a new mud brick pulpit was built in the usual position at the northeast corner of the nave, adjoining the west side of the nave pier. As preserved it was 1m wide, 2.4m long, and 90cm high. The upper portions had probably been added in later times, for the pulpit remained in use after the rebuilding of the church at Phase 4. It is certain however that it was first installed at the time of the Subphase 3c modifications, for its base rested on the Subphase 3c floor. Like all Nubian pulpits, it was ascended from the west side. The lowermost steps, which were buried in the course of later refloorings, were very much worn.

Beside the pulpit, at the point where it abutted against the *higab* wall, a section of ceramic pipe, 12cm in diameter, was set upright in the church floor. Only the lowermost 60cm were preserved *in situ*, but impressions in the mud plaster of the pulpit showed that the pipe had once extended upward as far as the top of the pulpit itself. Probably this was a socket into which a lamp stand or a lectern stand could be inserted.

There was no change elsewhere in the nave, except that a hand-made vessel was buried to its neck in the floor, at a point close to the southeast room corner. It is identified by the letter V in the plan (Figure 6).

The aisles. There was no change in either aisle, except that, as previously noted, a partition wall was run across the north aisle near its eastern end, creating a screened area through which the clergy could pass on their way from the sacristy to the *haikal*. Because the floor levels had been raised, there was no longer an extra step down from the exterior door thresholds to the floor of the church.

The western corner rooms. Preservation of the two western rooms was extremely poor, as they had been razed nearly to ground level when the church was rebuilt at Phase 4. Apart from the raising of the floor level, there appears to have been no change in the northwest corner room. In the southwest room, it looked as if the original entry door in the north wall had been blocked, and a new entry cut through the east wall, opening from the south aisle. This would have eliminated the previous asymmetry of the western rooms, one of which was entered from the east and the other from the north. The existence of the new doorway however could not be determined with absolute certainty. If it did exist, it was quite narrow, and had a raised threshold. These features suggest that it could have been a stair closet, beneath a flight of ascending steps in the southwest corner room. However, there were no actual surviving traces of a stairway within the room.

Exterior features

Outside the church, the adjoining platforms on the north, east, and south sides retained their previous configurations, but the floor levels all the way around were raised by about 40cm. In the process, nearly all of the previous parapet and partition walls were dismantled, and their stumps buried under the newly raised floor surface. As a result, the three parts now formed a single continuous platform, without any surface features, on the north, east, and south sides of the church. The narrow mastaba that had adjoined the west side of the church was buried by the natural buildup of sand on this side of the building.

The only segment of exterior wall that remained standing, apparently, was the 40-cm wall opposite the north doorway. Originally this was part of an antechamber adjoining the north church doorway, but at Subphase 3c the eastern and western walls of the antechamber were dismantled, and their stumps buried under the raised floor level. The north wall was perhaps left standing as a windbreak, to prevent the drifting of sand into the church doorway.

On the south side of the church, beside the doorway, the putative exterior pulpit was buried under the newly raised floor, as was the crypt alongside it. Former Building XXXVII, which had adjoined the southern platform, was entirely dismantled, leaving only the lowermost remnants of its walls buried under drifted sand. Thereafter, the church was never again adjoined by another building.

Finds in Church XXXVI

The ten registered finds from Church XXXVI are listed in Table 2. Of the ten, five are small votive lamps, and three others are Early Christian bowls that may also have been used as lamps. All of the deliberately made lamps are of the "candle-holder" form that was favored in Early Christian times (Forms P17-P20; see Adams 1986, 104 and 152). One bowl and four of the lamps were actually found on the eastern platform adjoining the church, which seems to have been a popular place to leave votive offerings.

Resting on the church floor were two finds of special interest. One was a complete, rather ornate bronze spoon (805), found in the apse. It is shown in Figure 7, and was

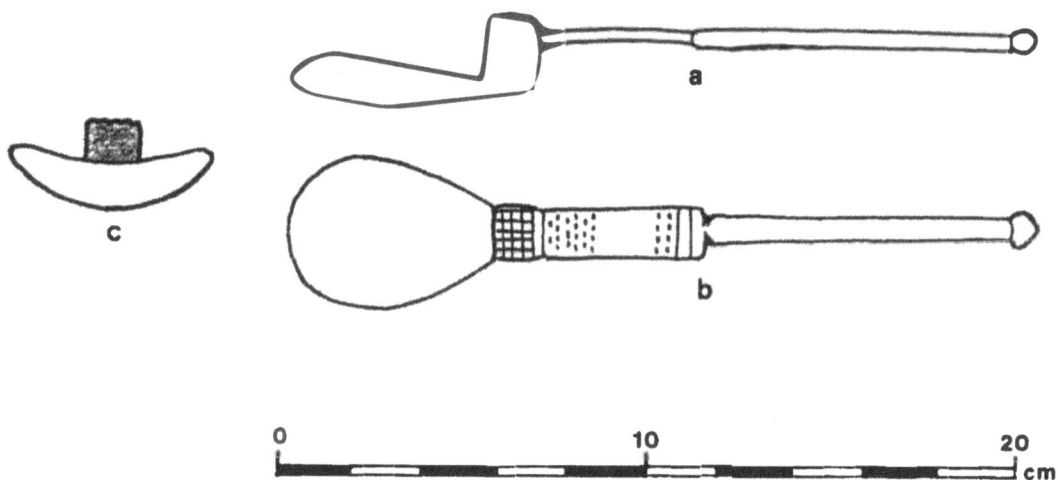

Figure 7. Bronze spoon (805) found on the floor of Church XXXVI, at Subphase 3d. It was cast in a single piece. **a**, side view; **b**, top view; **c**, end view.

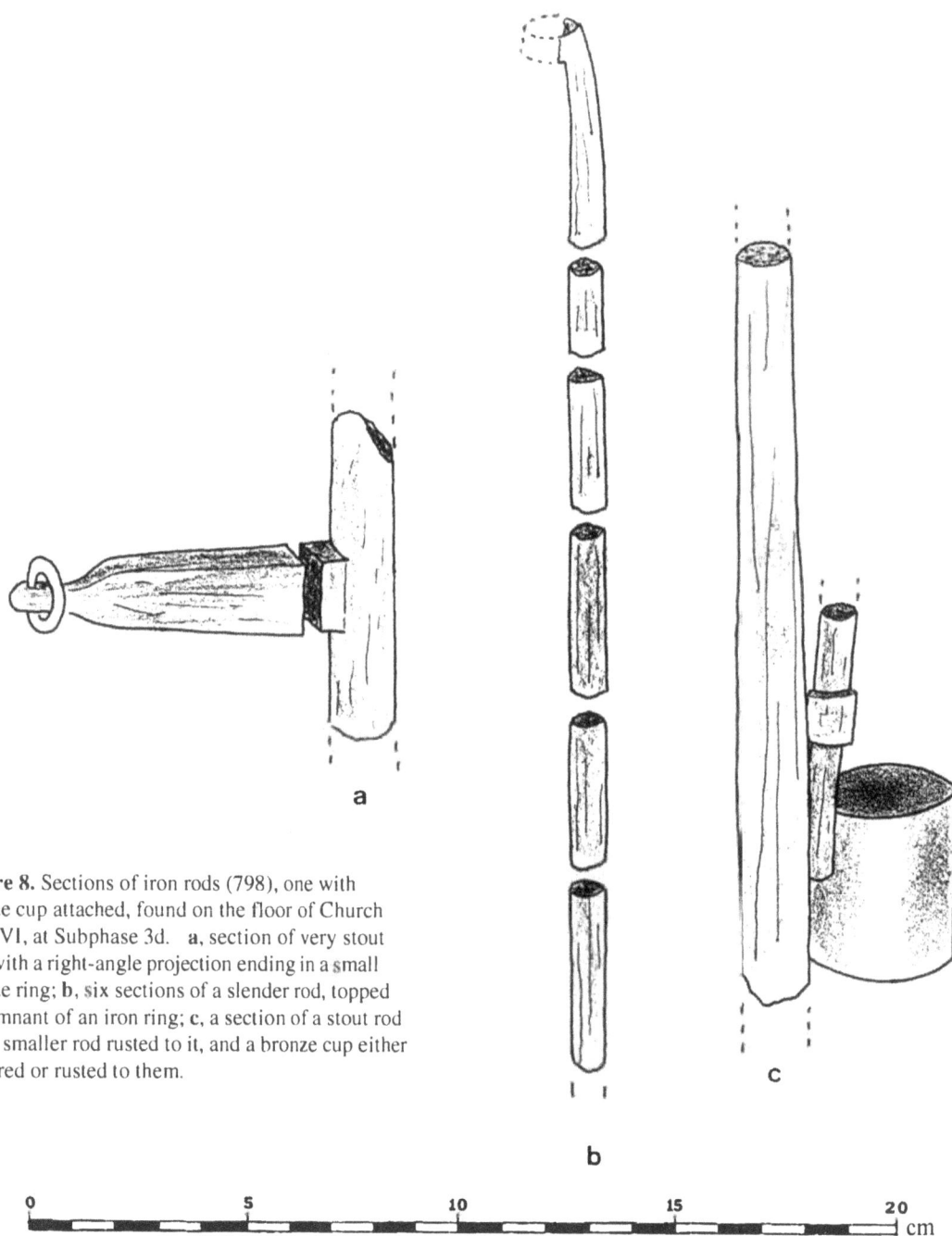

Figure 8. Sections of iron rods (798), one with bronze cup attached, found on the floor of Church XXXVI, at Subphase 3d. **a**, section of very stout rod, with a right-angle projection ending in a small bronze ring; **b**, six sections of a slender rod, topped by remnant of an iron ring; **c**, a section of a stout rod and a smaller rod rusted to it, and a bronze cup either soldered or rusted to them.

reported and illustrated also in *Meinarti II,* 44 and pls 14e-f. Another find, resting on the floor of the nave, was a collection of very rusty and fragmentary iron rods, one of which had a small bronze cup attached (789, shown in Figure 8 and Plate 6b). It is surmised that this may have been a candelabrum. Both objects were probably lost accidentally when the church was heavily damaged by flooding at the end of Phase 3.

Summary and comparisons of Church XXXVI

Church XXXVI was erected on the stumps of an older church during Subphase 3b, and most probably at its beginning, around A.D. 750. As originally constructed it was a fairly typical exemplar of Nubian church Type 2b, elsewhere called by me the Buhen Type (Adams 1965, 108-10). Its closest parallels, seemingly, were to the Western Church at Abdallah Nirqi (Castiglione *et al.* 1974, 324), Church 21-R-44 at Debeira West (Shinnie and Shinnie 1978, 29-33), and Church 11-I-1 at Murshid West (Mills and Nordström 1966, 14; author's unpublished field notes).

After a century or more, during Subphase 3c, various modifications were made whose effect was to convert the church from Type 2b to Type 3c, elsewhere called by me the Tamit Type (Adams 1965, 114-16). These included the installation of a tribune in the apse, the screening off of a *haikal* area both from the nave and from the aisles, the screening off of a passage in the north aisle, and the building of a new pulpit. Similar internal modifications were observed in the churches at Debeira (Shinnie and Shinnie 1978, 31) and Murshid (Mills and Nordström 1966, 14).

Church XXXVI lasted altogether about 250 years. Around A.D. 1000 it was heavily damaged by flood waters, as was the rest of Meinarti village, and was temporarily abandoned. After a hiatus of a generation or so, it was once again rebuilt, as Church VI.

Church VI: the third church

Subphase 4a

The entire village of Meinarti, including the church, was rebuilt at the beginning of Phase 4, after a period of abandonment of uncertain length (see *Meinarti II,* 51). The

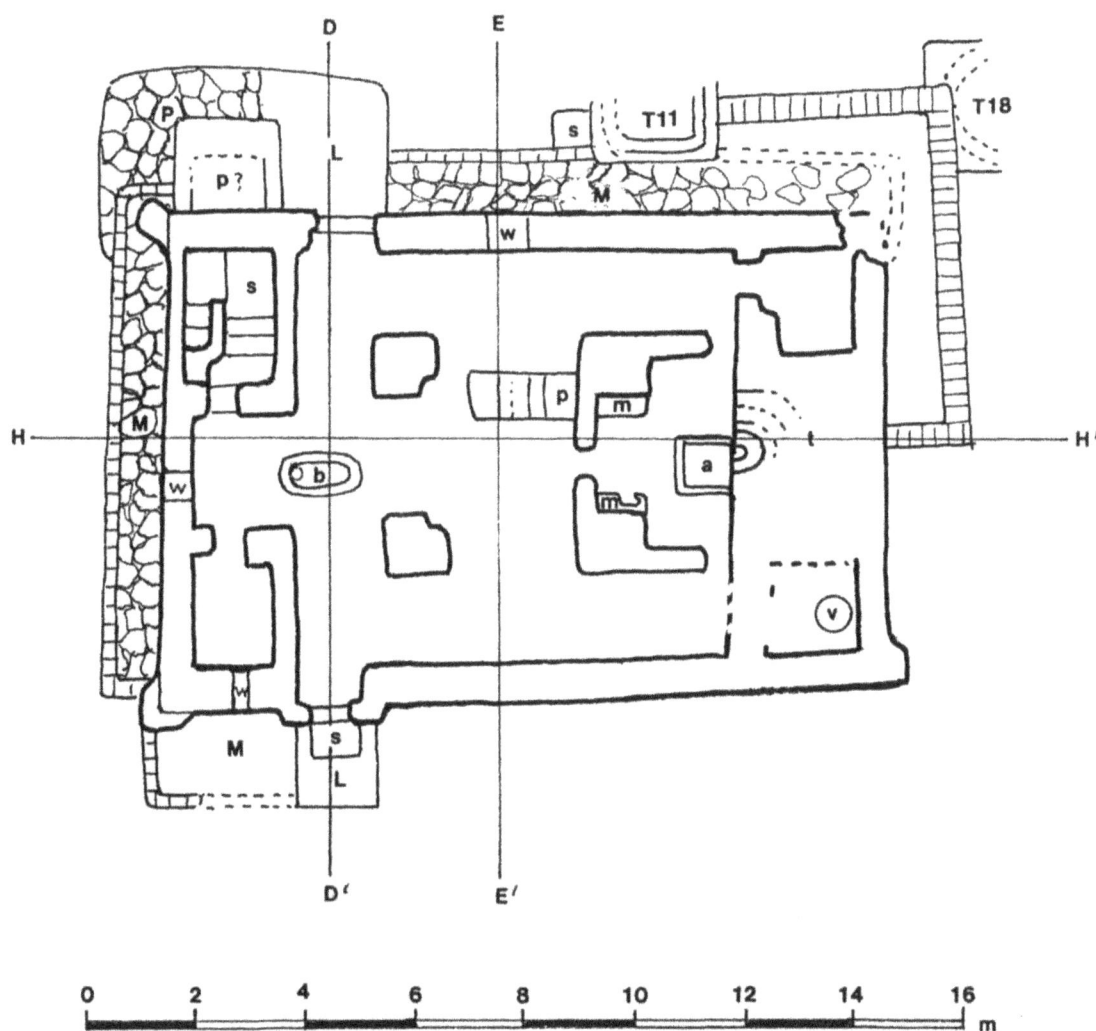

Figure 9. Plan of Church VI as first built, at Subphase 4a. **a**=altar; **b**=sunken basin; **L**=landing; **M**=external mastaba; **m**=internal mastaba; **P**=stone pavement; **p**=pulpit; **s**=steps; **T**=tomb superstructure (with number); **t**=tribune; **v**=buried pottery vessel; **w**=window. Only tombs immediately adjacent to the church are shown; for others see Figure 2. **D-D'**, **E-E'**, and **H-H'** are cross-section lines; see Figure 3.

newly rebuilt church was designated as Church VI (Figure 9; Plates 3-4). In the beginning it retained exactly the plan of its predecessor; it was the only building of Phase 4 that bore any relationship to an earlier structure. The stumps of the earlier walls were not systematically leveled prior to rebuilding; in most places, the new walls were simply built up on top of whatever the floods of earlier decades had left standing. In a few places where the older walls were very denuded, however – particularly at the eastern corners – a new foundation course of irregular granite blocks was laid on top of the older walls stumps, before the new brickwork was overbuilt (cf. Figure 3, Section E-E'). The line of juncture between older brickwork (surviving from Church XXXVI) and new construction could usually be recognized by differences in the brickwork, even where there were no intervening stone foundations.

The history of Church VI extended over about three and a half centuries, and involved a long series of internal and external modifications. More than anything else, its history involved an endless, and finally unsuccessful, battle against the accumulation of sand drifts, especially against the northern and western walls. Sand-restraining walls had to be installed outside the doorways already at Subphase 4b, and these were heightened again and again during subsequent phases, while the stairways descending to the church doors were repeatedly extended by adding steps to their upper ends. In due time it became necessary even to block the larger church windows, as drifted sand had reached the level of their sills. In its last years, Church VI was virtually a subterranean building.

Preservation

Church VI was finally abandoned, apparently, in the late fourteenth century. Thereafter for half a millennium it was subject to the ravages of flooding, surface slumpage, and vandalism. As a result, preservation in the building was highly variable, diminishing rapidly from west to east, as can be seen in Plates 3a-d and in Figure 3, Section H-H'. The walls at the west end – the windward side – stood nearly to their full original height (Plate 3a); indeed they had already been buried nearly to rooftop level before the church was abandoned. At the eastern end, always most subject to flood damage and surface slumpage, only a few centimeters of the apse and tribune were preserved, and no part of the eastern outer wall survived (Plates 3b-d).

Construction

Church VI was built throughout of mud bricks, measuring 40 x 20 x 7cm, the typical size of Classic and Late Christian bricks.

Walls. All load-bearing walls were 60cm thick except those which separated the two western rooms from the adjoining aisles; these were 40cm thick. The *haikal* screen walls on the north, south, and west were also 40-cm walls. The maximum surviving height of walls, at the southwest corner of the building, was 3.2m.

At the northwest and southwest corners of the church, the exterior walls were reinforced by brick buttresses which essentially "wrapped around" the corners of the building;

they can be seen in Plates 3a-c and Figure 9. At the base they projected outward about 50cm from the normal alignment of the wall, but above the base they diminished continually in thickness and width until, at a height of 1.5m above the base, they became flush with the regular wall surface. Such buttresses might have been present at the eastern church corners as well, but this could not be determined because of poor preservation.

The *haikal* enclosing walls and the pulpit employed numerous sections of broken ceramic pipe in their foundations, as did the exterior door thresholds.

Entryways. The original outside doorways of Church XXXVI were retained, but the threshold levels were substantially raised. Both doorways exhibited a rather complex construction, involving a flat, cut stone lintel on the outer side and a wider and taller arched aperture on the inner side. The presence of closing wooden doors was indicated by the presence of pivot stones in the thresholds and by bolt holes in the jambs of both doors.

The north doorway when found was fully preserved (Plate 3c). At the outer side it was 80cm wide and 2.4m high. The lintel, consisting of a cut sandstone block 25cm wide, rested on brick masonry jambs which were flush with the outer church wall. It is possible that the door originally had cut stone jambs like those in the south doorway; if so, they were removed and replaced by brick masonry in the course of some later rebuilding. At its inner side, behind the lintel and external jambs, the width of the doorway increased from 80 to 1.2m. This portion was crowned by a brick arch, whose crown was 65cm higher than the adjoining lintel, or in other words 3m above the original church floor.

The cut stone threshold of the north doorway was considerably above the level both of the church floor and of the outside ground surface, when first installed. It was adjoined on its outer side by a broad stoop, about 2m square, built up of hard mud.

The south doorway was not quite fully preserved; a portion of its sandstone lintel was broken away, along with the overlying wall (Plates 3b and 5b). The lintel was a reused piece of a Meroitic (or Pharaonic) uraeus lintel, installed with the carved side upward so that it was hidden under the overlying brickwork. Unlike the counterpart door on the north, the south doorway was equipped with cut sandstone jambs, rather crudely shaped (Plate 5b). They, and the lintel, were not flush with the church wall, but projected outward from it about 10cm. As usual in Nubian churches with stone-built doorways (as well as in pre-Christian temples), the jambs and lintels were scarred with innumerable deep grooves (visible in Plate 5b), where pious visitors had scraped away bits of the stone to commemorate their visits, and perhaps to use in protective amulets.

The southern doorway at its outer side, between the jambs, was 75cm wide; behind them it widened out, like the north doorway, to a width of 1.2m. The height of the doorway from sill to lintel was 2.6m. The cut stone threshold was adjoined by a landing and a small stoop on the outside, but there was no corresponding stoop on the inner side (cf. Figure 3, Section D-D').

20

Interior doorways. Only one of the original interior doorways in Church VI was fully preserved: the doorway from the western end of the nave to the southwest corner room. It was a narrow, arched opening 60cm wide and 2.9m high. The doorway opposite, leading to the northwest corner room, was of a similar width but was not preserved to its full height.

Windows. In the surviving walls of Church VI there were parts of four windows. Rectangular windows 60cm wide were located in the middle of the west wall, above the nave (Plates 3a and 4b), and in the middle of the north wall, above the north aisle (visible in Plate 3c). It seems very probable that there was a similarly placed window in the middle of the south wall, which however was not preserved up to sill height. The sill in the west window was 2.6m above the original floor level, while that in the north window was 2.3m above the floor. Neither window had survived to its full original height; the west window opening as preserved was 80cm high. In the course of later renovations both of these windows were blocked, because of the buildup of sand on the windward sides of the church.

Two narrower, "slot" windows were also partially preserved. Directly above the east jamb of the north doorway there was a window 20cm wide and at least 70cm high, which admitted light to the western end of the north aisle (visible in Plate 3c). The sill was at a level 3.2m above the original church floor. Near the western end of the south wall was another slot window, 20cm wide, which was preserved to its full original height of 60cm; it is visible in Plate 3b. It admitted light into the southwest corner room of the church. The sill, like that in the large western window, was 2.6m above the floor. Neither of the slot windows had been blocked.

Roofs. Church VI was unquestionably vaulted throughout, possibly but not certainly with a central cupola. Considerable portions of fallen vault material were found in the fill of the western rooms, and a portion of the vault was actually preserved *in situ* at one end of the southwest corner room. The crown was at a height of 3.6m above the floor, and the springing at 1.8m above the floor. The apse was probably covered by a semi-dome.

Floor. Church VI had a level floor of hard-packed mud throughout. As originally laid, it was only a few centimeters higher than the previous floor of Church XXXVI.

Plaster. The whole interior of Church VI was replastered and redecorated at least twice subsequent to the original building, in the course of which most of the original plaster was either covered over or removed. However, remnants of the original covering, pale grey to pale lavender in color, were preserved at a few places where buttresses were later built up against them (cf. Figure 15). They were observed here and there in the western portions of the church, except in the northwest and southwest corner rooms which apparently had only plain mud plaster. Because of flood destruction there were no surviving traces of plaster in the eastern rooms, but it seems a safe assumption that the whole church interior was originally plastered, except for the western corner rooms. There were also traces of pale grey plaster, which may or may not

have been original, on the church exterior.

The plan

The eastern rooms. Preservation in all three rooms was minimal. It is evident however that the apse and tribune from Church XXXVI were retained in Church VI (cf. Plate 4c), because a small altar was now built against the base of the tribune (see Figure 9). The northeast corner room seems to have remained unchanged, except for a slight raising of the floor level. The southeast corner room was not preserved up the level of the Phase 4 rebuilding.

The *haikal*. The *haikal* (sanctuary) retained *in toto* its earlier plan; both the nave piers and the enclosing screen walls were built back up from the stumps of their predecessors. The only major change was the installation of a small altar directly adjoining the base of the tribune. It was a column of brick masonry, roughly 1m square, resting on cut stone slabs. The original height could not be calculated, as only the lower 40cm survived. At the western side, the foundation slabs projected outward about 20cm beyond the base of the altar itself, providing a kind of low step on which the officiating priest could stand. There were very small and low mastabas adjoining the piers at the northern and southern sides of the *haikal;* that at the south side had a small bin or niche cut into it.

The nave. The mud brick pulpit from Church XXXVI was retained and built back up, at its traditional position adjoining the northeast nave pier. As preserved it was 1m wide, 2.4m long, and 90cm high (Plate 4d; also visible at far left in Plate 4a). The platform at the top was about 1m square, and was bordered all around by a raised ridge, 20cm higher than the remainder. The platform was ascended from the west by four steps. The two upper ones, with risers of about 30cm, were well preserved, while the two lower ones, with risers of about 15cm, were very much worn away. This suggests the possibility that the upper part of the pulpit was a later addition, made necessary by the raising of the floor level, and not an original feature of Church VI. Alongside the pulpit, on its south side, the section of upright ceramic pipe, installed already in Church XXXVI, remained *in situ.*

Near the western end of the nave, at a point midway between the two exterior doorways, an elongate oval basin was sunk into the floor. At the top it was 1m long from east to west and 40cm wide, with a depth of 50cm. The sloping sides were faced around the top with bricks set on edge, and below that with hard packed mud; the flat bottom was also formed of hard mud. A section of ceramic pipe was set upright into the floor of the basin at its western end; it projected upward for 50cm, so that its rim was flush with the surrounding church floor. The function of the basin and pipe is uncertain.

At the far western end of the nave, the doorways to the two western corner rooms were rearranged so that both were now entered from the nave rather than from the aisles.

The aisles. There was no change in the interior of the aisles, except that the former vestibule wall, screening off the east end of the north aisle, was removed. At the west end of both the north and south aisles, the former doorways giving access to the western corner rooms were eliminated when these rooms were rebuilt.

The western corner rooms. Both western corner rooms were rebuilt from the ground up, with 40-cm walls at their eastern sides but 60cm walls on the other three sides. In the process of rebuilding, the former doorways connecting the corner rooms with the north and south aisles were eliminated; both rooms were now entered from the west end of the nave.

The northwest corner room. The single most conspicuous change that took place in the rebuilt church was the installation of a stairway in the northwest corner room. This was a somewhat unusual location, as the great majority of Nubian church stairways were in the southwest corner room (Adams 1965, 99). It may have been chosen at Meinarti as a way of counteracting the weight of drifted sand against the northern church wall. The stairs, built entirely of mud brick, ascended northward along the east wall, to a landing adjoining the north wall. From here they returned southward along the west wall, the upper and lower sections being separated by a 20-cm balustrade wall. The lower steps were 90cm wide, and the upper ones 50cm wide; the landing halfway up was about 1.5m above the main church floor. There was no stair cupboard under the stairs, as in some Nubian churches. The steps when found were in extremely worn condition, the lower ones having become little more than a steeply sloping ramp. Some of the badly worn lower steps can be seen in Plate 4e.

The southwest corner room was entered through a low, arched doorway in its north wall, previously described. It was the best preserved room in the church, with the crown of its roof vault surviving intact at the southern end. The south wall was pierced by a narrow slot window, just below the vault crown, as previously described.

The floor of the room was featureless, but beam sockets in the east, west, and south walls suggested that there may once have been a loft within this room, at a level of 1.75m above the floor (i.e. just about at the level of the vault springing). There were three large sockets each in the east and west walls, and five smaller ones in the south wall, all at the same level. The eastern and western sockets were too large to suggest the presence of coat pegs; otherwise the southwest corner room might have been identified as a cloakroom. A series of small holes in the masonry at the northwest corner of the room might conceivably have been footholds to assist a person in climbing up to the loft, although they appeared too small to be effective for that purpose.

Decoration
Church VI was decorated, probably from the beginning, with colored murals as well as painted inscriptions. The original ones however were preserved only in very small remnants, where they had been protected by the building of later buttresses against them (see Figure 15). Elsewhere, they were covered over by later coats of plaster and decoration, applied at Phase 5. All of the murals will be described in a later section.

Exterior features
Platform. Unlike its predecessors, Church VI did not stand on an elevated platform, except at the northeast corner. Elsewhere, sand had accumulated to such a depth that the outside ground surface was now flush with what had been the top of the raised platform surrounding Church XXXVI; that is, essentially flush with the base of the Church VI walls. At the northeast corner, however, there was still an artificially raised area adjoining the new church. It was created by building a new brick retaining wall, 60cm thick and 70cm high, and filling in the enclosed area with sand. The wall paralleled a portion of the east church wall, at a distance of 1.6m from it, and the adjoining portion of the north wall, at a distance of 2.4m from it (see Figure 9). At its western end, the retaining wall closed against the side of a domed tomb superstructure (T11), which must have been built earlier (see below). The surface of the platform was paved over with hard mud. It is difficult to suggest any obvious reason for this feature; it might conceivably have been to protect the area immediately adjoining the church walls from grave digging, which could have undermined them.

Mastabas. From the time of its first building, Church VI was adjoined by low mastabas, 20cm high, running all along the north wall, all along the west wall, and along the south wall from the southwest corner as far as the doorway. Those adjoining the north and west walls were formed of roughly shaped granite blocks, cemented together with mud mortar and bordered at the outer edge by 20-cm brick retaining walls. These were the same blocks that, in a few places, ran underneath the rebuilt church walls, and served as foundations for them. The two mastabas had a hard, smooth mud paving on their upper surfaces. The mastaba adjoining the west wall (visible in Plate 3a) was about 1m wide, and was terminated at both ends where the brick retaining wall curved around to close against the outside church wall. The north mastaba varied in width between 1.3 and 1.4m. At the west end it closed against a built-up mud landing outside the church door. The east end was poorly preserved, and its actual point of termination could not be determined with certainty.

The short southern mastaba, 1.6m wide and 20cm high, was not formed of stone blocks but of hard-packed mud, behind its brick retaining wall. At the east end, it closed against a built-up landing outside the south church door.

Additional paved area. Adjoining the northwest corner of the rebuilt church, and extending about 3m from it to the north and to the west, there was an additional roughly square area formed of granite blocks set in mud mortar, and paved over with smooth mud at the top. The paved surface was more or less flush with the surrounding ground level, and it was not enclosed within a brick retaining wall, as were the mastabas. This feature antedated the building of the western church mastaba and of the external pulpit (described below), both of which rested partly on top of it.

Stair landings. In the first two Meinarti churches, the door thresholds were at a level considerably higher than the outside ground surface, so that it was necessary to pro-

22

vide built-up stoops at their outer sides. By the time of Church VI the opposite was true: the accumulation of drifted sand and refuse was such that the thresholds were 30 to 40cm below the outside ground level. From this time onward, entry to the church always involved a descent from the outside.

At the time of first rebuilding, Church VI was provided with landings of hard mud outside the north and south doors. Persons entering the church first stepped onto these, and then down into the church by two or three descending steps, one of which was the door threshold stone. The northern landing was about 2m square; that is, very much wider than the actual doorway. It was adjoined on its western side by the external pulpit (?) described below, and on its eastern side by the northern mastaba previously described. There was a step down from the landing to the stone door threshold, and a second step down to the church floor.

The southern landing was only slightly wider than the door itself; it measured 1.5m east-west by 1.8m north-south. At the western end it closed against the south mastaba. On the landing itself there was a step down of 15cm from the southern to the northern half, a second step down from this to the door threshold, and a third step down to the church floor.

External pulpit? Adjoining the north church wall, just west of the north doorway, was a solid mass of brick masonry measuring 1.75 x 2m, and standing to a height of 1.25m. Its east and west sides were vertical, while the northern face was slightly stepped, as can be seen in Plate 3c. The top of the structure seems to have been surrounded by a narrow parapet, 30cm higher than the space within. This feature was almost certainly coeval with the first building of Church VI, since its base was at the same level as that of the rebuilt church walls. It predated the building of the north church mastaba, which closed against its eastern side. It is just possible that this was a massive external buttress, meant to offset the thrust of the stairway built within the northwest corner room, but it may also have been an external pulpit. However, there was no surviving evidence as to how the top of the structure could have been reached.

Cemetery. From the time of its first building, Church VI was adjoined on the north, east, and south by the Meinarti cemetery. Many but not all of the graves had elaborate mud superstructures, the earliest of which stood in close proximity to the church walls. Features of the cemetery will be described in the following chapter.

Subphase 4b

Interior changes
There was almost no internal change in the church during Subphase 4b (Figure 10). Apparently, the floor level remained the same throughout the whole duration of Subphases 4a and 4b. The most conspicuous change was in the north doorway, where, because of sand accumulation on the outside, the threshold level was raised by no less than 40cm. Since there was no concurrent raising of the interior floor level, it was necessary to build a stoop adjoining the door on its inner side, providing an intermediate step between the threshold and the church floor. It was a small platform about 1.5m square, formed of mortared stone masonry with a hard mud upper surface. There was a step down of 25cm from the door threshold to the stoop, and a second step down of 15cm from the stoop to the church floor. It may have been in the course of this modification that the original sandstone jambs of the north door were removed, if indeed there ever were any.

Within the haikal, two low ridges of brick were built on the floor, extending westward from the corners of the altar toward the higab (ikonostasis). The more northerly ridge extended about halfway from the altar to the higab, while the more southerly one extended the full distance. What purpose was served by this feature is unclear; it was not retained at any later subphase.

There was some evidence of damage to the walls of the northwest corner room and to the northwestern nave pier, both of which had been undercut and then reinforced with large stones pushed under them.

Exterior changes
Exterior changes at Subphase 4b were much more conspicuous than those in the church interior, due to the steady, inexorable buildup of drifted sand on the northern and western sides. The earlier stone-built mastabas on those two sides were entirely sanded over, and a large, cruciform tomb superstructure (T120) was constructed directly on top of the buried northern mastaba (Figure 10 and Plates 11e-f). The putative external pulpit beside the north door continued to project above ground level, but not nearly as much as before.

The landing outside the north door, built at Subphase 4a, was now of necessity surrounded by a thin sand-restraining wall 60cm high, to prevent the drifting of sand against the door itself. Eventually, accumulated sand outside this structure reached as high as the tops of its walls. Consequently the enclosed landing surface, which at Subphase 4a was about 15cm higher than the adjoining ground surface, was 60cm below it by the end of Subphase 4b. In order to facilitate descent into this now-sunken area, two small steps were installed in its northeastern corner (visible in Figure 10).

Change on the southern or lee side of the church was much less conspicuous. The mud-built mastaba near the southwest corner continued to project a short distance above ground level. However, it was necessary here also to surround the steps leading to the south doorway with a low sand-restraining wall. Thus began the unending battle against sand that was to continue through the whole remaining history of Church VI.

Subphase 4c

Interior changes
Changes at Subphase 4c (Figure 11) were somewhat more numerous than at Subphase 4b. To begin with, the floor level throughout the building was raised by about 15cm, which had the effect of burying the former raised stoop

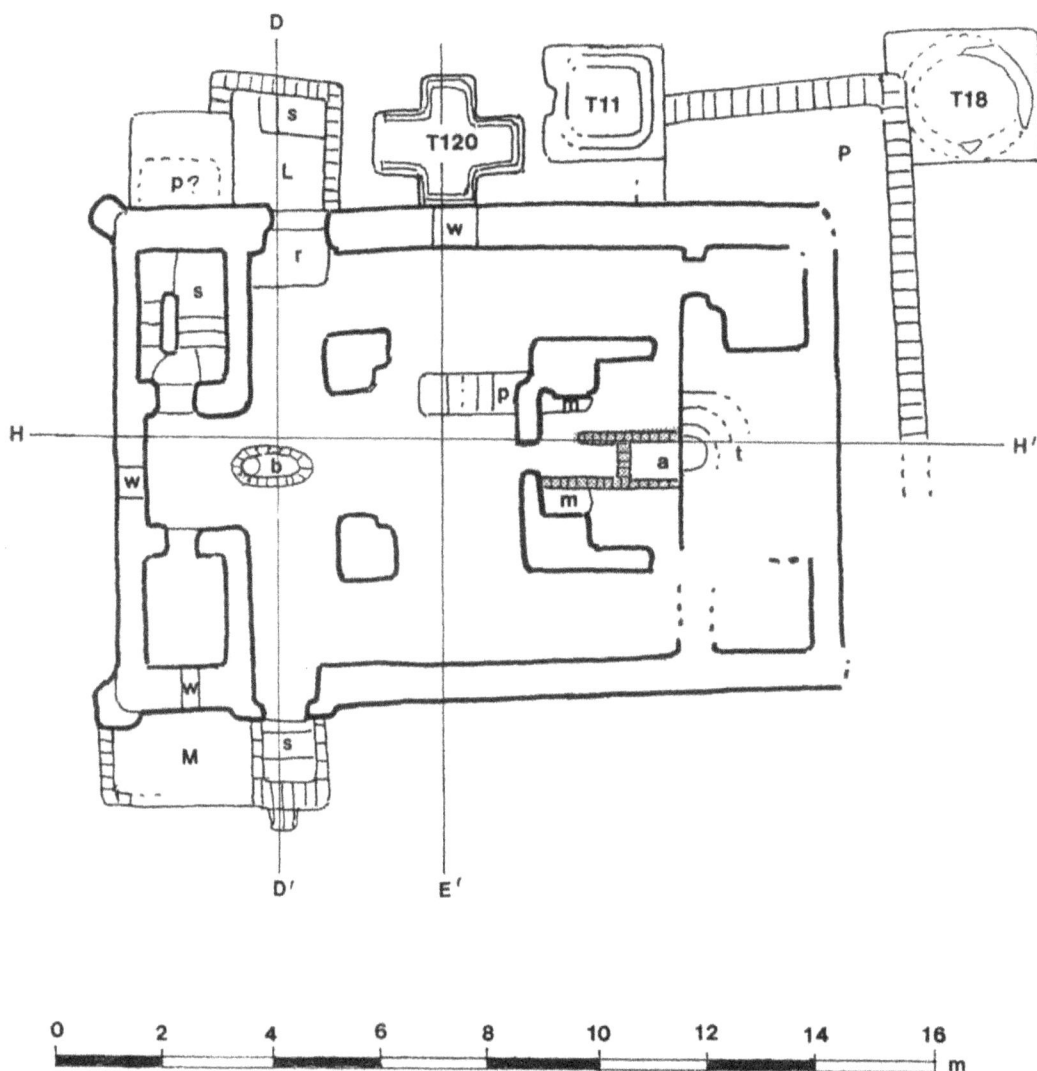

Figure 10. Plan of Church VI at Subphase 4b. Shading identifies features added at Subphase 4b. **a**=altar; **b**=sunken basin; **L**=landing; **M**=external mastaba; **m**=internal mastaba; **P**=platform; **p**=pulpit; **r**=recessed area; **s**=steps; **T**=tomb superstructure (with number); **t**=tribune; **w**=window. Only tombs immediately adjacent to the church are shown; for others see Figure 2. **D-D', E-E',** and **H-H'** are cross-section lines; see Figure 3.

beside the north doorway, and also the low ridges in the *haikal* floor.

The *haikal*. As just mentioned, the former ridges in the floor were buried when the floor level was raised, as also was the small and low mastaba adjoining the southeast nave pier. The small mastaba adjoining the northern pier however continued to project some distance above floor level. All three of the doorways to the *haikal,* from the nave and from the aisles, were newly equipped with raised stone thresholds, not present at the earlier subphases.

The nave. The most conspicuous addition to the nave was the building of a kind of broad, low brick bench, 30cm high and 1m wide, extending between the northwestern and northeastern nave piers and adjoining the base of the pulpit (see Figure 11). It had the effect of creating a separation between the nave and the north aisle. It is possible that this feature was originally higher, and was dismantled when the church was refloored at Phase 5. Its purpose is entirely unclear.

At the western end of the nave, the oval-shaped basin in the floor remained in use. Its sides were built upward with hard mud, to bring them level with the newly raised floor.

The aisles. Within the north aisle, and close to its eastern end, a small brick-walled enclosure was built adjoining the northern church wall (see Figure 11). The interior measured 2m east-west by 1.2m north-south, and was entered through a small doorway in the south wall. The enclosing walls were preserved only to a height of 30cm; the upper parts had almost certainly been dismantled when the church was refloored at Phase 5. A small pottery lamp, found on the floor in one corner, suggested that this might have been a votive chapel.

Farther to the west, a section of 20-cm wing wall was built, which partly closed off the western opening between the north aisle and the nave. Like the other features just named, it was mostly dismantled at Phase 5, leaving only its lowest portion buried under the floor. Taken together with the brick structure extending between the northeast and northwest nave piers, which also separated the north aisle from the nave, it suggests the possibility that the north aisle was a specially segregated area, perhaps for women

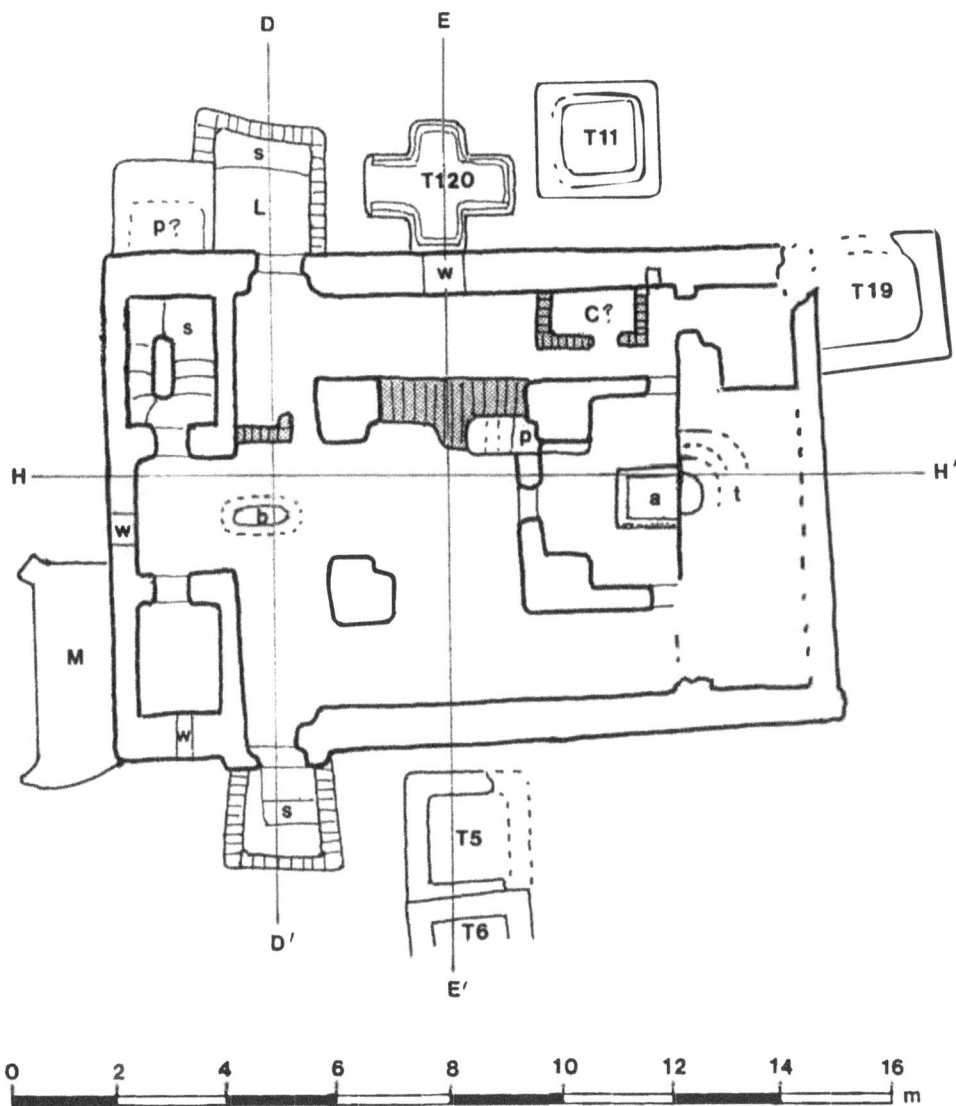

Figure 11. Plan of Church VI at Subphase 4c. Shading identifies features added at Subphase 4c. a=altar; b=sunken basin; C=votive chapel (?); L=landing; M=external mastaba; p=pulpit; s=steps; T=tomb superstructure (with number); t=tribune; w=window. Only tombs immediately adjacent to the church are shown; for others see Figure 2. D-D', E-E', and H-H' are cross-section lines; see Figure 3.

votaries.

There were no recognizable changes in the south aisle, or in the western corner rooms.

Exterior changes

Sand continued to drift inexorably against the outer walls of the building, and now covered the earlier southern mastaba as well as the previously covered northern and western ones. However, a new and rather oddly shaped mastaba, 25cm high, was now built against the southern half of the west church wall. Formed of hard packed mud, it was essentially rectangular in shape, but had projecting "ears" at both the outer corners, as well as a slightly curving southern end (Figure 11).

At the north side of the church, the sand-restraining wall surrounding the north door landing was considerably heightened, and so also was the landing within. Where there had formerly been two small steps leading down to the sunken area of the door landing, they were now replaced by a single wide step. The level of the door thresh-

old itself was heightened to such an extent that the full height of the north door was only 1.05m. From this time onward, anyone entering the church from the north would have had to bend down very considerably.

Beside the north door landing, the top of the old exterior pulpit, if such it was, still projected a few centimeters above ground level.

On the south side of the church, an additional step was added to the top of the stairs approaching the south doorway, and the steps were enclosed within a new sand-restraining wall.

Many new tomb superstructures were built close to the north and east church walls at Subphase 4c; they can be seen in Figure 19.

Subphase 5a

The Meinarti Church underwent its last major transformation at the beginning of Phase 5 (Figure 12; Plate 5), once again following an interval of abandonment during

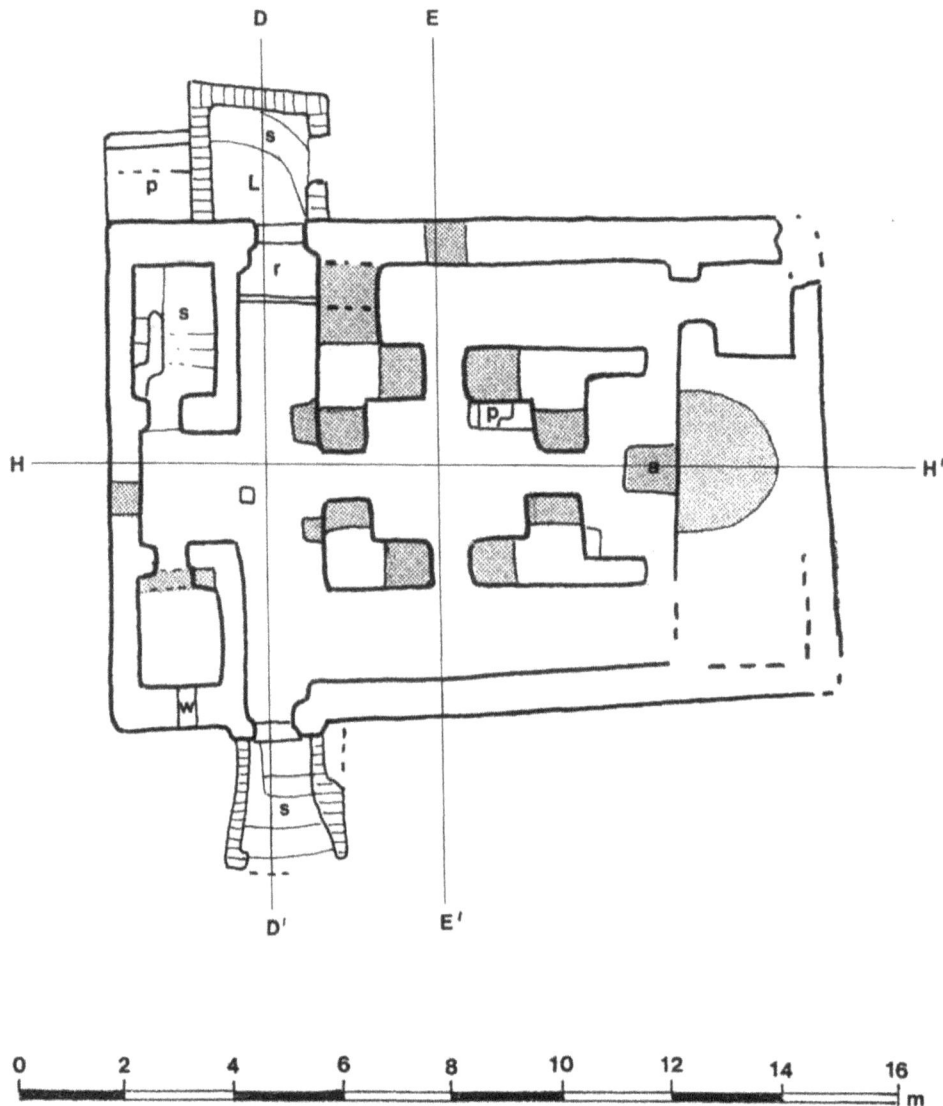

Figure 12. Plan of Church VI at Subphase 5a. Shading identifies features added at Subphase 5a. **a**=altar; **L**=landing; **p**=pulpit; **r**=recessed area; **s**=steps; **w**=window. **D-D'**, **E-E'**, and **H-H'** are cross-section lines; see Figure 3.

which it had suffered extensive damage, probably from Ayyubid raiders (see Adams 1977, 456). The changes somewhat altered the original plan, and also greatly reinforced the interior of the building - a recourse made necessary by the tremendous pressure of accumulated sand against the north and west walls. However, preservation was so poor at the eastern end of the building that some details could not be reconstructed.

While most of the changes at Subphase 5a were clearly required for purposes of reinforcement, there may have been two that were dictated by current architectural fashion. One was the elimination of the apse, leaving a rectangular sanctuary chamber, and the other was the construction of a central cupola projecting above the rest of the building. Both of these were common features of the Late Nubian Church Type 4, which made its appearance in the twelfth century (Adams 1965, 116-19).

Construction

Walls. Exterior walls remained unmodified, but the four L-shaped central piers were substantially lengthened and

thickened. In addition a massively thick wall was constructed across the north aisle, just east of the north doorway, to help relieve the pressure of drifted sand against the north wall (Plate 5d). A relieving arch was also built across the southwest corner room, at its northern end, to help bear the weight of sand against the west wall. These additions are indicated by shading in Figure 12.

Entryways. The earlier doorways in the north and south walls remained in use, and retained their original sandstone lintels. In the south doorway a new threshold stone, 25cm higher than the floor, was installed, to prevent the drifting of sand through the door. Since the lintel was not raised at the same time, the height of the doorway was now reduced to only 1.25m , thus requiring anyone who entered the church to bend down (cf. Plate 5a). A pivot stone in the church floor, just inside the doorway, showed that a pivoting wooden door had been installed when the church was refloored.

The north doorway was already so low that the threshold level could not be further raised, nor could the immediately adjoining floor surfaces. Instead, they were left at

26

their original levels while all the remaining floors inside and outside the church were raised. There were, as a result, small sunken areas adjoining the door threshold on both sides. A person entering the church from the north first stepped down into the deeply sunken door landing, then up to the threshold, then down again into a sunken area in the church interior, and up from this to the main church floor.

Interior doorways. The openings between the four nave piers, formerly about 2m wide, were reduced in width to less than 80cm by the lengthening of the piers. Curiously, all four of these doorways diminished somewhat in width from bottom to top. The one fully preserved example (seen in Plate 5c) was 2m high. The earlier, wider openings had probably been spanned by arches, but in the remodeled church these were replaced by flat stone lintels, one of which was preserved *in situ* and can be seen in Plate 5c. Set into the wall directly above the lintel there had been originally a small, decorative stone tablet (344), which is shown in Plate 6e, no. 2.

The newly built relieving wall across the north aisle was pierced, at its northern end, by a doorway 85cm wide and 1.85m high (Plate 5d). Doorways to the northwest and southwest corner rooms remained unaltered except that they were reduced in height when the floor level was raised. The fully preserved doorway to the southwest corner room was now about 2.5m high.

Windows. The two larger windows, in the north and west walls, were blocked up with bricks at some time during Phase 5, when drifted sand reached to the level of their sills. The smaller slot windows in the north and south walls were not blocked.

Roofs. Most rooms were presumably vaulted as before, and a portion of the vault survived intact in the southwest corner room. However, the reinforcement of the four central nave piers makes it a virtual certainty that these now supported a central cupola, which probably rose considerably higher than the adjoining roofs. As previously noted, this was a common feature of late Nubian churches of Type 4 (Adams 1965, 116-19).

Floors. Floor levels throughout the church were raised by an average 40cm above those of Subphase 4c. The new floor, like all its predecessors, had a hard, smooth surface of wet-laid mud. The result of reflooring was to bury the lower steps of the pulpit, at the northeast corner of the nave. The upper portion remained in use, but it now rose only about 90cm above the surrounding floor surface (Plate 5e). The stump of the original altar, at the east end of the nave, was entirely buried, but a new one was erected directly on top of it. Also buried was the deep oval depression in the floor near the west end of the nave, that had existed at Phase 4.

Plaster and decoration. Traces of hard, salmon-pink plaster, probably attributable to Subphase 5a, survived at various places in the western rooms; it is most clearly visible in Plate 5c. It was adorned with colored murals which will be described in a later section.

The plan

The apse. Although the remains were very denuded, it appeared that the former apse had been walled off across the front, and the area behind solidly filled with rubble. This was recognizable as deliberate fill and not simply fallen wall and roof material, for among the brick fragments it included also large fragments of stone mortars and columns, and one very large section of petrified tree trunk. This rather drastic alteration may have been made following extensive damage to the eastern end of the church, but it may also have reflected a desire to bring the church into conformity with other late Nubian churches (Type 4), nearly all of which lacked an apse (Adams 1965, 116-19).

The eastern corner rooms. The northeast corner room, conventionally called the sacristy, underwent no change except for the raising of its floor level. An Islamic tombstone (625) was set into the floor, face down, at the base of the east wall. (The inscribed side is shown in Plate 6f). Of the southeast corner room, tentatively identified earlier as a baptistry, nothing survived at the Subphase 5a level.

The *haikal*. After the filling of the apse, the *haikal* was left as a simple and rather small rectangular chamber. Its original area was further reduced by the thickening of the L-shaped piers at the northwest and southwest corners. At the west, it was not necessary to rebuild the *higab* (*ikonostasis*), for the newly extended nave piers formed a sufficient screen between *haikal* and nave. At the north and south, the *haikal* was still partially screened from the adjoining aisles by 20-cm wing walls, built upward from the earlier walls at the same locations.

An altar of brick masonry, about 75cm square, was built directly against the base of the east wall (i.e. the filled-in apse). This was a common position for altars in very late Nubian churches (Adams 1965, 116-20). It was not an upward extension of the previous altar of Phase 4, but was located slightly further to the north, so that its foundation rested only partly on the denuded top of its predecessor. The original height could not be determined, since the top of this altar also was denuded.

In the southwest corner of the *haikal,* in the angle formed by the southeast nave pier and the adjoining wing wall, there was a very small, slightly raised mastaba, which may have been a rest for a lamp.

The central nave and piers. In the church of Phase 4, the nave was separated from the adjoining north and south aisles by four L-shaped piers, which may or may not have supported a central cupola. In the course of rebuilding these were very much strengthened, both by adding to their thickness and by extending their outer ends. The effect of these extensions was to reduce the width of openings between the four piers, from 2m to only 80cm. The openings were now bridged by flat stone lintels, where formerly they had probably been spanned by brick arches (Plate 5c). Just above the lintel of the most westerly doorway, a small stone tablet with an incised floral design (344, shown in Plate 6e, no. 2) had been set into the brick masonry. It was found in the rubble just beneath the doorway, but the impression of its original locus was clearly visible in the masonry above. It seems most probable that the nave piers were reinforced in order to support a tall central cupola, like that found in other late Nubian churches of Type 4 (Adams 1965, 116-17).

In the northeast corner of the nave, only the top two steps and the upper landing of the pulpit continued to stand above the raised floor level (Plate 5e). The top was now about 50cm above the floor. A small lamp niche was cut into the southern face of the pulpit, at a level 30cm above the floor.

The western nave. The extension of the two western nave piers, leaving only a narrow, linteled doorway between them (Plate 5c), had the effect of converting the western portion of the nave into a separate room. The openings from it into the north and south aisles were also slightly reduced in width by the construction of short by stout buttresses adjoining the eastern walls. These were preserved only to a height of 20cm, for they seem to have been dismantled when the church was re-floored at Subphase 5b. There is however the alternate possibility that they were only very low lamp stands, and were never any higher.

In the center of the newly separated western nave, a small section of sandstone column, 20cm in diameter, was buried upright in the floor (Plate 5f). It was hollowed out at the top, to a depth of 25cm, the upper part of the hollowed area being square, but tapering to a round bottom. At the top, one side had been broken away. This object was buried deep beneath the Subphase 5a floor, but the top projected 20cm above it; i.e. to the level of the Subphase 5b floor. It is possible therefore that the object was installed at Subphase 5b rather than as part of the original renovation. Its function is unknown, but it is noteworthy that the stone column stood exactly above the spot where, at Phase 4, a section of ceramic pipe had been buried upright in the floor, within a sunken basin.

The north aisle. A very stout relieving wall, 1.4m thick, was run across the north aisle, just to the east of the north doorway. Beyond any doubt, it was inserted to help bear the pressure of drifted sand against the northern church wall. The newly created cross-wall was pierced, at its northern side, by an arched doorway 85cm wide and 1.85m high, which gave access to the more easterly portion of the north aisle (Plate 5d). The doorway had a slightly raised brick threshold on its western side. At the western end of the aisle, just inside the north doorway, there was a recessed area in the floor as previously noted. There were no features in the eastern portion of the aisle, where the former enclosure, interpreted as a votive chapel, was wholly dismantled.

The south aisle, No changes were noted in the south aisle, apart from the raising of the floor level.

The northwest corner room. There was no change in the northwest corner room, containing the stairway, except that the two lowest steps were now buried under the newly raised floor. There was however a step up of 15cm from the doorway to the lowest surviving step. The level of the

landing, halfway up the steps, was now 1.25m above the church floor.

The southwest corner room. In this room a kind of relieving arch was installed, spanning across the room from west to east, just inside the doorway. That is, a new brick buttress 40cm square was built in the northeast corner of the room, and from its top a brick arch passed above the doorway and closed against the west wall opposite. The arch was preserved intact. Its crown was 1.85m above the floor, i.e. about 30cm higher than the adjoining doorway. The purpose of this addition was undoubtedly to help relieve the pressure of drifted sand against the west church wall, by giving added internal support to the wall.

Exterior changes
Exterior changes were mostly those necessary to protect the access to the two church doors, as the levels of drifted sand continually increased.

The north door landing. The landing measuring 1.5 x 2m that had been installed outside the north doorway at Phase 4, continued in use at Phase 5. It was, as before, protected on all sides by a sand-restraining wall. Since the level of drifted sand had reached the top of the earlier, 20-cm wall, however, it was further heightened, this time by the addition of 40-cm masonry. The top of the newly heightened wall was no less than 1.25m above that of the landing within. To facilitate descent into this sunken area, a kind of sloping ramp, formed of loosely consolidated bricks and stones, was installed in its northeast corner. Some of the bricks bore traces of grey plaster, suggesting that they may have been taken from the dismantled tops of nearby tomb superstructures.

The external pulpit? A solid mass of brick masonry, measuring 1.75 x 2m, had been built just to the west of the north church doorway at Phase 4; it was tentatively identified as an external pulpit. By the time of Phase 5 drifted sand had reached as high as the original top, 1.25m above the base, but the structure was now heightened by at least 1m of additional brickwork. As before the northern side was slightly sloping, while the east and west walls were vertical. The added brickwork was rather crude, and was never plastered as was the original structure.

The stairs to the southern door. Outside the south doorway, a flight of three descending steps, enclosed by low wing walls, had already been installed at Subphase 4c. At the time of Subphase 5a, the further accumulation of sand required the addition of two and probably three more steps to the top of this stairway, and the enclosing sand-restraining walls were both thickened and heightened. These walls curved slightly away from each other toward the south, so that the upper steps were considerably wider than the original, lower ones. The total length of the stairway at Subphase 5a was at least 2.5m, with a descent of about 1m. The stair risers were formed partly of bricks set on edge, and partly of heavy stones.

Subphase 5b

At some point during Subphase 5b (Figure 13), or possi-

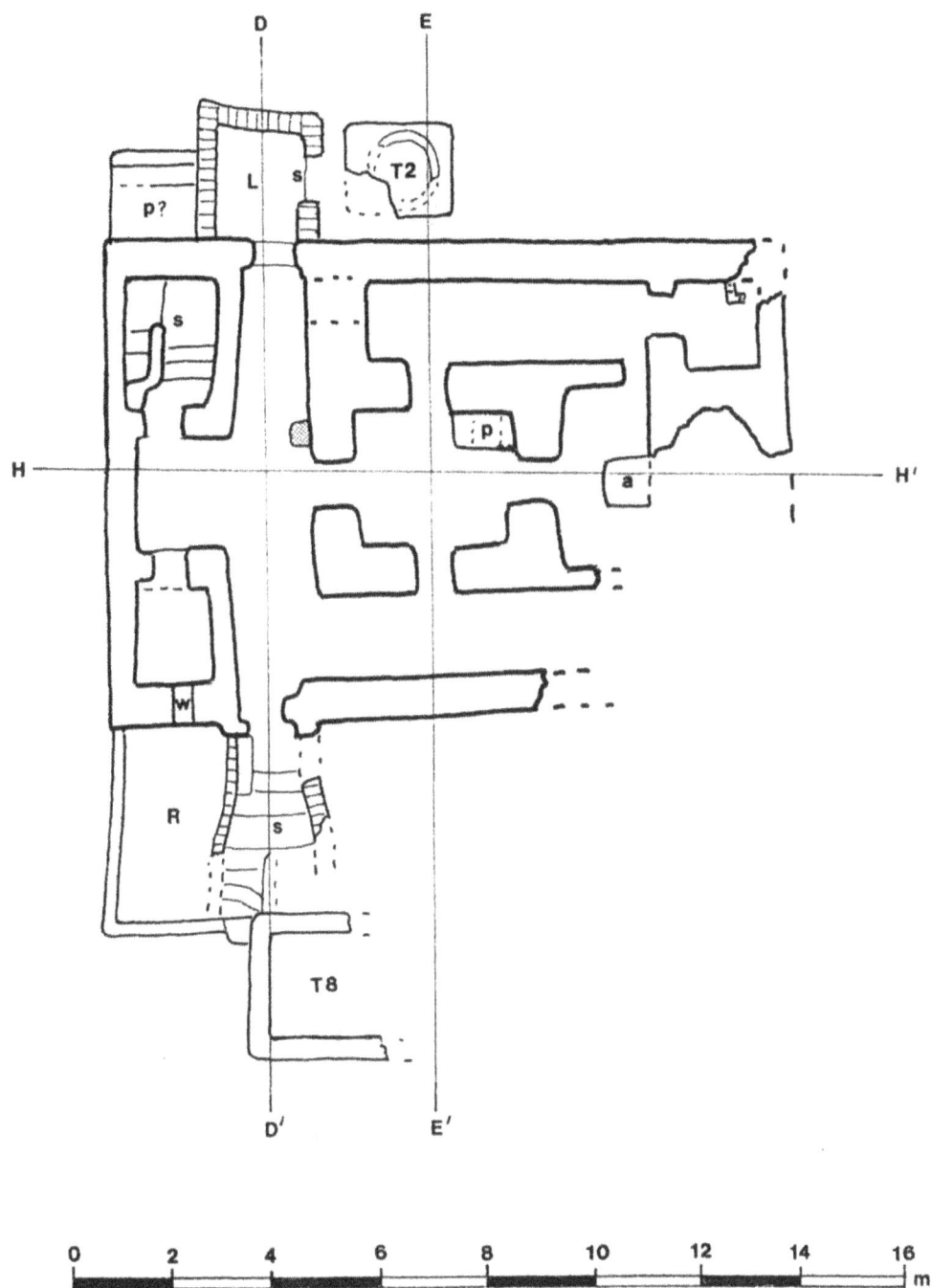

Figure 13. Plan of Church VI at Subphase 5b. Shading identifies feature added at Subphase 5b. a=altar; L=landing; p=pulpit; R=sand-restraining enclosure; s=steps; T=tomb superstructure (with number); w=window. Only tombs immediately adjacent to the church are shown; for others see Figure 2. **D-D'**, **E-E'**, and **H-H'** are cross-section lines; see Figure 3.

bly at its end, the villagers finally gave up the battle against drifting sand, and blocked the north church door. The blockage was done with rather loosely stacked bricks and was not plastered over, suggesting that there may have been some idea of removing it at a later date. In the event, this was never done.

Interior changes

Interior changes at Subphase 5b were minor. Floor levels throughout the church were raised by 20cm, except close to the west wall where the new floor sloped up slightly. Since the north doorway was no longer in use, the sunken area in the floor adjoining it was no longer needed, and

was filled over. The buttresses that had been built against the west ends of the western nave piers were removed, widening the passage from the nave to the west ends of the aisles. In the northwest corner of the church, the inner wall of the stair chamber had sagged inward to such an extent that it had to be partially rebuilt, and thereafter it had a slight curvature. A small lamp niche was newly cut into the masonry at the outside of its southeast corner. In the northeast corner room a very small, sunken bin was inserted; its floor was 20cm lower than the surrounding room floor. In the *haikal* and nave, the previous altar and pulpit remained in use, but the height of the pulpit was still further reduced when the floor level was raised.

Seven rather crudely formed lamps were found on the Subphase 5b floor, at various points in the church.

Exterior changes

The north door landing. Since the north doorway was no longer in use, the walled enclosure that had protected the access to it was allowed to fill with sand. Beside it, the presumed exterior pulpit at the northwest corner of the building still projected a few centimeters above ground level, but it probably served only as a mastaba.

The stairs to the southern door. On the south side of the church, the brick stairway giving access to the south doorway was considerably extended by adding at least five more steps at the top end. These were a good deal narrower than the lower steps, because they were "squeezed in" between a newly built tomb superstructure (T8) on the east and a newly built sand-restraining wall on the west, described below (see also Figure 13). The steps were rather rudely patched with stones, where they had become worn away.

Window-protecting walls. The wall which adjoined the steps of their west side was also the east wall of a large, empty enclosure that now adjoined the south church wall at its west end (see Figure 13). The 20-cm walls of this structure were built on soft sand, and there was no floor surface of any kind within them. The only function of this enclosure was evidently to prevent the drifting of sand into the window in the south church wall, which was never blocked.

Subphase 5c

In 1286, the Makourian king Shemamoun ordered the evacuation of Lower Nubia, in the face of a threatened

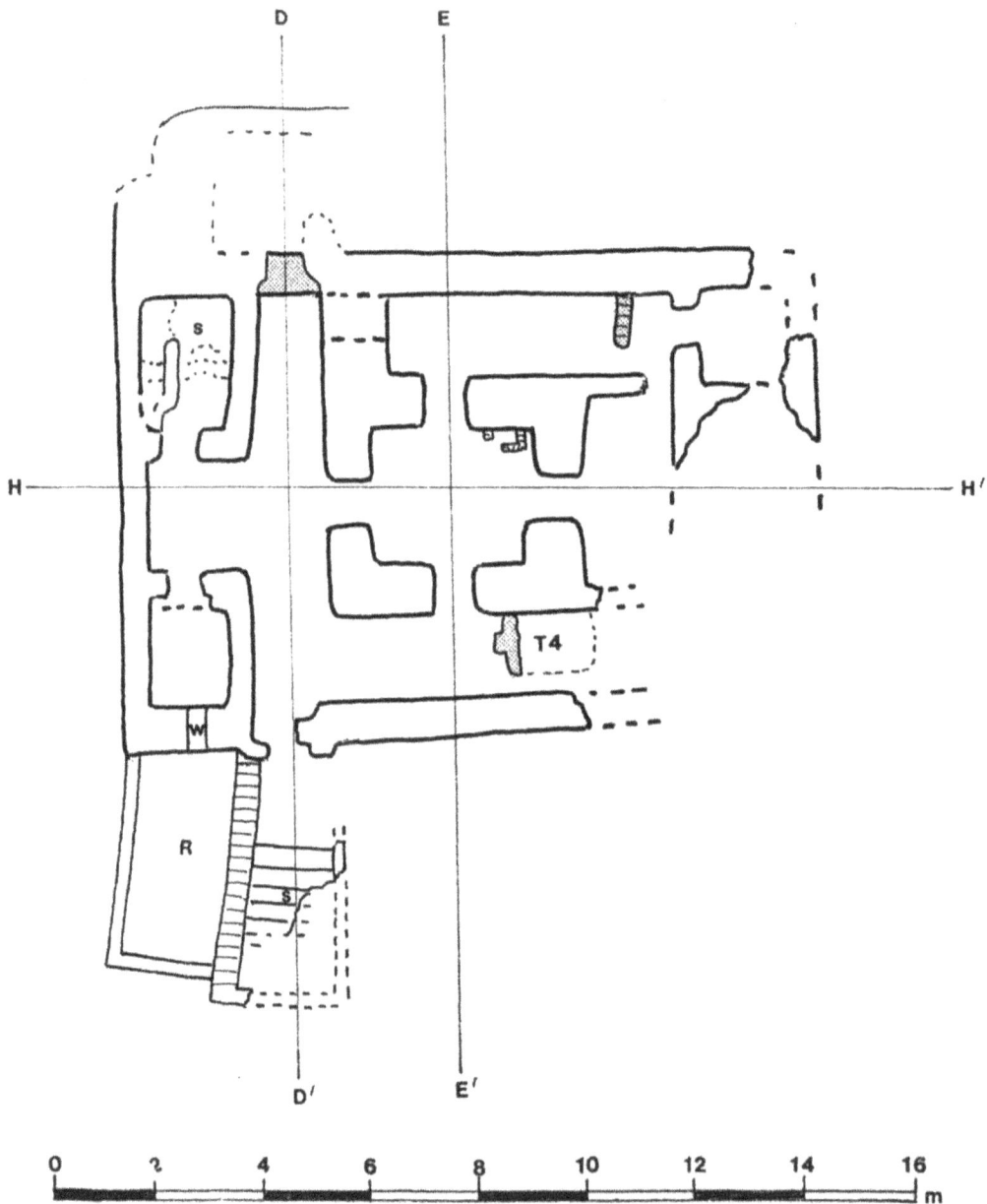

Figure 14. Plan of Church VI at Subphase 5c, its final phase. Shading identifies features added at Subphase 5c. **R**=sand-restraining enclosure; **s**=steps; **T**=tomb superstructure (with number); **w**=window. **D-D', E-E',** and **H-H'** are cross-section lines; see Figure 3.

30

Mamluk invasion. There was unmistakable evidence that the people of Meinarti, like all their neighbors, obeyed this decree (see *Meinarti III*, 32 and 41). Their return, a few years later, marks the beginning of Subphase 5c (Figure 14). It ended a little less than a century later, when Beni Ikrima nomads temporarily took possession of the island (see *Meinarti III*, 94).

That Subphase 5c was the final chapter in the history of the Meinarti Church can be inferred from the fact that the damaged murals, almost certainly defaced by the Beni Ikrima, were never repaired. I suspect that, at the time of Phase 6, the Meinarti parishioners were served by the small, newly-built church at Abdel Qadir, on the nearby west bank (reported in Griffith 1928, 63-80).

Interior changes

Floor levels throughout the church were raised by about 60cm, probably because a good deal of sand had drifted in during the interval of abandonment. This had the effect of burying all but the uppermost step of the pulpit, and the lower steps of the northwest corner staircase. Otherwise, architectural changes were minor. Near the east end of the north aisle a small area was screened off, creating once again a vestibule such as had existed at least twice previously. The eastern part of the church floor was not preserved at the Subphase 5c level, so that there was no surviving trace of an altar or other features of the *haikal*. The stairway in the northwest corner room, which had become very worn, was partly repaired with new mud paving. By far the most conspicuous change, however, was the whitewashing of the whole church interior, and the execution of a new set of murals which covered most of the older ones. These will be described in a later section.

Interior tomb. Tomb T4, which probably had a rectangular brick superstructure, was built in the south aisle, directly adjoining the southeast nave pier. Nothing survived except the extreme western end, including the lamp box. That it was installed while the church was still in use, and not after its abandonment, was suggested by the fact that it rested directly on the Subphase 5c floor, and that it was covered by the same whitewash that also covered the adjoining nave pier. Internal tombs were rare but not unknown in Nubian churches; this was the only one ever built at Meinarti.

Exterior changes

The stairs to the south door. All of the features formerly adjoining the north side of the church were now sanded over. On the south side, the stairway descending to the south door was entirely rebuilt, and considerably widened. However, only the middle and lower parts were preserved. There were seven surviving steps, of which the lower four were fully intact (Plate 5a). They were formed entirely of bricks set on edge, each with a tread width of about 25cm and a riser of 25cm. At the top of the steps, the superstructure of Tomb T8 was partially dismantled, and now served as the stair landing. The total descent from the landing to the church doorway was around 3m, which means that the top of the steps was nearly at the level of

the original church roof. For all practical purposes, Church VI had become an underground building.[9]

Window-protecting walls. The steps to the south doorway were bordered on their western side by a 40-cm retaining wall. This formed at the same time the east wall of an empty enclosure adjoining the south wall of the church at its west end. It was very nearly the same size and shape as the enclosure that had been built at Subphase 5b, but was in fact newly built on top of the sanded-up walls of its predecessor. As before, its only purpose must have been to keep sand from drifting into the southern church window.

Finds in Church VI

Altogether, 29 objects were registered from the various successive floor levels in Church VI, and from the adjoining platforms and mastabas. They are listed in Table 2. As in Church XXXVI, the vast majority of the finds (21 out of 29) are lamps. Some perhaps were used for illumination, but a larger number were probably used in votive contexts. In the church of Phase 4 most of the lamps were simple, open cups or small bowls, some of Aswan wares and some of hand-made wares. Some of these were still used during Phase 5, but the majority of the late lamps were simply the broken bases of footed bowls or vases.

Only a few of the non-pottery finds call for special remark. (Their registration numbers are given in parentheses for each object described.) The fragments of sculptured sandstone slab (809), shown in Plate 6d, were found in the fill material between the Subphase 4b and the Subphase 4c floor levels. They might be parts of an altar top. The small iron key (737) shown in Plate 6c, no. 1, was found lying on the Subphase 4b floor. The small bronze[10] object shown in Plate 6c, no. 2 (679) was found on the Subphase 5a floor, in the nave. It is most probably a kohl stick, although the form is somewhat aberrant (see *Meinarti III*, 83 and pl. 24b). The bronze pectoral cross (353) shown in Plate 6c, no. 3 was found in the fill material overlying the Subphase 5c tribune.

The small tablet of sculptured sandstone (344) shown in Plate 6e, no. 2, was originally a decorative element set into the wall, above the doorway at the west end of the nave. It was found among the fallen rubble on the floor, but the impression on the plaster above the door, where it was originally set, could be clearly seen. The Islamic tombstone (625), shown in Plate 6f, was set into the Subphase 5a floor in the northeast corner room, in a face down position. This was, obviously, a secondary context, and the date given in the inscription (equivalent to A.D. 1063) places its original carving well before the reconstruction of the church at Phase 5. It and other tombstones will be more fully discussed in the next chapter.

Summary and comparisons of Church VI

Church VI was built at the beginning of Phase 4, at the same time as the whole Meinarti village was reoccupied

---

[9] For a parallel situation at Abdallah Nirqi, see Van Moorsel *et al.* 1975, 9.

[10] The term "bronze" is here used to designate any alloy of copper, other than brass.

TABLE 2. REGISTERED FINDS FROM THE MEINARTI CHURCHES

Reg. no.	Material [1]	Object [2]	Condition [3]	Level (Phase)	Plate
Church XXXVIII					
827	Pottery (W2)	Footed bowl (D68)	Whole (R)	13 (3a)	
829	Pottery (W2)	Bowl (C74)	Whole	13 (3a)	
1046	Pottery (U2)	Amphorae (Z4)	Whole (R)	13 (3a)	
1107	Pottery (U4)	Amphorae (Z3)	Whole (R)	13 (3a)	
854	Ceramic	Incense stand	Portion	13 (3a)	6a
858	Bronze	Scrap	Scrap	13 (3a)	
Church XXXVI					
823	Pottery (R3)	Bowl (C83)	Whole (R)	12 (3b)	
812	Pottery (H3)	Bowl (C11)	Whole (R)	12? (3b)?	
826	Pottery (W2)	Lamp (P17)	Portion	12 (3b)	
830	Pottery (W2)	Lamp (P18)	Portion (R)	12 (3b)	
856	Pottery (U2)	Amphora (Z4)	Whole	12 (3b)	
811	Pottery (R7?)	Bowl (C18)	Almost whole	11a (3d)	
813	Pottery (W2)	Lamp (P18)	Almost whole	11a (3d)?	
814	Pottery (W2)	Lamp (P18)	Portion	11a (3d)	
815	Pottery (W2)	Lamp (P17)	Mostly whole	11a (3d)	
798	Iron and bronze	Candelabrum?	Many fragments	11a (3d)	6b
805	Bronze	Spoon	Whole	11a (3d)	6c, 4
Church VI					
809	Sandstone	Sculptured slab	Fragments	9 (4a)	6d
710	Pottery (H1)	Saucer lamp (P24)	Whole	8 (4b)	
739	Stone	Cylindrical plug	Portion	8 (4b)	
737	Iron	Key	Almost whole	8 (4b)	6c, 1
340	Pottery (Glaze)	Bowl (?)	Fragment	7 (4c)	
336	Pottery (W6)	Footed bowl (?)	Fragment	7 (4c)	
339	Pottery (W12)	Saucer lamp (P28)	Whole	7 (4c)	
686	Pottery (W12)	Saucer lamp (P28)	Whole	7 (4c)	
687	Pottery (W12)	Saucer lamp (P28)	Whole	7 (4c)	
338	Pottery (H4)	Saucer lamp (P24)	Almost whole	7 (4c)	
337	Pottery (H5?)	Saucer lamp (P26)	Whole	7 (4c)	
341	Shell	Lamp	Whole	7 (4c)	
1310	Pottery (W6)	Footed bowl (D23)	Fragment	6 (5a)	
538	Pottery (H1)	Saucer lamp (P26)	Whole	6 (5a)	
539	Pottery (H2)	Saucer lamp (P26)	Whole	6 (5a)	
625	Sandstone	Tombstone	Whole	6 (5a)	6f
353	Bronze	Cross pendant	Whole	6 (5a)	6c, 3
679	Bronze	Kohl stick?	Whole	6 (5a)	6c, 2
670	Pottery (W31)	Cup (A11)	Fragment	5 (5b)	
1357	Pottery (W15)	Vase (F23)	Fragment	5 (5b)	
588	Pottery (W6)	Lamp (P6)	Whole	5 (5b)	
589	Pottery (H8)	Saucer lamp (P27)	Whole	5 (5b)	
1484	Pottery (various)	7 lamps	Mostly whole	5 (5b)	
677	Bronze	Waster	Portion?	5 (5b)	
668	Pottery (R17)	Bowl (C23)	Whole	4 (5c)	
344	Sandstone	Decorated lintel	Whole	4 (5c)	6e
1339	Pottery (R11)	Footed bowl (D15)	Fragment	?	
1365	Pottery (R27)	Footed bowl (D23)	Portion	?	
1366	Pottery (W14)	Vase (?)	Fragment	?	

[1] Numbers in parentheses in this column identify pottery ware numbers.
[2] Numbers in parentheses in this column identify pottery vessel forms.
[3] (R) means restored.

after a considerably hiatus. It was erected directly on the denuded stumps of the previous Church XXXVI, and in the beginning reproduced almost exactly the plan of its predecessor. It was, as before, a typical example of Classic Nubian Type 3c (Adams 1965, 114-16). As with its predecessor, its closest parallels were to the Western Church at Abdallah Nirqi (Castiglione *et al.* 1974, 324), Church 21-R-44 at Debeira West (Shinnie and Shinnie 1978, 29-33), and Church 11-I-1 at Murshid West (Mills and Nordström 1966, 14; author's unpublished field notes).

The church was substantially modified when it was restored at the beginning of Phase 5, after an interval during which it had apparently suffered considerable damage. The reconstruction involved a number of interior changes meant to reinforce the building against the weight of drifted sand outside the north and west walls. There were also at least two changes that were, seemingly, meant to give the church the characteristics of other late Nubian churches of Type 4. The apse was abandoned and filled with rubble, providing the *haikal* with a straight eastern wall, and the church was apparently provided with a tall central cupola, projecting above the roof line of the surrounding rooms. These innovations, characteristic of nearly all churches of Type 4, are believed to have been inspired by contemporary architectural trends in Greece and the Levant (Adams 1965, 118).

Thus, while the church of Phases 3 and 4 had conformed to the basilican Type 3c, the modifications of Phase 5 had the effect of converting it, at least in part, to a church of Type 4. Early Nubian churches were frequently converted in the course of time, from Type 1 to Type 2 and from Type 2 to Type 3, but Meinarti represents the only known instance in which a Type 3 church was converted to Type 4. There are, as a result, no close parallels to the church in its final stage of transformation.

Murals and inscriptions

Murals and inscriptions, found in several buildings at Meinarti, were assigned numbers in a single series. Numbers 60 to 75 were assigned to the murals in the church.

Church VI was decorated with murals at least three times, the later paintings being executed on plaster laid directly over the earlier ones. It seems a reasonable inference that the entire church interior was decorated, except for the two western corner rooms where no traces of either painting or whitewash were observable. The paintings however were preserved only in the western portions of the nave and aisles, where the walls still stood to a considerable height, and even in these places they were in very fragmentary condition. The uppermost part was not preserved in any painting, and the lower portions of several showed extensive water damage, as the church was apparently invaded by a flood at least once subsequent to its abandonment.

The second and third layers of decoration were done during Phase 5, but the earliest was clearly done when the church was first built, at Phase 4. This was demonstrated by the fact that the surviving remnants of the earliest murals were preserved underneath buttresses that had been built up against them when the church was reinforced at

the beginning of Phase 5. Locations of all the murals are shown in Figure 15.

Reproductions of four of the paintings are shown in colored Plate I. These are not direct photographs; they are copies of miniature painted reproductions that were made by Sayyed Abdel Rahim Hag el-Amin, while the paintings were still *in situ* on the walls. Subsequently, a few of the better-preserved ones (specifically, nos 64, 66, and 72-74) were removed and conserved by Mr. Jozef Gazy, of the Polish Archaeological Mission at Faras. They are now in the National Museum in Khartoum

Phase 4 murals and inscriptions

Five fragments attributable to Phase 4 were preserved. They were almost certainly executed when Church VI was first constructed, at Subphase 4a, and thereafter remained visible until the church was reconstructed at Subphase 5a. The designs were executed mainly in red and yellow, with a sparing use of black for outlining and detail, on a pale lavender or grey background.[11]

No. 60 was located on the south face of the northeast nave pier, prior to the time when it was reinforced at Phase 5. All that survived was a small fragment of painting in red and yellow; the design could not be made out. Probably, like many murals on narrow piers, it showed a single standing figure. Beneath it was an inscription, in black letters 2cm high, which was not decipherable.

No. 63 was executed on the north wall of the north aisle, where it was later partly cut away and partly covered over by a reinforcing arch. The surviving remnant showed part of the body and wings of a robed, winged figure. The robe was red, with folds indicated in black, and was bordered by a yellow band with superimposed red spots. The wings had vertical stripes of red and yellow. Only the middle part of the torso was preserved. The upper part had been destroyed by erosion, and the lower part was deliberately cut away to provide a bonding surface for a relieving arch built at Phase 5. The location and size of the surviving portion suggested that the original painting must have been very tall.

No. 66 , shown in Plate Ia, was preserved behind a later reinforcing wall in the north aisle. It is by far the most interesting of the Phase 4 paintings. The surviving portion shows two or more figures, of indeterminable sex, wearing red skirts but with bare arms. In front of them to the right are two apparent males wearing red and white robes, and still further to the right is the remnant of a winged figure with a halo. The figures at the center seem to be holding between them either a severed, bearded human head, or the head of a supine man being carried, or possibly lying on a bed. The upper part of the painting had been destroyed by erosion, and the lower part by water damage. The painting is remarkable for the crude execution of the figures' hands, as well as of the supine head. Beneath the painting was a short, complete inscription of two lines, which was unfortunately destroyed in the process of conservation. The painting was removed and

---

[11] For additional discussion of the murals see Adams 1999.

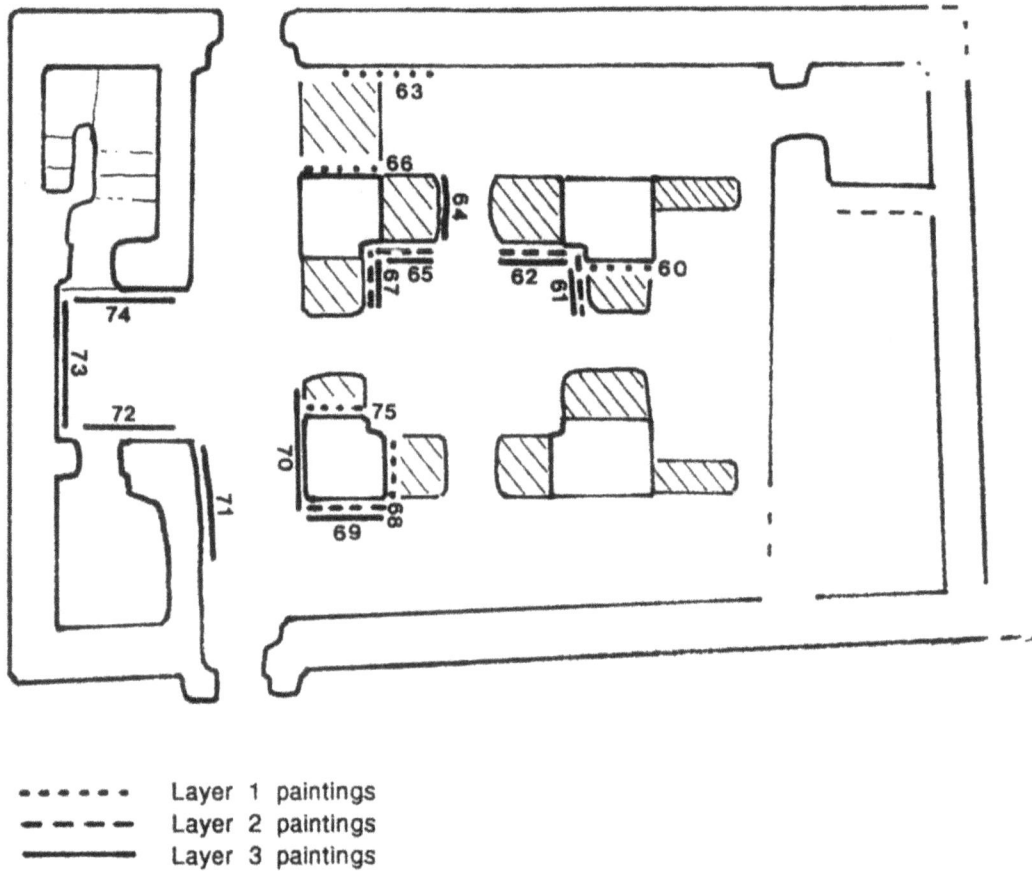

Figure 15. Plan of Church VI, to show locations of mural paintings. Paintings of Layer 1 were executed at Phase 4; those of Layers 2 and 3 were overpainted at Phase 5.

conserved by Mr. Gazy.[12]

No. 68. Removal of a later buttress adjoining the southwest nave pier revealed lavender or grey plaster having part of an incised graffito, but no traces of painting.

No. 75 was also preserved on the southwest nave pier, on its north face. The remnant appeared to show part of a standing figure, whose robe was decorated down the center with a yellow band bordered by pairs of red lines, and with superimposed red circles outlined in black.

Subphase 5a murals and inscriptions

Church VI was replastered throughout with a hard, salmon-pink plaster when it was rebuilt at Subphase 5a, and the second set of murals was presumably executed at that time. Their remains only came to light when the later paintings of Subphase 5c had been removed, and they were, for obvious reasons, extremely fragmentary. In no case is it possible to give a complete description of the original design.[13]

No. 61 was an inscription of five or more lines, on the inner side of the northeast nave pier, just at the top of the pulpit. The letters were in black, about 5cm high. The full text seems to have been preserved, but only a few remnants could be deciphered. Professor G. M. Browne writes

that "I think that it is Greek. I see tos and pros (in lines 3 and 5 respectively), and it is just possible that line 1 should read tou ou(ran)ou."[14]

No. 62 was a mural, also on the inner side of the northeast nave pier, alongside the pulpit. Only a few very faded scraps survived. The painting seems to have shown a robed figure wearing a garment of purplish red, with darker outlining in the same color.

No. 65 was a mural on the inner face of the northwest nave pier, facing south. The tiny surviving fragment seemed to show a round object, possibly a shield or a flower, executed in red, black, and blue.

No. 67 , also on the inner face of the northwest nave pier, had been a mural showing a standing figure wearing a cape, and with a halo. The face was not preserved. The colors were the same as in No. 65, and it is possible that these two paintings were parts of the same original composition, since they occupied adjoining sections of wall.

No. 69a was a mural painted on the outer side of the southwest nave pier. Nothing survived except a small fragment of a design in red.

Subphase 5c murals and inscriptions

These, like their predecessors, survived only in the western part of the building, where the walls were preserved to a sufficient height. All of them were fragmentary, and

[12] For colored illustrations see Colored Plate 1a, and Adams 1999, pl. 1.

[13] Some of the paintings were previously discussed in Adams 1999, 8-9.

[14] Personal communication of 17 May 1999.

all had been defaced by marauders. They were nevertheless more complete than any of the earlier paintings, and three of them were deemed worthy of conservation by Mr. Jozef Gazy. They are now in the National Museum in Khartoum. Positions of the surviving paintings in the church are shown in Figure 15.[15]

No. 64, shown in Plate Ib, was painted on the outer end of an extension that had been added to the northwest nave pier. The surviving portion shows the head and upper body of a standing man, holding a lance or staff vertically in his right hand and possibly a large round shield in his left. The figure is shown in full face and wears some kind of a tight-fitting headdress, with a streamer flying out from it at the figure's left. The lower part of the figure was preserved at least down to the knees, but was too water-damaged to be recognizable. The eyes had been gouged out by vandals.[16]

The colors are predominantly red and yellow, but include also blue and black. There was an inscription of at least six lines, in Old Nubian, to the right of the head (Plate 7a), and parts of two others to the left. The name of St. Menas was recognized by Prof. Fritz Hintze, who saw the painting *in situ*, yet the figure is clearly lacking a halo. Prof. G. Michael Browne, who saw a photograph of a part of the inscription, writes that it "...is clearly Old Nubian: the plural marker -*gou*- appears twice in [the inscription to the right of the figure], and [the inscription at the left] has *eissn*, "behold," four lines from the end. I cannot see any indication that Menas is mentioned."[17] The painting was removed and conserved by Mr. Jozef Gazy, and is now in the National Museum in Khartoum.

No. 69b, on the south side of the southwest nave pier, was painted directly over No. 69a. Nothing survived except some streaks of yellow on a white background.

No. 70 occupied the whole west face of the southwest nave pier, but was very faded and indistinct. The surviving fragments apparently showed the robe of a standing figure, the garment being dark red edged in black. To the figure's right as well as below it were remnants of one or more long inscriptions in black, but little could be made of them. Professor Browne has written that it "is also Old Nubian, I believe; at least the appearance of -*oul*- in line 5 so suggests."[18]

No. 71 occupied a considerable part of the west wall of the south aisle, but was also very indistinct. There were large areas of red hatching on a yellow background, which almost certainly represented part of a garment. In the surviving portion, black was used only for outlining.

No. 72 was painted high on the south wall at the west end of the nave, directly over the doorway to the southwest corner room. The surviving portion showed the upper torso of a figure having very large, pale yellow wings outlined in black. Only the middle parts of the wings and the left side of the torso were preserved. The figure wore a robe which was elaborately designed in red and yellow. To the figure's right were fragments of at least two fairly long inscriptions, in black (Plate 7b). This painting and inscriptions were removed and conserved by Mr. Gazy.

Of the inscriptions, Professor Browne writes: "The upper, larger inscription, in Old Nubian, concerns the archangel Michael. Line 3 runs '. . . let us do . . . , and my Michael will (save?) me;' line 5 may be translated: 'no one who is in . . . will be separated from Michael.' Line 6 is a Greek insert: 'Lord Jesus Christ, guard, protect, and help . . .,' and 'of Michael' (in Old Nubian) appears in line 8. The next 6 lines are in Old Nubian and Greek, but I can make little out of them.

"The lower part of [no. 72], mainly in Old Nubian, begins with an invocation in Greek: 'Master, my God and my Lord and my fathers' <Lord> sail with me . . .' Old Nubian follows, but I can give a translation only of a small part: ' . . . if he hopes in you, if he is in a form of . . ., if he is in illness, an envious person . . . I will save (him), in the power . . . .' The last line is in Greek: ' . . . compassionate and only-begotten Son and Holy Spirit: Michael has . . . .' It is followed by a subscription in Greek: 'I, Raphaelaña son of Abraham, the Priest, wrote (this).' To the right of the text there is a similar note: 'I, Raphaelaña, the son <of Abraham>, the Great Priest, wrote this.'" [19]

No. 73, shown in Plate Ic, was located high on the west wall of the nave, and was the best preserved of the Meinarti murals. It was painted directly over the blockage that had been inserted in the original west window. The painting shows the head and upper body of what was perhaps a winged figure, executed almost entirely in red and yellow. The face is largely framed by red hair, apparently with a topknot, and this in turn is surrounded by a yellow halo. The figure wears a gown of yellow, with red piping, and with a kind of red bib at the upper front. In terms of its stylistic simplicity this painting stands out from the other Church VI murals, and the absence of black is surprising. This painting also was conserved by Mr. Gazy.[20]

No. 74, shown in Plate Id, was painted on the north wall at the west end of the nave, directly above the doorway to the stair chamber. It is the most iconographically familiar of the Meinarti paintings, showing the traditional head and shoulders of Christ in a *mandorla*, with wing-like figures radiating outward from it and crossing one another.[21] The painting is nevertheless unusual in that it lacks the heads of the Four Living Creatures, which are usually shown adjoining the *mandorla* at its four corners.[22]

The face and bare upper chest of Christ are white, with the facial features indicated in black, although these had been largely defaced. Black hair surrounds the face all around, and this is surrounded in turn by a golden halo, with white cross arms radiating at the sides and, probably, the top. The figure wears a dark red robe with fine black

---

[15] Some of the paintings were previously discussed in Adams 1999, 9-10,

[16] For an illustration see Colored Plate 1b.

[17] Personal communication.

[18] *Ibid*.

[19] *Ibid*.

[20] For an illustration see Colored Plate 1c.

[21] For many parallel examples see Donadoni 1970, pl. 192; Griffith 1928, pl. XXXIX; Michałowski and Gerster 1967, pls. 44, 87-89; Monneret de Villard 1957, vol. IV, pls. CLIV, CLXXI; Van Moorsel *et al.* 1975, pls. 57, 69, 78; and Adams 1994b, pl. 3.3f.

[22] For an illustration see Colored Plate 1d.

stripes. The wing-like elements radiating outward from the *mandorla* are executed in yellow, with red cross-hatching and black bordering. Unique to this painting is the use of pale lavender as a background color within the *mandorla*, and also in some but not all of the areas between the radiating wings. There were fragments of a large inscription in black directly below the painting, and other shorter ones, possibly done later, at its left. This painting also was conserved by Mr. Gazy.

Of the inscription Professor Browne writes that "74 is likewise Old Nubian: the derivative suffix -*ka* appears in line 1, and the future marker -*dra* appears in the penultimate line."[23]

Comparisons and discussion of the murals

The few and fragmentary murals at Meinarti do not afford much basis for comparison with other churches. The figure in No. 64, with its lance in hand and its head scarf streaming out in the wind, bears some resemblance to the cavalier saints that were popular in late Nubian church art (see Adams 1977, 484).[24] If this is true, then the identification with St. Menas, tentatively suggested by Prof. Fritz Hintze, would be appropriate (cf. du Bourguet 1991, 534). On the other hand this painting was made on the narrow end of one of the nave piers, where there was almost surely no room for a representation of a horse.

The winged (?) figure shown in No. 73 seems to have a large topknot at the top of the head; in this and other respects it bears a considerable resemblance to two archangels, identified by name as Michael and Gabriel, painted in the Faras Cathedral (Michałowski and Gerster 1967, esp. pls 23-25). Similarities in the representation of the facial features are particularly striking. However the figures at Faras are without haloes, while at Meinarti the halo is unmistakable.

No. 74, the head of Christ within a *mandorla*, surrounded by radiating, wing-like elements, is the most immediately recognizable of the Meinarti murals. Variants of the design have been found in just about every decorated church in Nubia, including Tamit (Monneret de Villard 1957, pl. CLIV), the Faras Rivergate Church (Griffith 1926, pl. LVII), the Faras Cathedral (Michałowski and Gerster 1967, pls 44, 87-89), Abdel Qadir (Griffith 1928, pl. XXXIX; Monneret de Villard 1957, pl. CLXXX), Sonqi Tino (Donadoni 1970, pl. 192), and Kulubnarti (Adams 1994b, 161 and pl. 3.3f). The Meinarti representation is however unique in lacking the heads of the Four Living Creatures (man, eagle, bull, and lion) who are usually thought to symbolize the four evangelists (for discussion see Van Moorsel *et al.* 1975, 99, 112).

No. 66, with its representation of a supine, bearded human head, is surely the most unusual and most interesting of the Meinarti murals. At the time of its discovery it was believed to be unique among Nubian church murals (cf. Adams 1999, 8). However, it bears some affinity to two paintings recently discovered at Old Dongola, which

are believed to represent the preparation of a body for burial (Martens-Czarnecka 1998, 100-102). The resemblance is by no means exact, for in the Dongola paintings the full body of the deceased is visible, while in the Meinarti example only the head is visible, while the remainder is hidden behind the attendants. Nevertheless, the preparation of a body for burial is perhaps the likeliest explanation for the Meinarti painting as well.

No. 66 is the only painting from the original program of church decoration (at Subphase 4a) of which any substantial portion survived. Apart from the subject matter, it is remarkable also for the crudeness of is execution.

The stylistic features of late Nubian church decoration, subsequent to the abandonment of the Faras Cathedral, have yet to be fully studied.[25] However, numerous examples have been recorded from Tamit (Monneret de Villard 1957, pls CLVII-CLXV),[26] from Faras (Griffith 1926, pls 34-5; Michałowski 1961, pl. 66), from Abdel Qadir (Griffith 1928, 69-78 and pls. XXXI-XLVII; Monneret de Villard 1957, pls CLXXIV-CLXXX), from Qasr Ico (Presedo Velo 1963, 36-9 and pls I-V); from Kulubnarti (Adams 1994b, 155-65 and pls 3.3a-f and 3.4a-d) and Old Dongola (Martens-Czarnecka 1997; 1998). None of these paintings show more than a small fraction of the stylistic elaboration seen in the latest Faras Cathedral paintings, which Michałowski identified as exhibiting the Multicolored Style (Michałowski 1970, 15). It may be doubted however if the Faras Cathedral was ever typical; as the most important cathedral in its region it was probably far more elaborately decorated than were contemporary parish churches.

Martens-Czarnecka has observed that "The late period features the activity of many local painters, which is made obvious by the different styles of decoration in certain particular churches. The artistic value of the paintings of that period is very different, which makes it very difficult to investigate the style of that painting" (Martens-Czarnecka 1992, 307). This seems adequately to characterize the problem raised by the Meinarti paintings. Apart from the lack of minute elaboration (particularly in the rendering of garments), the single most conspicuous characteristic of all the late paintings would appear to be the preponderance of yellow. Red appears as the most common secondary color, with black used mainly for outlining, and blue comparatively rare (cf. Adams 1994b, 164).

Concluding summary and discussion

As an institution, the Meinarti Church had one of the longest histories of any church in Nubia. Its total life span was about seven hundred years, beginning probably within the first century of Nubian Christianity, and persisting until

[23] *Ibid.*

[24] cf. in particular paintings nos 30 and 41 at Abdel Qadir (Griffith 1928, pls XXXV and XLIII).

[25] The valuable survey undertaken by Martens-Czarnecka (1992) includes Classic as well as Late Christian painting under the heading "late."

[26] Monneret de Villard (1935, 158) dated the Church of the Angels at Tamit between the ninth and eleventh centuries, but this is almost certainly incorrect. I identified the church as a late type on architectural grounds (Adams 1965, 138), and this seems to be confirmed also by the style of the paintings.

nearly the last century. It may have been the only church in the region that was totally rebuilt not once but twice.

Evolution of the plan

Subphase 3a. The earliest version of the church (Church XXXVIII) was built at the beginning of Phase 3, when Meinarti was reoccupied after an interval of abandonment. It was atypical for its time, both because of its notably skewed plan and because of the unusual arrangement of western rooms, where there may have been a narthex. The skewed plan was exhibited also in three very early churches in the Faras area,[27] but it was more extreme at Meinarti than in any of the others. The angle between end walls and side walls departed from a true right angle by almost 20°. Another highly unusual feature of the first church was the cobblestone floor, having a "mosaic" cross design in the middle of the nave.[28] In other respects, however, the interior arrangements at the east end of Church XXXVIII were typical of early Nubian churches of Type 2b (Adams 1965, 108-10).

The skewed plan at Meinarti and at the three Faras churches was certainly not a reflection of architectural incompetence, for many of the houses built at Meinarti at the same time had regularly rectangular plans, as did most early Nubian churches. It must therefore have had some symbolic or iconic significance, which today cannot be guessed. However, it must have been perceived later as undesirable, since both the first Meinarti church and the first Faras Cathedral were torn down and rebuilt from scratch, after a century or so. The two other churches in the Faras area however were never rebuilt.

Subphases 3b-3d. After perhaps a century, the original church was leveled almost to the foundations, and was overbuilt by a regularly rectangular building (Church XXXVI). As originally constructed at Subphase 3b this was a typical example of Type 2b, except perhaps for the absence of a pulpit and of a western stairway. At Subphase 3c the interior was modified by the building of a tribune in the apse, the screening off of the *haikal* and of a vestibule in the north aisle, and the construction of a pulpit beside the northeast nave pier. These changes in effect converted the church from Type 2b to Type 3c (Adams 1965, 114-16). Similar changes were made in many other Lower Nubian churches at about the same time; specifically at Arminna (Trigger 1967, 12-14), Qustul (Clarke 1912, 73; Monneret de Villard 1935, 181-3), Faras West (Mileham 1910, 27-36; Griffith 1927, 93-4; Monneret de Villard 1935, 190-93), Faras East (Mileham 1910, 36-8; Clarke 1912, 66-70; Monneret de Villard 1935, 188), Serra (Mileham 1910, 45-7; Clarke 1912, 59-62; Monneret de Villard 1935, 204-5; Gardberg 1970, 24-5), Debeira West (Mileham 1910, 14-21; Clarke 1912, 59-62; Monneret de Villard 1935, 206-9; Shinnie and Shinnie 1970, 17-19), Sahaba (Monneret de Villard 1935, 211; Gardberg 1970, 27-35), and Meili Island (Adams and Nordström 1963,

34, 41). Presumably, they reflected a change in the basic nature of the holy service, a portion of which was hereafter performed behind the closed door of the *haikal,* out of sight of the congregation (Adams 1965, 121).

Whether or not the first two Meinarti churches were decorated with murals could not be determined, due to the very denuded condition of the walls.

Phase 4. At the end of Phase 3 Meinarti was once again abandoned for a time, possibly as a result of extensive flood damage. When the inhabitants returned, at the beginning of Phase 4, they rebuilt the church for a second time (as Church VI), directly on the denuded stumps of its predecessor. In the beginning the new building reproduced almost exactly the plan of the old, the main innovation being the installation of a stairway in the northwest corner room. The earliest identifiable altar also belongs to Church VI, although it seems likely that there were altars in the previous churches also. The building interior was whitewashed and adorned with colored murals, though only a few small remnants of these had survived through later alterations. After its reconstruction the church persisted in use for about three and a half centuries, through the whole of Phases 4 and 5.

Subphase 4c. There were no significant changes at Subphase 4b, but at Subphase 4c a number of minor interior alterations were made. A broad brick bench, or possibly a partition wall, was built between the northeastern and northwestern nave piers, so that it separated most of the north aisle from the nave. At the west end of the nave, an additional short section of wall was built, which closed off most of the passage from the north aisle to the nave here as well. These changes suggest the possibility that the north aisle at this time was reserved for votaries who were not allowed access to the remainder of the church. Additionally, a small enclosure like a votive chapel was built adjoining the north wall of the north aisle, near its eastern end. None of these changes however was retained when the church was renovated for the last time at Phase 5.

Phase 5. The last major modifications in the church took place at the beginning of Phase 5; once again following a period of abandonment when the building had suffered damage. The most conspicuous changes were those required to reinforce the building against the deep buildup of sand along the exterior walls, particularly on the north and west. A very stout cross-wall was run across the north aisle, relieving the pressure on the north wall, and a relieving arch was installed in the southwest corner room, to help bear the pressure of sand against the west wall. In addition, the larger windows in the north and west walls were solidly blocked with brick masonry, since sand had accumulated on the outside up to the level of their sills.

Two major changes were made that seem to have been dictated by current architectural fashion rather than by structural requirements. These were the closing off of the former apse, leaving the church with a rectangular *haikal,* and, apparently, the building of a tall central cupola, projecting above the rest of the roof line. These were characteristic features of the late Nubian churches of Type 4 (Adams 1965, 116-19). All or nearly all of the churches

---

[27] The first cathedral (Michałowski and Gerster 1967, 48), the South Desert Church (Mileham 1910, pl. 17), and the North Church at Faras East (Mileham 1910, pl. 23)

[28] A few other examples of mosaic church floors are known in the Old Dongola area; see Welsby 2002, 224.

built in Nubia after the twelfth century were of this type, which seems to have been influenced by concurrent architectural developments in Greece and the Levant (Adams 1965, 123). The Type 4 churches were sufficiently distinct from all of their predecessors so that they were already recognized as a separate type (Type B) by Somers Clarke, at the beginning of the twentieth century (Clarke 1912, 32). Especially well preserved exemplars of the type were the Cupola Church at Qasr Ibrim (Clarke 1912, 81 and pl. 19; Monneret de Villard 1935, vol. 1, 109-10; vol. 2, pl. LV); the North Church at Serra East (Mileham 1910, 32-5 and pls. 32-5; Clarke 1912, 64-5; Griffith 1927, 100 and pl. 78, 2; Monneret de Villard 1935, vol. 1, 192, 196; vol. 2, 90); and the churches at Qasr Ico (Presedo Velo 1963, 16-28), and Kulubnarti (Clarke 1912, 49-50; Monneret de Villard 1935, 234; Adams 1994b, 149-83).

At the time of rebuilding, the whole church interior was given a coat of hard salmon-pink plaster, on which new murals were painted, largely obscuring the earlier ones. These remained through Subphases 5a and 5b, but at Subphase 5c the building was given a new coat of whitewash, on which a final set of murals was executed.

Most of the churches of Early and Classic Christian types (i.e. Types 2 and 3) were abandoned at the beginning of the Late Christian period. A few remained in use, alongside the newly built structures of Type 4. The Meinarti church was however the only one in which there was any effort to convert the building, from Type 3 to Type 4. In the last centuries of its use, it was thus unique in its combination of Type 3c and Type 4 characteristics.

Phase 6. The island of Meinarti was temporarily seized by Beni Ikrima nomads in 1365. They seem to have penned their sheep and goats in some of the Late Christian houses, and it was surely they who defaced the murals both in the church and in one of the secular buildings (Building III; see *Meinarti III*, 34). That this took place during the Beni Ikrima incursion, and not after the final abandonment of the site, was demonstrated by the fact that the sanded-up remains of Building III were later overbuilt by the "castle-house" (Building I) of Phase 6, which itself bore Christian inscriptions.

The Beni Ikrima occupation may not have lasted very long, but it seemed that the Meinarti villagers remained away for at least a generation (see *Meinarti III*, 97). On their return, they built the "castle-house" directly on top of the sanded-up Building III. The defaced murals in the church however were never repaired, and this suggests the probability that the building was not restored to use after the villagers returned.

When found, the doorways from the nave to the two western corner rooms were partially blocked with crudely piled stones, probably indicative of their use as animal pens. This was a common fate of Nubian churches in the post-Christian period (cf. Adams 1994b, 155). Whether the stones at Meinarti were the work of the Beni Ikrima, or were put in at a later date, could not of course be determined.

I suspect that, during the last century of Nubian Christianity, the Meinarti parishioners were served by the little church newly built at Abdel Qadir, on the nearby West Bank (Griffith 1928). This building, of a very late type which I have called Type 5 (Adams 1965, 119-20) stood by itself on a rocky shelf, and there were no other structures of Late Christian date anywhere within ten kilometers.[29] A somewhat detached location, apart from any settlement, was characteristic of many late Nubian churches of Type 4; it was perhaps a response to the fact that the churches were subject to depredation by Muslim raiders. An isolated location might therefore serve to deflect attention away from the actual villages (Adams 1977, 519).

External changes

Unlike internal modifications, which were often dictated by liturgical concerns, changes around the outside of the church were the result purely of pragmatic considerations. They seem to have gone on more or less continually throughout the entire history of the three Meinarti churches. First and foremost, they were necessitated by the continual and inexorable buildup of drifted sand, especially against the windward (north and west) walls. The earliest Meinarti church, when first built, had stood on a raised platform well above the natural ground level. Seven centuries later, the thresholds of the last church doorways were three meters below the surrounding ground level. The church had become to all intents and purposes a subterranean building.

Because of the sloping ground on which it was built, Church XXXVIII was constructed on a raised platform of hard mud, which at the eastern end stood about 1.5m above the natural ground level. At the western end however it was essentially flush with the natural ground. The doorways in the north and south walls, although they were near the western end of the building, were in the beginning well above ground level, and it was necessary to provide them with built-up approach ramps, so that persons entering the church would not have a long step up.

When the church was rebuilt as Church XXXVI, at Subphase 3b, it was still on an elevated platform, and the approach ramps to the doorways were still needed. They were in fact extended eastward until they adjoined the full length of the north and south walls. By the final rebuilding at Subphase 4a (as Church VI), however, sand had accumulated up to the tops of the surrounding platform, except at the southeast corner. Elsewhere, the base of the church walls was effectively at the level of the ground surface outside. The north and south doorways had now to be provided with new, elevated thresholds to prevent the drifting of sand into the building, and each was therefore adjoined on the outside by a small landing of packed mud.

From that time onward, the story was one of continual and increasingly drastic steps to protect the church doorways. The landing adjoining the north doorway, originally at ground level, was later surrounded on three sides by a sand-restraining wall, and in later centuries this was heightened at least twice, until its top was over 1.6m above the

[29] We were able to establish this with confidence because we surveyed the area around Abdel Qadir very intensely in the course of the West Bank Survey; see Adams and Nordström 1963, 10-15.

original level of the landing. The height of the doorway itself was reduced several times by raising the threshold, until in the end it was no more than 1.05m high. Finally, at Subphase 5c, the villagers gave up the fight altogether, and blocked the north doorway with masonry.

Sand accumulation on the southern, lee side of the church was somewhat slower, but here also an increasingly long descent was necessary to reach the doorway. At Subphase 5a, when Church VI was first built, there were two descending steps into the doorway, and thereafter they were continually added to. There were three steps at Subphase 4b, four steps at Subphase 4c, at least six steps at Subphase 5a, and at least eight steps at Subphase 5b. At Subphase 5c, the final episode of occupation, the entire stairway was rebuilt, at a much steeper angle than before. There were surviving portions of eight steps, but the extent of the retaining wall surrounding them showed that several additional steps had been lost at the top end (Plate 5a). The height of the south doorway was also reduced more than once, until at the end it was 1.25m high.

Other measures of defense against the sand included the blocking of the original, large windows in the north and west walls, and the building, and subsequent heightening, of a restraining wall to prevent the drifting of sand into the small window in the southwest corner of the church.

Not all the exterior changes were related to sand defense. At several stages in its history the church was adjoined by either platforms or slightly raised mastabas, especially along its north, west, and south walls. There was an elevated platform extending all around the north, east, and south walls of Church XXXVI at Subphases 3b, 3c, and 3d. By the time when Church VI was overbuilt, at Subphase 4a, these had disappeared under drifted sand, but the new church was adjoined by low, stone-built mastabas along its north and west sides, and along the south side as far as the doorway. These in their turn were buried by the time of Subphase 4c, and a new mud-built mastaba was then constructed along the southern half of the west wall. After this was buried, at Phase 5, no more mastabas were built. It is surmised that these features were meant simply to provide convenient seating for persons wishing to sit against the church wall – as many persons do today in the Coptic churches of Ethiopia. However, they may also have served to prevent grave-digging immediately alongside the walls or they might have provided some protection against flood damage.

In the church of Subphases 3b and 3c (Church XXXVI), there was a small rectangular mass of brick masonry, 80cm wide and 1.2m long, adjoining the church wall beside the south doorway. By the time of Phase 4 it was sanded over, but a larger mass of masonry, measuring 1.75 x 2m, was built beside the north doorway of the new Church VI. As originally constructed it was 1.25m high, but the height was increased when, at Phase 5, drifted sand had reached the level of the original top. It is surmised that these features may have been external pulpits, where a lesson could be read to persons outside the church - again by analogy with a feature found in Ethiopian churches.

Tomb superstructures began to be built close to the northern, eastern, and southern church walls at Subphase 4a, and their number steadily increased thereafter, apparently reaching a maximum at Subphase 4c. Thereafter one after another they were sanded over and buried, and at a later date new graves were often intruded into them. It appears however that most of the later tombs, built at Phases 5 and 6, did not have superstructures. Only two superstructures were ever built directly adjoining the church wall. Tomb superstructures and other funerary features will be much more fully discussed in the next chapter.

Overall comparisons

Overall, the two churches that exhibit the most suggestive comparisons with Meinarti are those of Sahaba (Gardberg 1970, 27-37) and Abdallah Nirqi (Van Moorsel et al. 1975), simply because they too had very long histories.

Sahaba began its life as a church of Type 2a, a very distinctive early type having direct passages from the eastern corner rooms to the nave. Only a few examples of this type were ever built (Adams 1965, 107-8, 135). The Sahaba church later underwent the usual conversions, having a tribune built within the apse, and the *haikal* screened off at the west, north, and south, which converted it to a church of Type 3a (Adams 1965, 110-12). In addition an eastern passage, behind the apse, seems to have been built at some time after the original construction (Gardberg 1970, 33-4), and doorways were then cut through the original east wall. This may have been the case at Meinarti also when Church XXXVI was built, although the evidence was not conclusive. Sahaba, like Meinarti, originally had asymmetrically placed entrances to the western corner rooms. As at Meinarti, the original entrance to the northwest corner room was at the west end of the north aisle, but this was relocated to the nave when a stairway was later built in the northwest corner room.

There were nevertheless important differences between the Sahaba and Meinarti churches. At Sahaba the nave was separated from the aisles by elongate piers, which undoubtedly supported arcading, as was the case in the first Meinarti church (Church XXXVIII). However, the original piers at Sahaba were never replaced at a later date by short, L-shaped piers, as they were at Meinarti, indicating that the Sahaba church never had a central cupola. There was also no final closing off of the apse, as there was at Meinarti at Phase 5.

The author suggested an original building date at Sahaba (as I had also done independently) of A.D. 700 (Gardberg 1970, 27). On the basis of pottery finds I suggested, very tentatively, an abandonment date in the twelfth century (Adams 1965, 136).

Abdallah Nirqi resembled Meinarti more in its external than in its internal characteristics. It was built originally as a church of Type 2b, and the only later modification in the east end of the church was the screening of the *haikal*, which converted it to a church of Type 3b (Van Moorsel et al. 1975, 9). This paralleled the change at Meinarti, when Church XXXVI was converted at Subphase 3c (around A.D. 850). At Abdallah Nirqi however there was no later construction of a tribune, and the altar remained in its original location within the apse throughout the history of the building. An odd peculiarity, not observed in any other Nubian church, was that a passage was cut through directly from the northeast corner room to the apse, at some time after the original building (cf. Van Moorsel *et al.* 1975, 8, fig. 1). At the same time the original doorway to the northeast room from the aisle was blocked (*ibid.*, 14). This was the precise opposite of developments in other early Nubian churches (of Type 2a), where original doorways from the eastern corner rooms to the apse were later blocked (cf. Adams 1965, 112).

Like both Sahaba and Meinarti, the Abdallah Nirqi church originally had asymmetrically placed doorways to the western rooms, and here again the asymmetry was later corrected when the doorway to the northwest room was relocated from the north aisle to the nave. In this case however the change was not necessitated by the building of a stairway, because at Abdallah Nirqi the stairway was always in the southwest corner room (Van Moorsel *et al.* 1975, 15-17).

Externally, Abdallah Nirqi like Meinarti ended up deeply buried in sand, with a long descending stairway to the south doorway, while the north doorway was finally blocked altogether (*ibid.*, 9). Sahaba, despite its long history, did not have a similar problem, because like all structures on the East Bank it was on the lee side of the Nile, protected from the drifting dunes on the west side.[30]

The excavators have estimated that the Abdallah Nirqi church was built in the middle of the eighth century, and may have remained in use until the fifteenth (*ibid.*, 5). This dating seems consistent with the published pottery finds, which include types from every period from Early Christian to Terminal Christian (*ibid.*, pls 30-40). The building had, if this is true, the longest history of any church in Nubia, perhaps exceeding even that of the three Meinarti churches combined.

[30] The wind in Lower Nubia blows directly out of the north during most of the year. Since the Nile here flows in a northeasterly direction, however, sand piles up all along the west bank but does not carry across to the east bank (see Adams 1977, 34-5).

THE CEMETERY

Introduction

The Meinarti cemetery adjoined Church VI on its north, east, and south sides. On the north however its growth was always limited by the presence of neighboring buildings, and it never extended more than about 5m from the north church wall. On the east, the preserved remains extended eastward for about 15m, but there may have been additional tombs and/or burials farther east, that were destroyed by flooding. Since the cemetery ground had at all times a considerable downward slope from west to east, the tombs at the eastern end were exceptionally prone to flood destruction (see Plates 8a and 8d). On the south, the preserved tombs and burials extended southward from the church wall for a little over 30m at the time of maximum expansion, at the end of Subphase 4b (Figure 17 and Plate 8e).

From Subphase 4b onward, the growth of the cemetery was "upward" rather than outward. That is, later graves were dug directly into the sand that had accumulated over earlier ones, very frequently intruding upon the buried superstructures of earlier graves (cf. Plate 9). At the end, the latest graves were at a level at least 4m higher than the earliest ones. This pattern of vertical growth was a unique feature of the Meinarti cemetery, and called for an unorthodox excavation strategy that will be described in a later section.

We investigated the whole of the cemetery, insofar as it was preserved, except for a portion at the eastern end that was overgrown by dom palms. Our excavations uncovered 119 tombs with superstructures, 234 burials without superstructures, and three foetal burials in pots. All but one of the superstructures covered only a single interment; only Tomb 8 contained three bodies. It was also the only tomb at Meinarti having a subterranean vault, although Tombs T5, T6, and T7 all had vaulted chambers within the superstructure itself. In all other cases, burial was made in the usual excavated shaft.

Although Meinarti had been occupied since Meroitic times, and the first two churches were built at Phase 3, none of the graves uncovered by us could be dated before Phase 4. There are several possible explanations for this anomaly. One is that the superstructures of earlier tombs[1] were entirely swept away by the high floods that were prevalent during Early Christian times (see *Meinarti II*, 48-9). The burials themselves might also have been swept away, or they might have been at a greater depth than was reached by our excavations. If the latter were true, however, they would have been within the alluvial floodplain, which seems unlikely.

A more probable supposition is that the earlier inhabitants at Meinarti buried their dead at another locality. It might have been elsewhere on the island, although our

survey did not find any trace of it, or it might have been at the nearby site of Kor, on the West Bank, where there were already extensive cemeteries at the time when Meinarti was first settled.[2] In any case, the Early Christian inhabitants presumably continued to use the same cemetery as had their pagan ancestors until the time when Church VI was built, after which they began to bury their dead near that church. Once established, the cemetery beside Church VI remained in use at least through Phases 4 and 5, and probably also through Phase 6 – that is, until the final abandonment of the settlement.

Throughout its history of five or more centuries, the cemetery was subject to the same processes both of continual sand buildup and of periodic flood destruction that affected the houses and churches. As a result, it acquired a complex stratigraphy of its own, which was its most extraordinary feature (cf. Figure 3). The graves of Phase 4 were mostly dug into virgin soil, except on the immediate south side of the church where they were intruded into the sanded-up remains of Building XXXVII (described in the previous chapter). By the time of Phase 5, however, the earlier superstructures were nearly all sanded over, and the burials of Phase 5 were dug directly into the sand overlying the earlier graves. As a result of this process, no fewer than 15 of the Phase 4 superstructures had been disturbed by the subsequent intrusion of Phase 5 graves (cf. Plate 9). Although preservation at the uppermost levels was very poor, there was some evidence that the same process was repeated at Phase 6; that is, the Phase 6 graves were dug into deposit overlying the Phase 5 graves.

There is also a possibility that, in the latter part of Phase 5, the deeply buried graves at the southern end of the cemetery were overbuilt by Buildings VII and VIII. This would have been true had those two buildings had the usual rectangular plan. It could not be confirmed, however, because the more easterly portions of Buildings VII and VIII were not preserved (see *Meinarti III,* 28 and figure 8).

Preservation

The superstructures. All but one of the 119 Meinarti tomb superstructures were built of mud brick. Conditions of preservation were highly variable, as can be seen in Table 3 and in Plate 8. Thirty-one superstructures were intact or very nearly so, because they had become sanded over before they had suffered much damage. Another nine were intact except for the intrusion of later grave shafts into their tops (Plates 9b-9f). In the largest number of cases (38), however, the tops were partially denuded, evidently because they had become somewhat worn away before they were completely buried. This was probably due more

---

[1] The use of superstructures was usual in Early Christian cemeteries; see Adams 1998b, 19-20.

[2] Vercoutter (1955, 15) reported at Kor a cemetery "...de très basse époque, sans doute romaine."

to normal processes of surface deflation (a combination of wind and passing traffic) than to flooding. However, 11 tombs at the lower (eastern) end of the cemetery were extremely denuded, and this was probably due to flooding (see Plates 8a and 8d). Sixteen tombs had had large parts destroyed, either by flooding or by the intrusion of later graves, and fourteen survived only in small fragments.

TABLE 3. CONDITION OF SUPERSTRUCTURES IN THE MEINARTI CEMETERY

Intact or nearly intact	31
Intact except for intruded grave shaft	9
Top somewhat denuded	38
Very denuded	11
Partly destroyed	16
Only fragments remained	14

The burials. Conditions of preservation were variable in the case of the burials as well. All of the Phase 4 burials, and probably also those of Phase 5, had been subjected to intermittent soaking from high floods, so that the bones were often very soft and brittle. A number of burials had also been disturbed by the intrusion of later graves. The condition of preservation in the largest number of burials could be described as poor to fair. Good preservation was found mainly in the late burials of Phases 5 and 6, but a few of these were incomplete because they had been disturbed by surface deflation. It was nevertheless possible to carry out routine osteological examination in all but six of the interments, and in most cases to determine the sex and approximate age at death. Conditions of preservation for the burials are indicated in Table 9, far right column.

The excavation of the cemetery
The existence of the Meinarti cemetery did not become apparent until the second excavation season, because no grave superstructures were preserved at or near the pre-excavation ground surface. As we removed sand from the exterior walls of the church, however, we began encountering burials here and there. In most cases we could not recognize the existence of grave shafts until the bones themselves began to appear, because the late interments were made in soft, windblown sand fill.

Before long however we noted that some of the late burials had been intruded into buried brick structures, and these on further investigation proved to be the superstructures of much earlier graves. It then became apparent that the excavation of the cemetery could not proceed in the conventional way, by digging out individual graves while leaving the surrounding earth matrix undisturbed. If the earlier, buried superstructures were to be fully revealed and recorded, the entire overburden of sand, including whatever late burials it contained, would have to be removed. Accordingly, I adopted a somewhat unorthodox excavation procedure, in which the graves were dug out, and the surrounding earth matrix was removed, in one single operation. As soon as a grave shaft was identified, it was given a number, and one laborer was detailed to work within it. At the same time however other laborers were digging away the sand on either side of the grave. In this way it was possible fully to uncover the earlier superstructures, and to photograph and map the cemetery surface as it had existed at Phase 4 (shown especially in Plate 8).

The excavation of burials having superstructures proceeded as follows. Each superstructure was assigned a number, preceded by the letter "T," and this was written on a wooden stake driven into the ground just to the west of the structure. After demolition of the superstructure, as the excavation of the grave shaft proceeded downward, the stake was also progressively driven downward until the burial was encountered. This procedure made it possible to identify which burials went with which superstructures – something that might not otherwise have been easy, since many of the burials were crowded close together (cf. Plates 14e-f).

The procedure in the case of burials without superstructures was similar. As soon as a grave shaft was recognized, the burial was assigned a number, preceded by the letter "B." This again was written on a stake, driven into the ground just to the west of the shaft, and the stake was driven downward as the excavation proceeded, until the burial was reached.

This unorthodox method very much speeded up the work of excavation, but it had two other practical advantages as well. First, it allowed the burials, after cleaning, to be photographed, without the obscuring shadows that are inevitably present when burials are photographed in the bottom of a grave pit (cf. Plate 14). Second, it was infinitely more convenient for physical anthropologists to take anthropometric measurements and observations, without having to squat within the narrow confines of a grave. There was, of course, one disadvantage: the original depth of the grave shafts could not be recorded.

Because of the extreme time pressure confronting the Meinarti excavations, it was not my original intention to excavate the burials beneath the Phase 4 superstructures. I planned only to clear the ground surface on which they stood, and to photograph and map the structures. However, my anthropologist colleagues from the University of Colorado Expedition expressed a keen interest in studying the Meinarti skeletons, to augment a series of post-pharaonic skeletal material that they were assembling from their own excavations, a few kilometers to the north (see Armelagos et al. 1965). The unique stratification of the Meinarti cemetery offered them an unparalleled opportunity, not elsewhere possible, to place the graves in a chronological sequence, and hence to study differences in pathology and mortality between Early and Late Christian populations.

To accommodate their wish, I agreed to detail a part of the Meinarti labor force to the excavation of the graves, provided that my colleagues would undertake all the work of excavation supervision, exposing the bones, and collecting anthropometric information. Work proceeded in this fashion throughout the early weeks of 1964, and it is to my colleagues, Messrs. George Armelagos, George Ewing, and David Greene, that I owe the anthropometric information presented in this volume. All mapping and photography however was done by me.

Chronology and dating

Tombs with superstructures. The dating of tombs is usually a more difficult business than is the dating of houses – particularly in the case of Christian Nubian burials that contain no grave goods. At Meinarti, however, the dating of tombs with superstructures was facilitated by four factors. First, compacted occupation surfaces that had been identified and dated within the townsite could be followed into the cemetery as well; that is, they were the surfaces on which the superstructures were built. Second, those surfaces were liberally strewn with potsherds which further facilitated the dating process (cf. Adams 1986, 617-33). Third, a majority of tombs had a "lamp box" at the western end (especially visible in Plate 8f), and this in many cases still contained a votive lamp of a datable type. Failing any such evidence, a good many tombs could still be dated on the basis of direct superposition: Phase 4 tombs because they were overlain and sometimes disturbed by Phase 5 and Phase 6 tombs, and Phase 5 and 6 tombs because they were underlain by Phase 4 tombs. Only one tomb (T12) however could be precisely dated, because it still bore an affixed tombstone (Plate 13a).

With such evidence available, most of the Meinarti tombs with superstructures could be dated not only to a phase but to a subphase. The main exception occurred in the case of Subphases 4a and 4b, because Subphase 4a only lasted about a generation, and during that interval there was very little accumulation of sand. As a result, the superstructures of the two subphases were built essentially on the same ground surface, the growth of the cemetery having been horizontal rather than vertical. It is assumed that the tombs closest to the church walls were the earliest, while later burials were made at successively greater distances, but it was impossible to say where the tombs of Subphase 4a ended and those of Subphase 4b began. Throughout the discussion that follows, tombs and burials from the earlier part of Phase 4 will be described as belonging to "Subphase 4ab."

Only Tomb T11 could be assigned unequivocally to Subphase 4a, because it was built prior to the construction of an early reinforcing wall around the church. All the remainder of the stratigraphically earliest tomb superstructures were assigned only to Subphase 4ab, without more specific attribution to a subphase. By the time of Subphase 4c, however, sand had accumulated in the cemetery to a sufficient depth so that the Subphase 4c superstructures were built on a higher ground surface than their predecessors; they could therefore be distinguished on stratigraphic grounds (cf. especially Plate 9a). Burials

underlying the superstructures could, obviously, be assigned the same date as the superstructures, and they were given the same numbers as the superstructures, prefixed by the letter "T."

Burials without superstructures. The dating of graves without superstructures (about two-thirds of the total) was more problematical. Earlier burials, from Phase 4, could sometimes be dated by the ground surface from which they had been dug down. That is, if a grave shaft first became visible when the Subphase 4c surface was cleared, the burial was presumed to belong to Subphase 4c. If the shaft did not become visible until the Subphase 4ab ground surface was cleared, we assumed that the grave had been dug at Subphase 4ab and was already sanded over by the time of Subphase 4c. Some burials were also dated on the basis of their proximity to other burials at the same depth, that had been dated by their superstructures. Sometimes too it was evident that a grave shaft had been dug so as not to disturb an extant superstructure, which must therefore still have been exposed at the surface when the new grave was dug.

Later burials could sometimes be assigned to Phase 5 if they were intruded into Phase 4 superstructures (Plate 9), or were at the same depth as other burials that were. However, only about a score of burials could be assigned with some degree of confidence to Subphase 5a, and only three to Subphases 5b or 5c. None could be assigned with certainty to Phase 6. The burials in loose sand, encountered highest in the fill, could only be identified as "late," meaning probably either Subphases 5b or 5c, or Phase 6.

In sum, then, the Meinarti burials fall into four main chronological groups: a large group made up of burials attributable to Subphases 4a and 4b; a second large group attributable to Subphase 4c; a smaller group attributable to Subphase 5a; and a large group attributable only to Phases 5 and 6, but not to any specific subphase. There is also a small group of burials attributable to Phase 4 but not to a specific subphase. The totals for each group are shown in Table 4.

General features of the cemetery

The superstructures

Superstructures were by far the most interesting features of the Meinarti cemetery. Not only did the site exhibit a much greater variety of types than did any other Nubian cemetery, but most of them were types unique to this site (Plates 10-13).

Of the 119 surviving tomb superstructures, all but five

TABLE 4. NUMBERS OF DATED BURIALS, BY SUBPHASE OR PHASE

Subphases	With superstructures	Without superstructure	Foetus in pot	Total
Subphases 4ab	63	94	2	159
Subphase 4c	43	60	1	104
Subphase 5a	5	13		18
Late (Phase 5-6)	2	67		69
Uncertain	6			6
Totals	**119**	**234**	**3**	**356**

dated from Phase 4; that is, from the earlier period of the cemetery's use. Sixty-three structures could be assigned to Subphase 4a or 4b, and 43 structures to Subphase 4c. There is good evidence that the use of superstructures became less prevalent everywhere in Late Christian times (Adams 1998b, 19, 36), but it is nevertheless probable that some later superstructures at Meinarti were destroyed by surface erosion, or by *sebbakh* diggers, during and after Phase 6.

All but one of the Meinarti superstructures were built of mud and/or mud brick. The single most prevalent type, unique to Meinarti, was the cross-embossed mastaba, to be described below. There was a notable scarcity of flat brick or stone pavements, of the type predominant further south in Nubia (Adams *et al.* 1999, 16, 30-36), and also of the kind of loaf-shaped superstructures illustrated by Monneret de Villard from several sites (Monneret de Villard 1935, 127, 134, 136-7, 164). In addition to brick structures, one grave was covered by a flat pavement of stones.

Superstructures were used with almost equal frequency for male and for female adult burials; in fact, some of the most elaborate of all the superstructures were associated with females. There was a definite correlation between superstructures and age: the older the person at death, the more likelihood that he or she would be buried under a superstructure. It is an extraordinary fact nevertheless that nearly all of the largest superstructures (those of Type 1) were associated with the burials of young individuals, in their 20s or early 30s. Superstructures were used infrequently for adolescents and for infants at Subphases 4a and 4b, while thereafter they were almost entirely lacking in the case of infant burials. The distribution of tomb burials (i.e. those having superstructures) by age and sex is shown in Table 5.

Most but not all of the largest and most elaborate tomb superstructures were built close to the church walls, and all those that survived from Subphases 4a and 4b were on the north or northeast side of the building.

Structure types

The Meinarti tomb superstructures have been subdivided for descriptive convenience into eight major categories, and 25 subtypes, as shown in Figure 16 and described

TABLE 5. DISTRIBUTION OF TOMB BURIALS BY AGE AND SEX

Tomb type	Males	- Adults - Females	???	Adolescents	Infants	Total
1A	1	1				2
1B	1	3				4
1C	2	1				3
1X	2	2	1			5
2A	13	10	4	1		28
2B	1					1
2C		1				1
2D	1					1
2E	2					2
2F	1					1
2G	1					1
2X	2					2
3	2					2
4A			1		1	2
4X	15	14	6	2	1	38
5					5	5
6				2	1	3
7A					1	1
7B	1				1	2
7C					1	1
7D					1	1
8A		1				1
8B		1				1
Stone					1	1
Uncertain	2	1			1	4
Totals	47	35	13	5	14	114*

* This figure does not correspond to the total of superstructures because in five cases the burial was not found.

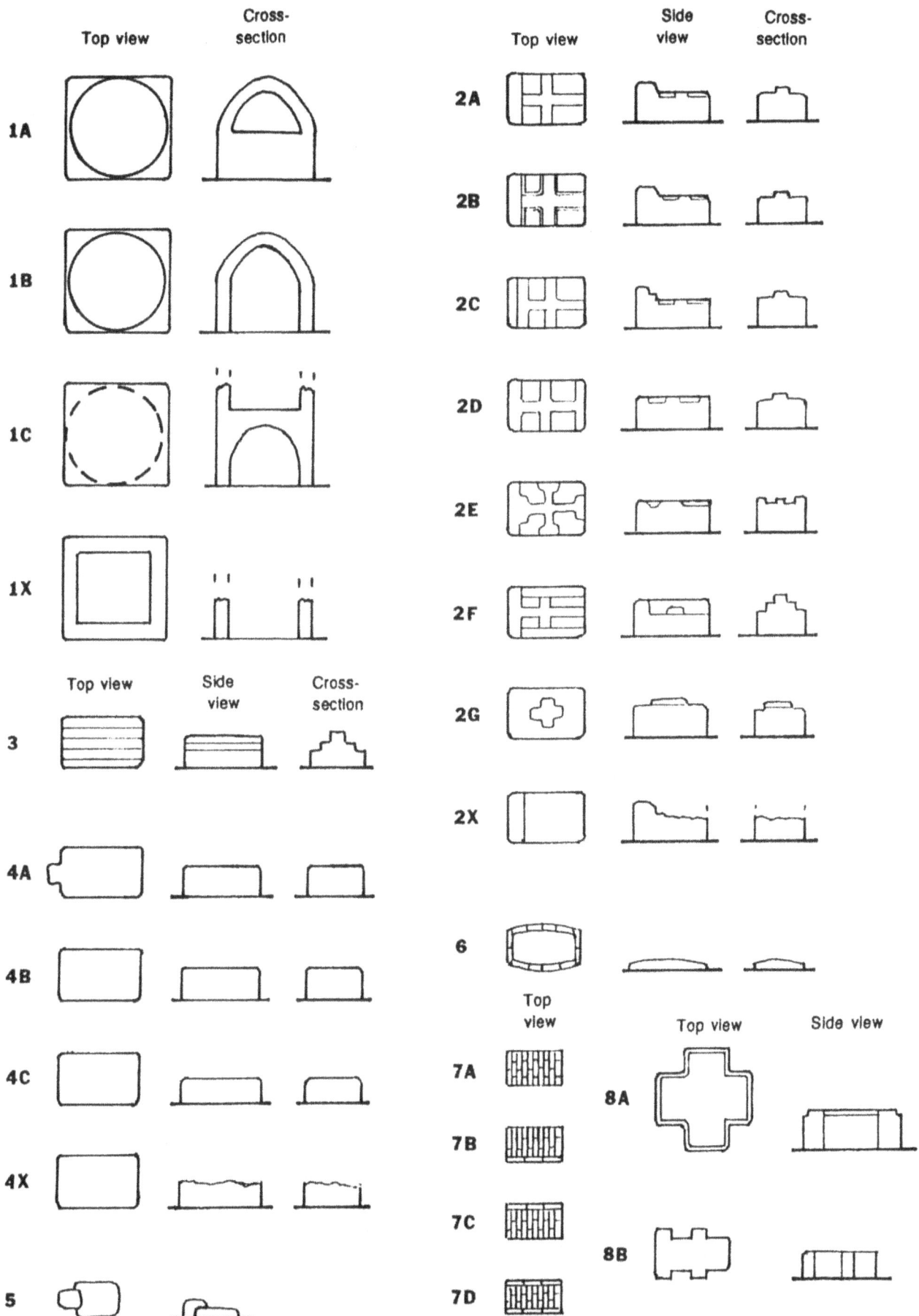

Figure 16. Meinarti tomb superstructure types. **1A-1X**, *qubba* types; **2A-2X**, cross-topped mastaba types, **3**, stepped mastaba type; **4A-4X**, plain mastaba types, **5**, loaf-shaped mastaba for child's tomb; **6**, brick-outlined mud pavement; **7A-D**, brick pavement types; **8A-B**, cruciform types.

below. The distribution of the different types in different phases and subphases is shown in Table 6. A complete listing of superstructures, grouped by period and by type, is given in Table 7.

masonry, surmounted by a dome (Plate 10a). There were only two specimens of this type, both from Phase 5. Both had pink plaster, of the same kind that was prevalent throughout the neighboring Buildings II-III at Subphases

TABLE 6. DISTRIBUTION OF SUPERSTRUCTURES BY TYPE AND SUBPHASE

Types	Subphases						Total
	4a	4ab	4c	5a	5b	5c	
Type 1 *Qubbas*							
1A				1	1		2
1B	1	2	1				4
1C				1			1
1X			3	1		1	5
Total							12
Type 2 Cross- topped							
2A		14	11				26
2B			1				1
2C			1				1
2D		1					1
2E			2				2
2F			1				1
2G		1					1
2X		2	2				4
Total							37
Type 3 Stepped			2				2
Type 4 Rectangular							
4A		3					3
4X		28	15				43
Total							46
Type 5 Pillow		4	1				5
Type 6 Oval		3					3
Type 7 Brick pavement							
7A		2					2
7B		1	1				2
7C			1				1
7D		1					1
Total							6
Type 8 Cruciform							
8A		1					1
8B			1				1
Total							2

Type 1: *qubbas* (Plate 9). These were the most elaborate of Meinarti tomb superstructures, numbering 12 in all. They consisted either of a solid square or, more commonly, of a hollow square of brick masonry, surmounted by a dome. All the known examples were covered with colored plaster. Interestingly, all of the four sub-types were used both for male and for female burials, in about equal numbers. At least three of the *qubba* tombs were chambers in which burials were placed on a floor within the super-structure, rather than in a shaft below it. The group of *qubbas,* though small, included both some of the earliest and some of the latest tombs in the cemetery.

Type 1A consisted of a solid square platform of brick

5b and 5c (see *Meinarti III,* 22-3).

Type 1B consisted of a hollow square of brick masonry surmounted by a dome (Plates 10b and 10c). The four surviving specimens all dated from Phase 4. Three speci-mens had pink plaster, and one had grey plaster. One may have had a tombstone attached, but this was not certain.

Type 1C consisted of a hollow square of brick masonry, which may have been surmounted by a dome, resting atop a subterranean vault. The one surviving example of this type, from Subphase 5a, had golden pink plaster, and origi-nally bore a tombstone on its west side. The subterranean vault (shown in Plate 10d) contained three burials (shown in Plates 14b and 14c); it was the only example of a multiple-burial tomb at Meinarti.

Type 1X is the designation given to tombs having at the base a hollow square of brick masonry, but with the upper part too destroyed for definite identification.

Type 2: cross-topped mastabas (Plate 10)

The term 'mastaba' as used here does not have the same meaning as in Dynastic Egyptian archaeology. It refers to a small, solid rectangle of brick masonry, typically about 2m long, 1m wide, and 60 to 80cm high at the top. Of the various sub-types described below, most had a western pylon: an area at the west end of the structure, typically about 35cm long, which stood 10 to 15cm higher than the remainder. These were by far the most common super-structures at Meinarti, accounting for over 55% of all the tombs of identifiable type. It is probable that a high percentage of the mastaba tombs of unidentifiable sub-type ("Type 4X") were also of this type. All of the known specimens of Type 2 tombs dated from Phase 4; they were about equally divided between Subphase 4ab and Subphase 4c. Despite their abundance at Meinarti, cross-topped mastabas have elsewhere been identified only at Old Dongola, far to the south (Welsby 2002, figs 25-26).

A few cross-topped tombs appear to have had a thin whitewash all over, although the evidence was not absolutely clear in any case. A slightly larger number had white-wash on the western pylon only; in at least some of these cases the evidence was unmistakable. Virtually all the cross-topped tombs had a lamp box at the western end, but only one had a tombstone. Cross-topped tombs were used almost exclusively for adult burials, and about equally for males and females (cf. Table 5).

Type 2A was by far the most common sub-type of cross-topped tomb, accounting for about two-thirds of the known specimens. These tombs had a slightly raised western pylon, while the remainder of the top was embossed with a simple cross, one brick (18cm) wide and raised one brick (9-10cm) higher than the surrounding surface (Plates 11a and 11c). In some tombs the east and west arms of the cross were of about equal length; in others the transept was situated slightly west of the centerpoint of the cross, so that the eastern arm was longer than the western. There was only one clear-cut instance in which a tomb of this type had been accompanied by a tombstone (Tomb T12; Plate 13a). In most other cases it would not have been possible, as the western face was not tall enough to accommodate a tombstone.

Type 2B. The single tomb of this type (T122) differed from tombs of Type 2A only in that the embossed cross had slightly stepped edges; that is, a slightly narrower upper cross was superimposed over a slightly wider lower one. This effect was achieved entirely with sculptured mud plaster, not by the use of bricks of different sizes.

Type 2C. The single tomb of this type (T89) differed from Type 2A only in that the western pylon was taller, and was stepped down on its eastern side, in a series of three steps, to the point where the cross adjoined (Plate 11b).

Type 2D. The single tomb of this type (T23) differed from Type 2A only in that the embossed cross was "footed;" that is, the cross was adjoined at the bottom

(east end) by a second transept running across the full width of the mastaba.

Type 2E. The two tombs of this type (T28 and T105) were the most elaborate of the cross-topped tombs, and fortunately one was perfectly preserved. The embossed cross was formed not of bricks but of molded mud plaster in the form of an elaborate Greek cross (Plates 11c and 11d), which in one case had stepped-up sides. That is, a smaller cross was superimposed on a larger one.

Type 2F. The single tomb of this type (T78) had stepped sides: that is, a central ridge with two descending steps on either side (Plate 11e). The central ridge was in fact the central member of the cross, while the transept extended outward as far as the outer edge of the middle step, but did not extend across the lower step. The arms of the cross in this case were considerably wider than in most other embossed crosses.

Type 2G. This exceptionally wide tomb (T31) was embossed at the top with a small equilateral cross, like a + sign, whose arms did not extend outward as far as the edges of the superstructure (Plate 11f). Because of poor preservation it is not certain if the tomb had a western pylon.

Type 2X is the designation given to three tombs that had a western pylon, but no surviving remnants of a cross to the east of it. It is not certain in any of these cases, however, that the cross had not been destroyed by erosion.

Type 3: stepped mastabas (Plate 12a). Type 3 tombs are described as stepped mastaba tombs. The two tombs of this type (T14 and T15) were similar in outline to the cross-topped tombs, but they lacked an embossed cross, and probably also a western pylon. They had, instead, a rather narrow central ridge running the full length of the tomb from west to east, and three descending steps on either side of it. Because the western ends of both surviving tombs had been partly destroyed by the intrusion of later burials, it could not be stated with certainty that they lacked pylons. The two tombs were built side-by-side at Subphase 4c (Plate 12a), and almost certainly were for members of the same family. Both interments were male.

Type 4: plain rectangular mastabas. Type 4 is the designation given to plain rectangular mastabas, without either pylons or adornment on the top.

Type 4A. The two tombs of this type (T68 and T95) had a small square projection at the western end, which however was of solid masonry and therefore was not a lamp box.

Type 4B. The single tomb of this type (T96) was a plain rectangle or masonry, having a lamp box rather than a solid western projection.

Type 4X was the designation given to mastaba tombs whose tops were too denuded to retain any evidence of embellishment. This was considerably the most common category of tombs at Meinarti, numbering 43 examples in all. It is probable that the great majority of these were originally cross-topped tombs of one type or another.

Type 5: "pillow" mastabas (Plate 12b). The Type 5 tomb was a small and rather low rectangle of brick masonry, usually with slightly rounded corners, and having at the

western end a small, square "pillow" rising 10 to 15cm above the level of the remainder of the tomb. The "pillow" was always of solid masonry; it was not a lamp box. All five superstructures of this type covered infant burials.

Type 6: ovate pavements (Plate 12c). Type 6 tombs had a low superstructure, formed of molded mud with bricks around the edge. The form was an oblate oval, having outward curving sides but squared-off ends. Of the three known specimens of this type (T114, T115, and T116), one covered an infant and two covered adolescents.

Type 7: brick pavements (Plate 12d). Superstructures formed by a rectangular pavement of rollag brickwork (i.e. bricks set on edge) were relatively common at Kulubnarti (Adams *et al.* 1999, 30, 44) and at many other sites (Adams 1998b, 22). At Meinarti however they were extraordinarily rare, and all but one of them were used with infant burials.

The pavement in all cases was formed chiefly of brick rows running at right angles to the long axis; that is, in a north-south direction. The four subtypes were differentiated solely by the presence or absence of one or more rows of brick running parallel to the long axis. In Type 7A the pavement consisted entirely of bricks running transversely to the long axis. In Type 7B the transverse bricks were bordered along the south side by a single row of bricks running longitudinally, and in Type 7C they were bordered along the north side only by a row of bricks running longitudinally. In Type 7D the transverse bricks were bordered on both sides by a single row of bricks running longitudinally. There was a notable absence of pavements having a central "spine" of bricks running longitudinally – the most common form at Kulubnarti and elsewhere (Adams 1998b, 22; Adams *et al.* 1999, 30).

Type 8: cruciform superstructures. Type 8 is the designation given to two cruciform superstructures, both of which covered the burials of females of mature age.

Type 8A was represented by a very large superstructure in the form of a cross, in which the west-east axis was slightly longer than the transept (T120; Plates 12e and 12f). Although the top was mostly flat, the edges all the way around were stepped down in three small steps. The tomb apparently was whitewashed, although this was very poorly preserved.

Type 8B. The single tomb of this type (T119) had a very unusual shape (Plate 12e). The main body of the tomb was a regular mastaba of brick, about 80cm wide, but there were two narrow transepts, projecting north and south for 20cm. One was at the western end of the tomb, and the other at a point somewhat west of the middle. The uppermost part of this tomb had been leveled at a later date, so that the original shape of the top could not be determined. The tomb had apparently only mud plaster, without coloring.

Plaster

The great majority of superstructures had a plain but very smooth mud plaster coating. However, all the *qubbas* (Type 1 tombs) were covered with a thick and hard plaster, made of sand mixed with lime. Of the seven *qubbas*

built at Phase 4, five had a light grey plaster, similar to the earliest coat of plaster applied in Church VI, and two had a salmon pink plaster, similar to the second coat of plaster in the church. All three of the *qubbas* that could be attributed to Subphase 5a had a distinctive plaster of a dark golden pink color, which otherwise was found only in one room of Building III, clearly datable also to Subphase 5a (*Meinarti III*, 16). The two *qubbas* attributed to the latter part of Phase 5 had pale pink plaster.

Among the cross-topped and rectangular mastabas (Types 2-4) only four specimens had a hard plaster similar to that found on the *qubbas;* it was pink in three cases and grey in one. Tomb T12, the only mastaba tomb to bear a tombstone, had pink plaster. Most of the mastaba superstructures retained no trace of coloring, but a few had unmistakably been whitewashed, and there were surviving traces of whitewash on several others. Eight of the cross-topped mastabas had apparently been whitewashed only on the pylon; i.e. the western end.

Lamp boxes

The great majority of Meinarti tomb superstructures had a small box attached to, or occasionally set into, the western end, to contain a votive lamp. These features were nearly universal in the case of mastaba tombs (Types 2, 3, and 4); they were not always present in the case of *qubba* tombs, or on either of the two cruciform tombs. However, lamp boxes were definitely lacking in only 14 of the 119 Meinarti tomb superstructures; in another 19 cases their presence could not be definitely confirmed because the western end of the structure was not preserved. The boxes can be divided into three types. In a good many cases where a lamp box was present, however, the state of preservation did not permit a definitely identification of the type.

Covered boxes were the most common, numbering 45 definitely identifiable examples (Plates 8f, 11c-f). These boxes projected westward from the middle of the west end of the tomb superstructure, at ground level. They were constructed of two upright, square bricks, spanned across the top by a horizontal brick, the whole being then plastered over. The typical dimensions were about 25 x 25 x 25cm.

Open boxes differed from covered boxes only in that they lacked a horizontal, covering brick over the top. There were 13 definitely identifiable examples of this type.

Inset boxes comprised a square recess within the brick masonry of the superstructure itself; usually but not always at ground level. There were 13 examples of inset boxes.

Lamps

Lamps (Plate 15) were encountered *in situ* in 29 tomb boxes. Twenty of the specimens were small vessels of Aswan Ware W12, and of these 15 were "saucers" of Form P28 (see Adams 1986, 153) (Plate 15a). There were also five other saucer lamps (Form P24; Plates 15c and 15d) and two "candle-holder" lamps (Forms P19 and P20; Plate 15b) of Classic Christian Nubian wares, one fragment of a large imported pottery bottle, and one oyster shell. In

TABLE 7. REGISTER OF TOMB SUPERSTRUCTURES IN THE MEINARTI CEMETERY

In chronological order by subphase

Tomb no.	Sub-phase	Type	Plaster[1]	Tomb-stone	Lamp box	Lamp[2]	Condition/remarks
T11	4a	1B	Grey	Removed			Top dug away
T12	4a	2A	Pink	Yes		U6 bowl	T14 partly cut in
T18	4ab	1B	Pink		Covered box	W10 bowl	Fairly well preserved
T19	4ab	1B	Grey	?	?		Mostly disturbed
T16	4ab	2A	Wh/mud		Covered box		Intact
T34	4ab	2A?	Mud		?		Both ends destroyed
T36	4ab	2A?	Mud				Top denuded
T39	4ab	2A	Mud		?	W12 bowl	Burial B6 cut into top
T46	4ab	2A	Mud		Covered box	U6 bowl	Top slightly denuded
T50	4ab	2A	White?		Inset	W12 bowl	Partly under T49
T53	4ab	2A?	Grey?		Covered box	U6 bowl	Top slightly denuded
T56	4ab	2A	Mud		Covered box	U6 bowl	East end denuded
T85	4ab	2A	Mud		Covered box		Well preserved
T88	4ab	2A	Wh/mud?		Covered box		Well preserved
T91	4ab	2A	Mud		Covered box	W10 bowl	Very wide top cross
T94	4ab	2A	Wh/mud?		Covered box		Well preserved
T123	4ab	2A	Mud		Covered box		Well preserved
T126	4ab	2A	Mud		Covered box	W6 bowl	Somewhat denuded
T23	4ab	2D	Mud		Covered box	U6 bowl	Burial B4 cut into top
T31	4ab	2G	Mud		Covered box		Well preserved
T92	4ab	2X	Mud		Open box		Somewhat denuded
T98	4ab	2X	Mud		Covered box		Well preserved
T68	4ab	4A	Mud		Covered box	Shell	B26 cut into top
T95	4ab	4A	Mud		Inset		Well preserved
T96	4ab	4B	Mud		Open box		Top partly denuded
T30	4ab	4X	?		?		Only fragment found
T32	4ab	4X	Pink		Covered box		Burial B5 cut into top
T33	4ab	4X	Mud		Open box?	U6 bowl	Burial B7 cut into top
T38	4ab	4X	Mud		?		Denuded
T40	4ab	4X	Mud		Covered box		T41 partly over top
T44	4ab	4X	Mud		Inset		Top very denuded
T47	4ab	4X	White?		Inset	U6 cup	Top denuded
T48	4ab	4X	Mud		Inset	U6 bowl	Top denuded
T54	4ab	4X	Mud		?		Top, ends denuded
T55	4ab	4X	Mud		?		Denuded; B19 cut in
T57	4ab	4X	Mud		Covered box		Top denuded
T58	4ab	4X	Mud		Covered box	U6 bowl	Top, east end denuded
T59	4ab	4X	Mud		Covered box		Badly destroyed
T60	4ab	4X	Mud		Box	R5 lamp	Badly destroyed
T65	4ab	4X	Mud		?		B23 cut into top
T67	4ab	4X	Mud		?		West end missing
T69	4ab	4X	Mud		Covered box	U5 lamp	Top denuded
T70	4ab	4X	Mud		Covered box		Only west end left
T71	4ab	4X	Mud		Open box		East end missing
T72	4ab	4X	Mud		Open box	U6 goblet	Partly under T80
T86	4ab	4X	Mud		Covered box	U6 bowl	East end missing
T97	4ab	4X	Mud		Inset		Denuded, east end gone
T99	4ab	4X	Mud				Top denuded
T102	4ab?	4X	Mud		Box	W10 lamp	Top very denuded
T109	4ab	4X	White		Inset?		Partly under T42
T110	4ab	4X	Mud		Covered box		Top denuded
T121	4ab	4X	Mud		Covered box		Somewhat denuded
T125	4ab	4X	Mud		Covered box	U6 footed bowl	Only West end exposed
T73	4ab	5	Mud?		?		Partly denuded
T66	4ab	5	Mud				Somewhat denuded
T90	4ab	5?	White?		Inset?		Made from kiln bricks
T22	4ab	5?	Mud		Open box		Largely destroyed
T114	4ab	6	Mud		Open box?		Fairly well preserved
T115	4ab	6	Mud		Inset?		Well preserved

[1] Wh/mud means white pylon, remainder with plain mud plaster
[2] Letter and number entries identify the pottery ware of the lamp. See Adams 1986, 103-4.

In chronological order by subphase

Tomb no.	Sub-phase	Type	Plaster[1]	Tomb-stone	Lamp box	Lamp[2]	Condition/remarks
T116	4ab	6	Mud		Inset?		West end eroded
T113	4ab	7A					Stone pavement
T117	4ab	7A	Mud		Open box		Top denuded
T100	4ab	7B	Mud				Denuded, west end gone
T81	4ab	7C	Mud		Box?		Considerably denuded
T118	4ab	7C	Mud				Well preserved?
T93	4ab	7D	Mud?				All plaster gone
T120	4ab	8A	Pink				T2 burial cut in
T124	4ab	?	Mud		?		Under T41 and T42
T26	4ab?	?	Pink		?		Very eroded
T87	4c	1B	Pink				Perfectly preserved
T5	4c	1X	Grey				Top leveled at Phase 6
T6	4c	1X	Grey				Top leveled at Phase 6
T7	4c	1X	Grey				Top leveled at Phase 6
T10	4c	2A	White?		Inset		Well preserved
T17	4c	2A	Mud		Covered box	W10 bowl	Well preserved
T74	4c	2A	Mud		Covered box		Somewhat denuded
T75	4c	2A	White?		Covered box		Slightly denuded
T76	4c	2A	Mud		Covered box	U6 bowl	Well preserved
T77	4c	2A	Mud		Open box		Well preserved
T79	4c	2A	Mud		Covered box		Well preserved
T80	4c	2A	Mud		Covered box		Slightly denuded
T84	4c	2A	Wh/mud		Covered box		Well preserved
T103	4c	2A	Wh/mud		Covered box	W12 bowl	Sloping sides
T104	4c	2A	Wh/mud		Covered box	U6 bowl	Well preserved
T122	4c	2B	Mud		Covered box		T9 burial cut in
T89	4c	2C	Wh/mud		Covered box	W12 bowl	Well preserved
T28	4c	2E	Mud		Covered box	W10 bowl	East end denuded
T105	4c	2E	Wh/mud		Covered box		Perfectly preserved
T78	4c	2F	Grey?		Covered box		Well preserved
T25	4c	2X	White	?	Open box		Top denuded
T29	4c	2X	Mud		Covered box		Top denuded
T14	4c	3	Mud				Cut by late burial
T15	4c	3	Mud		Box		Cut by late burial
T20	4c	4X	Mud		?		West end cut by B2
T21	4c	4X	Mud		Open box	U6 lamp	B3 cut into top
T24	4c	4X	White?				Top denuded
T37	4c	4X	Mud		?		Only one corner left
T41	4c	4X	Mud		?		B8 cut into west end
T42	4c	4X	Mud				Top denuded
T43	4c	4X	Mud		Inset?		Very denuded
T45	4c	4X	Mud		?		Only east end left
T49	4c	4X	Mud		Open box		Top denuded
T61	4c	4X	Mud		Open box		Very denuded
T64	4c	4X	Mud		Open box	U6 bowl	Top cut away
T82	4c	4X	Mud		Covered box		Top denuded
T101	4c	4X	Mud		Box		Only remnants left
T106	4c	4X	Wh/mud		Covered box		Top denuded
T108	4c	4X	Mud		?		Made of reused bricks
T83	4c	5	Mud		Inset	W9 bowl	Well preserved
T107	4c	7B	Wh/mud		?		Partly destroyed
T119	4c	8B	Mud?				Top leveled at Phase 6
T51	4c?	?	?				Only small fragment left
T52	4c?	?	?				Only small fragment left
T111	4c	?	?				Only small fragment left
T9	5a	1A	Gold pink	?	Covered box		Top leveled at Phase 6
T2	5b	1A	Pale pink	?			Top worn down
T8	5a	1C	Gold pink	Removed	Within vault		Top partly destroyed
T3	5a	1X	Gold pink	?	Open box		Only west end left
T4	5c	1X	Pink?	?	Covered box	Bottle frag.	Very little left

[1] Wh/mud means white pylon, remainder with plain mud plaster

[2] Letter and number entries identify the pottery ware of the lamp. See Adams 1986, 103-4.

addition, a dish lamp probably of Ware R21 was found within the vaulted chamber of Tomb T8 (visible in Plate 14b).

Tombstones (Plate 17)

Only one tombstone (832) was found *in situ* at Meinarti, on Tomb T12 of Subphase 4a (see Plate 13a). It bore a conventional Coptic mortuary formula, and a date equivalent to A.D. 1045 (Plate 17a). Only two other tomb superstructures, respectively of Types 1B and 1C, bore evidence that they had originally borne tombstones, which were subsequently detached. However, a number of complete Christian tombstones were collected at Meinarti by earlier visitors, and several detached fragments were also found by us. It was not possible in any case to determine where these had come from. The same was true in regard to two complete and four fragmentary Islamic tombstones, found in reused contexts in the houses. They probably did not come from this cemetery, since nearly all of the superstructures were of recognizable Christian types, and none of the excavated burials was in the usual Muslim position. The tombstones will be much more fully discussed in a later section.

The burials

The Meinarti Cemetery as excavated contained 114 bodies found beneath (or in three cases within) superstructures, and 237 burials for which no superstructures were preserved. As previously noted, the dating of burials without superstructures was not as secure as in the case of the tomb burials. However, burials could be assigned to subphases or groups of subphases as follows:

TABLE 8. DISTRIBUTION OF BURIALS BY SUBPHASE

Subphases	Tomb burials	Burials without tombs	Total
Subphases 4ab	63	85	148
Subphases 4abc		11	11
Subphase 4c	44	61	105
Subphase 5a	5	13	18
Subphase 5b	1	1	2
Subphase 5c	1		1
Phases 5-6		66	66
Totals	114	237	351

Grave shafts

Some of the latest burials at Meinarti were encountered just below the pre-excavation surface, and in these cases the original shape of the grave shaft could not be determined. Among the remaining burials, whether with or without superstructures, all but ten were placed at the bottom of shafts, typically about 2m long and 60cm wide. The exceptions included *qubba* Tombs T5-T7, in which the body was placed on a pavement within the superstructure; Tomb T8, in which three bodies were buried in a subterranean vault; mastaba Tombs T33 and T61, where the burial was found immediately below the bricks of the superstructure; and Tomb T25, in which two interments

were encased within the mud of the superstructure itself.

Among the graves with shafts, all but six involved a simple vertical shaft, designated in Table 9 as a "slot." The exceptions were five cases in which the body was placed in a lateral offset niche on the north side of the shaft, and one in which the lateral niche was on the south side of the shaft. In all these six cases, the body was protected by bricks laid all along its outer side (that is, adjoining the main shaft). Graves shafts with neatly squared corners, such as were present in a number of graves at Kulubnarti (Adams *et al*. 1999, 17), were not observed.

Body coverings

The great majority of Meinarti burials had some kind of covering, consisting nearly always of brick, placed over all or part of the body. The largest number, 151 specimens, had only a structure of three bricks covering the head: one upright brick on each side of the face, and one horizontal brick bridging across the top (most clearly seen in Plate 14a). Three burials had a head covering made similarly, but of flat stones. In addition to the bricks over the face, seven bodies had a brick covering extending down to the waist, six had bricks laid all along the right side, and two had bricks all along the left side. In 44 cases there were bricks laid along the full length of the body, on both sides, and in two cases there were stones along the full length. In these latter cases, the bricks or stones from each side were laid in a slanting position so as to meet in the middle, forming an inverted "V" over the body. One body had bricks over the face, while the remainder of the body was covered with a casing of mud. There were 64 bodies which definitely had no covering, as well as a fair number in which the presence or absence of a covering could not be determined. There was no discernible pattern of variation in the use of different covering practices at different phases.

In addition to normal interments, there were three foetus burials in pottery vessels. This practice seems to have been less common at Meinarti than at other Nubian sites (cf. Adams *et al*. 1999, 23). The vessels employed were hand-made pots (Ware H1) in two cases, and an Aswan-made pot (Ware U6) in one case.

Burial positions (Plate 14)

All burials in the Meinarti Cemetery were in extended position, oriented east and west, except that in a few cases the knees were somewhat flexed to fit into a grave shaft that was too short. All heads were toward the west. The largest number of individuals lay on their backs, but 32 were on their right sides, and 11 on their left sides. This preference for burial on the right rather than the left side was observed in other cemeteries in Lower Nubia, but was distinctly different from the situation at Kulubnarti, where there was a strong preference for burial on the left side (Adams 1998b, 29). The practice of burying individuals on their sides seems to have been a good deal more prevalent during Phase 4 than it was in Phases 5 and 6.

Among the dorsally extended individuals, the head in most cases was facing straight up. In 22 cases however it was turned toward the right (south), as in Plate 14b, and

TABLE 9. COMPREHENSIVE REGISTER OF MEINARTI BURIALS

Grouped by subphase or phase

Burial no.	Phase	Shaft type[1]	Body position[2]	Head position[3]	Head cover[4]	Body cover	Age	Sex	Condition
T11	4a	Slot	Dorsal	Up	3 bricks	None	Mature	F?	Poor
T12	4a?	Slot	Right side	Right	3 bricks	None	34	F	Good
T112	4a	(burial not found)							
B184	4a	Slot	Right side	Right	None	None	25+	F	Fair
B197	4a	Slot	Dorsal	Up	3 stones	None	Adult	M?	Poor
B204	4a?	Slot	Dorsal	Up	3 bricks	None	27-30	F	Good
B207	4a?	Slot	Dorsal	Right	3 bricks	None	17-18	F	Fair
B211	4a?	Slot	Dorsal	Up	3 bricks	None	18-21	F?	Very frag.
T16	4ab	Slot	Dorsal	Up	3 bricks	None	30-40	F	Good
T18	4ab	Slot	Dorsal	Up	None	None	30+	F	Fair
T19	4ab	Slot	Dorsal	Up	3 bricks	None	Adult	F	Very bad
T22	4ab	Slot	Right side	Right	3 bricks	None	8	?	Fair
T23	4ab	Slot	Dorsal	Up	3 bricks	Bricks all along	c. 30	M	Poor
T26	4ab?	(burial not found)							
T30	4ab	Slot	Dorsal	Up	3 bricks	None	30+	M	Good
T31	4ab	Slot	Dorsal	Up	3 bricks	None	40+	M	Very bad
T32	4ab	Slot	Dorsal	Up	3 bricks	Bricks to waist	25-30	M	Fair
T33	4ab	Slot	Dorsal	Right	3 bricks	None	18-19	F	Good
T34	4ab	Slot	Dorsal	Up	3 bricks	None	30-35	M	Fair
T36	4ab?	Slot	Dorsal	Up	3 bricks	None	11-12	?	Fair
T38	4ab	Slot	Dorsal	Up	3 bricks	None	40-50	M	Poor
T39	4ab	Slot	Dorsal	Up	3 bricks	None	30-40	F	Good
T40	4ab	Slot	Dorsal	Up	3 bricks	None	c. 30	M	Fair
T44	4ab	Slot	Dorsal	Right	3 bricks	None	18-19	F	Good
T46	4ab	Slot	Dorsal	Up	3 bricks	None	Adult	F	Very poor
T47	4ab	Slot	Dorsal	Up	3 bricks	None	40-45	M	Very poor
T48	4ab	Slot	Dorsal	Up	3 bricks	None	40-42	F	Fair
T50	4ab	Slot	Dorsal	Up	3 bricks	None	30-35	M	Fair
T53	4ab?	Slot	Dorsal	Up	3 bricks	None	Young ad.	?	Good
T54	4ab	Slot	Dorsal	Up	None	None	30+	?	Poor
T55	4ab	Slot	Right side	Right	None	None	30-35	F	Good
T56	4ab	Slot	Dorsal	Up	3 bricks	None	?	?	Fair
T57	4ab	Slot	Dorsal	Right	3 bricks	None	15-18	M	Fair
T58	4ab	(burial not found)							
T59	4ab?	Slot	Right side	Right	3 bricks	None	30-35	F	Fair
T60	4ab	(burial not found)							
T65	4ab	Slot	Right side	Right	3 bricks	None	Adoles.	?	Fair
T66	4ab	Slot	Dorsal	Up	3 bricks	None	8	?	Good
T67	4ab	Slot	Right side	Up	3 bricks	None	Adult	F	Fair
T68	4ab	Slot	Dorsal	Up	None	None	25+	F	Poor
T69	4ab	Slot	Dorsal	Up	None?	None	20-25	F	Poor
T70	4ab	Slot	Dorsal	Right	3 bricks	None	40+	?	Good
T71	4ab	Slot	Dorsal	Up	3 bricks	None	Young ad.	M	Fair
T72	4ab	Slot	Right side	Right	3 bricks	None	?	?	Fair
T73	4ab	Slot	Left side	Left	3 bricks	None	4	?	Fair
T81	4ab	(burial not found)							
T85	4ab	Slot	Dorsal	Up	3 bricks	Bricks all along	Adult	?	Poor
T86	4ab	Slot	Dorsal	Up	3 bricks	Bricks to waist	Adult	?	Poor
T88	4ab	Slot	Dorsal	Up	3 bricks	Bricks all along	20-22	M	Fair
T90	4ab	Slot	Dorsal	Up	3 bricks	Bricks all along	7 months	?	Good
T91	4ab	Slot	Dorsal	Up	3 bricks	Bricks right side	27-30	F	Fair
T92	4ab	Slot	Dorsal	Up	3 bricks	Bricks all along	23-25	M	Good
T93	4ab	?	Right side	Right	?	?	17 months	?	Very bad
T94	4ab	Slot	Dorsal	Right	3 bricks	Bricks all along	25+	M	Good
T95	4ab	Slot	Dorsal	Up	3 bricks	None	8	?	Fair
T96	4ab	Slot	Dorsal	Right	3 bricks	None	Adult	?	Very bad
T97	4ab	Slot	Dorsal	Up	3 bricks	None	c. 19	F	Fair
T98	4ab	(burial totally destroyed)							

[1] Slot = plain vertical shaft; Niche = slot with offset niche to north or south
[2] All bodies, whether dorsal or on sides, were extended with heads to west
[3] Up = looking straight up; Right = head turned to right; Left = head turned to left
[4] 2 bricks = bricks at sides of head only; 3 bricks = bricks at sides and over the top of head

Burial no.	Phase	Shaft type[1]	Body position[2]	Head position[3]	Head cover[4]	Body cover	Age	Sex	Condition
T99	4ab	Slot	Right side	Right	3 bricks	None	2-6	?	Poor
T100	4ab	Slot	Dorsal	Up	3 bricks	None	6	?	Poor
T102	4ab	Niche	Right side	Right	3 bricks	Bricks all along	29-30	M	Good
T109	4ab	Slot	Dorsal	Up	3 bricks	None	50-60	F	Fair
T110	4ab	Slot	Dorsal	Right	3 bricks	None	Young ad.	F	Very poor
T113	4ab	Slot	Right side	Right	3 bricks	None	2-3	?	Good
T114	4ab	Slot	Right side	Right	None	None	2-6	?	Poor
T115	4ab	Slot	Right side	Right	3 bricks	None	12-14	?	Fair
T116	4ab	Slot	Dorsal	Up	3 bricks	None	15-17	?	Fair
T117	4ab	Slot	Dorsal	Right	3 bricks	None	2-3	?	Fair
T118	4ab	Slot	Dorsal	Up	3 bricks	Bricks all along	2-6	?	Very bad
T120	4ab	Slot	Dorsal	Up	3 bricks	None	45+	F	Fair
T121	4ab	Slot	Dorsal	Left	3 bricks	None	25-30	?	Fair
T123	4ab	Slot	Dorsal	Up	3 bricks	None	17-25	F	Good
T124	4ab	Slot	Right side	Right	3 bricks	None	2-6	?	Very poor
T125	4ab	(not excavated)							
T126	4ab	Slot	Dorsal	Up	3 bricks	None	Adult	?	Good
B68	4ab	Slot	Left side	Left	3 bricks	Bricks left side	Young ad	M	Fair
B69	4ab	Slot	Dorsal	Up	3 bricks	None	10-12	?	Good
B70	4ab	Slot	Dorsal	Up	None	None	c. 4	?	Poor
B83	4ab	Slot	Dorsal	Up	3 bricks	None	c. 25	F	Poor
B86	4ab	Slot	Dorsal	Up	3 bricks	Bricks all along	Adult	?	Fair
B87	4ab	?	Left side	Left	None	None	Sub-adult?	Very bad	
B88	4ab	Slot	Dorsal	Up	3 bricks	Bricks all along	c. 25?	F	Bad
B89	4ab	Slot	Right side	Right	None	None	c. 5	?	Fair
B90	4ab	Slot	Right side	Right	2 bricks	None	2-6	?	Good
B91	4ab	Slot	Left side	Left	3 bricks	Bricks all along	6-8	?	Fair
B92	4ab	Slot	Dorsal	Left	3 bricks	Bricks all along	20-25	?	Poor
B93	4ab	Slot	Dorsal	Up	None	None	Sub-adult ?	Very frag.	
B96	4ab	Slot	Dorsal	Up	None	None	c. 20	?	Poor
B100	4ab	Niche	Left side	Left	3 bricks	Bricks left side	c. 12	?	Good
B101	4ab	?	Left side	Left	None	None	2-6	?	Poor
B113	4ab?	Slot	Dorsal	Up	None	None	Child	?	Poor
B116	4ab?	Slot	Dorsal	Right	None	None	40+	F	Poor
B117	4ab	Slot	Dorsal	Up	None	None	5-6	?	Fair
B119	4ab	Niche	Dorsal	Up	None?	None	Adult	?	Poor
B123	4ab	Slot	Dorsal	Up	None	None	20+	?	Poor
B125	4ab	Slot	Dorsal	Left	?	?	Adult	F	Part dist.
B126	4ab	Slot	Dorsal	Up	None	None	2-6	?	Poor
B127	4ab	Slot	Right side	Right	None	None	c. 6	?	Poor
B128	4ab	Slot	Right side	Right	None	None	18-20	F	Poor
B129	4ab?	Slot	Dorsal	Up	3 bricks	None	Adult	?	Poor
B131	4ab	Slot?	Left side	Left	1 brick	Bricks along back	?	Poor	
B132	4ab	Slot	Dorsal	Up	None	None	2	?	Fair
B135	4ab	Slot	Right side	Right	3 bricks	None	6-7	?	Poor
B136	4ab?	Slot	Dorsal	Up	3 bricks	None	2+	?	Poor
B137	4ab?	Slot	Right side	Right	None	None	17-25	F	Fair
B141	4ab	Slot	Right side	Right	None	None	14 months	?	Poor
B149	4ab	Slot	Right side	Right	None	None	11 months	?	Fair
B151	4ab	Slot	Right side	Right	3 bricks	None	2-6	?	Fair
B152	4ab	Slot	Dorsal	Up	3 bricks	None	2-6	?	Fair
B154	4ab?	Slot	Right side	Right	None	None	c. 1	?	Crushed
B157	4ab	Slot	Dorsal	Up	3 bricks	None	Adult	F	Fair
B158	4ab	Slot	Dorsal	Up	3 bricks	None	c. 40	M	Good
B159	4ab	Slot	Dorsal	Up	3 bricks	None	5-6	?	Very poor
B164	4ab	Slot	Dorsal	Up	None?	None?	20-25	F	Fair
B165	4ab	Slot	Dorsal	Up	3 bricks	None	35-40	F	Poor
B166	4ab?	?	Right side	Right	None	None	7 months	?	Poor
B167	4ab	Slot	Dorsal	Left	3 bricks	Bricks all along	2-6	?	Poor

[1] Slot = plain vertical shaft; Niche = slot with offset niche to north or south

[2] All bodies, whether dorsal or on sides, were extended with heads to west

[3] Up = looking straight up; Right = head turned to right; Left = head turned to left

[4] 2 bricks = bricks at sides of head only; 3 bricks = bricks at sides and over the top of head

Burial no.	Phase	Shaft type[1]	Body position[2]	Head position[3]	Head cover[4]	Body cover	Age	Sex	Condition
B170	4ab	Slot	Dorsal	Up	3 bricks	None	2-6	?	Poor
B171	4ab	Slot	Dorsal	Up	3 bricks	None	20-24	M	Poor
B172	4ab	Slot	Dorsal	Up	3 bricks	None	17-25	M	Fair
B173	4ab?	Slot	Dorsal	Left	3 bricks	None	14 months	?	Poor
B174	4ab?	Slot	Dorsal	Up	3 bricks	None	25-26	M	Poor
B177	4ab?	?	Left side	Left	None	None	14 months	?	Poor
B178	4ab	?	Dorsal	Up	None	None	15 months	?	Fair
B179	4ab	Slot	Dorsal	Up	3 bricks	None	Adult	M?	Fair
B180	4ab	Slot	Dorsal	Up	3 bricks	None	30-35	F	Fair
B181	4ab?	Slot	Right side	Right	3 bricks	None	2-6	?	Fair
B185	4ab	?	On ? side	?	None	None	c. 2	?	Very dist.
B186	4ab	Slot	Dorsal	Up	None	None	2-6	?	Poor
B191	4ab	Slot	Dorsal	Right	3 bricks	None	30-35	M	Fair
B192	4ab	Slot	Dorsal	Up	3 bricks	None	12-15	F?	Fair
B193	4ab	Slot	Dorsal	Up	None	None	4-5	?	Very poor
B194	4ab	Slot	Right side	Right	3 bricks	None	5-6	?	Fair
B195	4ab	Slot	Dorsal	Up	None	None	6-7	?	Poor
B196	4ab	Slot	Dorsal	?	?	Bricks all along	Adult	?	Very dist.
B198	4ab	Slot	Dorsal	Up	None	None	?	?	Very dist.
B200	4ab	Slot	Dorsal	Up	3 bricks	None	Adult	?	Poor
B201	4ab	Slot	Dorsal	Left	None	None	6-7	?	Fair
B202	4ab	Slot	Dorsal	Left	3 bricks	None	1-2	?	Poor
B203	4ab	Slot	Right side	Right	3 bricks	None	40-45	?	Good
B205	4ab	Slot	Dorsal	Right	3 bricks	None	Adult	F	Poor
B206	4ab	Slot	Dorsal	Up	3 bricks	Bricks to waist	Adult	F	Poor
B208	4ab	Slot	Dorsal	Right	None	None	8-10	?	Very frag.
B209	4ab	Slot	Dorsal	Up	3 bricks	None	30+	F	Poor
B212	4ab	Slot	Dorsal	Up	None	None	Adoles.	?	Poor
B213	4ab?	Slot	Dorsal	Up	None	None	40-45	F	Very frag.
B214	4ab	Slot	Dorsal	Up	3 bricks	Bricks all along	7-8	?	Fair
B215	4ab	Slot	Right side	Right	3 bricks	Bricks all along	Adult	M	Poor
B216	4ab	Slot	Dorsal?	?	?	?	?	?	Legs only
B217	4ab	Slot	Dorsal	Right	3 bricks	None	Adult	?	Very frag.
B218	4ab	Slot	Dorsal	Up	3 bricks	Bricks all along	35-40	F	Poor
B230	4ab	Slot	Dorsal	Left	?	?	45-50	M	Very bad
B231	4ab	Slot	Dorsal	Up	?	?	22-25	F	Very poor
F2	4ab?	Foetus burial in Ware U6 pot							
F3	4ab	Foetus burial in Ware III pot							
T5	4c	Slot	Dorsal	Up	3 bricks	Bricks all along	c. 20	F	Good
T6	4c	Slot	Dorsal	Up	3 bricks	Bricks to waist	c. 20	M	Poor
T7	4c	Slot	Left side	Left	3 bricks	Bricks all along	Young ad.	M?	Good
T10	4c	Slot	Dorsal	Up	3 bricks	None	30-35	M	Good
T14	4c	Slot	Dorsal	Right	3 bricks	Mud all along	Adult	M	Good
T15	4c	Slot	Dorsal	Up	3 bricks	None	40+	M	Fair
T17	4c	Slot	Dorsal	Up	3 bricks	None	30-35	M	Good
T20	4c	Slot	Dorsal	Up	3 bricks	None	25-27	M	Fair
T21	4c	Slot	Dorsal	Up	3 bricks	None	35-39	F	Good
T24	4c	(burial not found)							
T25	4c	Slot	Dorsal	Up	3 bricks	Bricks to waist	25-30	M	Poor
T28	4c	Slot	Dorsal	Up	3 bricks	None	22-24	M	Good
T29	4c	Slot	Right side	Right	3 bricks	None	45+	F	Good
T37	4c	Slot	Right side	Right	3 bricks	None	20-25	F	Fair
T41	4c	Slot	Dorsal	Up	3 bricks	None	27-30	M	Poor
T42	4c	Slot	Dorsal	Up	3 bricks	None	30-35	M	Fair
T43	4c	Slot	Dorsal	Up	3 bricks	None	30-35	M	Fair
T45	4c	Slot	Dorsal	Up	3 bricks	None	25-30	M	Good
T49	4c	Slot	Left side	Left	3 bricks	None	39-44	F	Fair
T51	4c?	Slot	Dorsal	Up	2 bricks	None	25-30	M	Fair

[1] Slot = plain vertical shaft; Niche = slot with offset niche to north or south

[2] All bodies, whether dorsal or on sides, were extended with heads to west

[3] Up = looking straight up; Right = head turned to right; Left = head turned to left

[4] 2 bricks = bricks at sides of head only; 3 bricks = bricks at sides and over the top of head

Burial no.	Phase	Shaft type[1]	Body position[2]	Head position[3]	Head cover[4]	Body cover	Age	Sex	Condition
T52	4c?	Slot	Dorsal	Up	3 bricks	None	c. 20	F	Poor
T61	4c	None	Dorsal	Up	Superst.	Superstructure	22-25	F	Very bad
T64	4c	Slot	Dorsal	Up	3 bricks	None	Mature	F	Good
T74	4c	Slot	Dorsal	Up	3 bricks	None	40+	M	Fair
T75	4c	Slot	Dorsal	Up	3 bricks	Bricks left side	25+	M	Good
T76	4c	Slot	Dorsal	Up	3 bricks	None	20-25	F	Good
T77	4c	Slot	Dorsal	Up	3 bricks	None	30-40	F	Fair
T78	4c	Slot	Dorsal	Up	3 bricks	Bricks to waist	c. 50	M	Poor
T79	4c	Slot	Dorsal	Up	3 bricks	None	Adult	F	Fair
T80	4c	Slot	Dorsal	Up	3 bricks	None	17-25	M	Poor
T82	4c	Slot	Dorsal	Up	3 bricks	None	Adult	F	Fair
T83	4c	Slot	Dorsal	Up	3 bricks	None	8-9	?	Good
T84	4c	Slot	Dorsal	Up	3 bricks	None	40+	M	Poor
T87	4c	Slot	Dorsal	Up	3 bricks	Bricks all along	22-24	M	Good
T89	4c	Slot	Dorsal	Up	3 bricks	None	45-50	F	Poor
T101	4c	Slot	Right side	Right	3 bricks	Bricks right side	Adult	M	Fair
T103	4c	Slot	Dorsal	Up	3 bricks	None	25+	M	Fair
T104	4c	Slot	Dorsal	Up	3 bricks	None	25+	M	Fair
T105	4c	Slot	Dorsal	Right	3 bricks	None	25+	M	Poor
T106	4c	Slot	Dorsal	Up	3 bricks	None	40+	M	Fair
T107	4c	Slot	Dorsal	Up	3 bricks	Bricks to waist	20-25	M	Good
T108	4c	Slot	Dorsal	Up	3 bricks	None	45+	M?	Poor
T111	4c	Slot	Dorsal?	?	3 bricks	Bricks right side	Adult	M	Very bad
T119	4c	Slot	Dorsal	Up	3 bricks	None	39-44	F	Very bad
T122	4c	Slot	Dorsal	Up	3 bricks	None	20-24	M	Good
B61	4c	Slot	Dorsal	Up	3 bricks	None	35-40	F	Fair
B62	4c	Slot	Dorsal	Right	None?	Stones right side	2-6	?	Poor
B63	4c	Slot	Dorsal	Up	None	None	Sub-adult	?	Very bad
B65	4c	Slot	Left side	Left	3 bricks	Bricks left side	6-8	?	Fair
B67	4c	?	Dorsal?	Up?	?	?	8-10	?	Very dist.
B74	4c	Niche	Dorsal	Up	3 bricks	Bricks all along	20-25	F	Fair
B75	4c	Slot	Left side	Left	None	None	6-8	?	Poor
B76	4c	Slot	Dorsal	Up	3 bricks	Bricks all along	24-30	?	Good
B77	4c	Slot	Dorsal	Up	3 bricks	Bricks all along	15-18	?	Fair
B78	4c	Slot	Dorsal	Up	3 bricks	Bricks all along	25-30	F?	Fair
B80	4c?	Slot	Dorsal	Up	3 bricks	Bricks all along	35+	F?	Fair
B81	4c?	Slot	Left side	Left	3 bricks	None	c. 25	F	Poor
B82	4c?	Slot	Dorsal	Up	3 bricks	None	Adult	M?	Poor
B84	4c	?	Right side	Right	None	None	Adult	?	Poor
B85	4c?	Slot	Right side	Right	3 bricks	None	2-6	?	Poor
B94	4c	Slot	Dorsal	Up	None	None	Adult	F	Fair
B95	4c	?	Left side	Left	None	None	16-18	F	Good
B97	4c	Slot	Right side	Right	3 bricks	None	20-25	F	Good
B99	4c	Slot	Right side	Right	3 bricks	None	7-9 month	?	Good
B102	4c	?	Ventral	?	None	None	25-26	M	Fair
B103	4c	?	Dorsal	Up	3 bricks	Bricks all along	2-6	?	Fair
B105	4c?	?	Dorsal	Up	None	None	22-24	M	Fair
B106	4c?	?	Dorsal	Right	None	None	6	?	Poor
B107	4c?	?	Dorsal	Up	None	None	10-12	?	Very frag.
B108	4c	?	Dorsal	Up	None	None	c. 12	?	Poor
B109	4c	Slot	Right side	Right	3 bricks	None	25+	M	Good
B110	4c	Slot	Dorsal	Up	None	None	c. 40	F	Fair
B111	4c	Slot	?	?		Brick + stone	Infant	?	Very frag.
B112	4c	?	Dorsal	Up	None	None	20-24	F	Poor
B114	4c	Slot	Dorsal	Up	?	?	35-39	?	Very bad
B115	4c	Slot	Dorsal	Up	3 bricks	None	11 months	?	Poor
B118	4c	Slot	Right side	Right	None	None	11-12	?	Very frag.
B120	4c	Slot	Dorsal	Up	None	None	11 months	?	Very bad
B121	4c	Slot	Dorsal	Up	3 bricks	None	c. 2	?	Fair

[1] Slot = plain vertical shaft; Niche = slot with offset niche to north or south

[2] All bodies, whether dorsal or on sides, were extended with heads to west

[3] Up = looking straight up; Right = head turned to right; Left = head turned to left

[4] 2 bricks = bricks at sides of head only; 3 bricks = bricks at sides and over the top of head

Burial no.	Phase	Shaft type[1]	Body position[2]	Head position[3]	Head cover[4]	Body cover	Age	Sex	Condition
B122	4c	Slot	Right side	Right	3 bricks	None	25	M	Good
B124	4c	Slot	Left side	Left	2 bricks	None	6	?	Fair
B130	4c?	Slot	Right side	Right	3 bricks	None	11 months	?	Poor
B133	4c	?	Right side	Right	None	None	2+	?	Poor
B140	4c	Slot	Dorsal	Right	3 bricks	None	c. 20	M	Good
B142	4c?	Slot	Right side	Right	2 bricks	None	c. 20	F	Fair
B143	4c	Slot	Dorsal	Up	2 bricks	None	2-6	?	Poor
B144	4c	Slot	Right side	Right	None	None	2-6	?	Fair
B145	4c	Slot	Dorsal	Up	3 bricks	None	2+	?	Fair
B146	4c	None?	Dorsal	Right	Superst.	Superstructure	27-30	M	Poor
B147	4c	None?	Dorsal	Up	Superst.	Superstructure	35-39	F	Poor
B150	4c	Slot	Dorsal	Right	3 bricks	None	30-40	M	Poor
B153	4c	Slot	Right side	Right	3 bricks	Bricks all along	14 months	?	Good
B155	4c?	Slot	Right side	Right	3 bricks	None	2	?	Poor
B156	4c	Slot	Dorsal	Right	3 bricks	None	c. 7	?	Poor
B160	4c	Slot	Dorsal	Right	3 bricks	None	30-35	M	Fair
B161	4c	Slot	Right side	Right	3 bricks	None	27-30	M	Fair
B162	4c	Slot	Right side	Right	None	None	25+	F	Fair
B163	4c	Slot	Dorsal	Up	3 bricks	Bricks right side	Adult	F	Poor
B168	4c	Slot	Left side	Left	2 stones	None	12-14	?	Fair
B169	4c	Slot	Dorsal	Up	None	None	c. 7	?	Poor
B175	4c?	Slot	Dorsal	Up	None	None	Adult	F	Fair
B176	4c?	Slot	Dorsal	Up	3 bricks	None	Adult	F	Fair
B182	4c?	Slot	Dorsal	Up	3 bricks	None	c. 1	?	Fair
B183	4c?	Slot	Dorsal	Up	3 bricks	None	c. 2	?	Poor
B187	4c	Slot	Dorsal	Right	3 bricks	Bricks all along	Mature	F	Fair
B188	4c?	Slot	Dorsal	Up	3 bricks	Bricks all along	2-6	?	Fair
B189	4c?	Niche	Dorsal	Up	3 bricks	Bricks right side	8	?	Good
B190	4c?	Slot	Dorsal	Up	2 bricks	None	Adult	M	Good
B199	4c	(burial not found)							
B210	4c?	Slot	Dorsal	Up	3 bricks	None	Adult	?	Fair
F1	4c	Foetus burial in Ware H1 pot							
B219	4abc	Slot	Dorsal	Up	?	?	30-35	F	Very bad
B220	4abc	Slot	Dorsal	Up	?	?	1-2	?	Very bad
B221	4abc	Slot	Dorsal	Up	?	?	45-50	M	Very bad
B222	4abc	Slot	Dorsal	Up	?	?	27-30	F	Very bad
B223	4abc	Slot	?	?	?	?	6-7	?	Skull only
B224	4abc	Slot	Right side	Right	?	?	23-25	F	Very bad
B225	4abc	Slot	Dorsal	Up	?	?	27-30	F	Very bad
B226	4abc	Slot	Dorsal	Up	?	?	30-35	F	Very bad
B227	4abc	Slot	?	?	?	?	?	?	Total dist.
B228	4abc	Slot	Right side	Right	?	?	45-50	F	Very dist.
B229	4abc	Slot	?	?	?	?	?	?	Total dist.
T3	5a	Slot	Dorsal	Up	3 bricks	None	29-35	F	Poor
T8:1	5a	Vault	Dorsal	Up	2 bricks	None	27-30	M	Good
T8:2	5a	Vault	Dorsal	Up	None	None	30-35	F	Good
T8:3	5a	Vault	Dorsal	Up	2 bricks	None	?	M	Very poor
T9	5a	Slot	Dorsal	Up	3 bricks	None	27-30	M	Good
B59	5a	?	Dorsal	Up	3 bricks	None	Adult	M	Fair
B64	5a?	Slot	Dorsal	Up	None	None	c. 6	?	Fair
B66	5a	?	Dorsal	Up	None	None	Child	?	Bad
B71	5a?	Slot	Left side	Left	None	None	Infant	?	Very bad
B72	5a?	Slot	Dorsal	Up	None	None	6-8	?	Very frag.
B73	5a?	Slot	Dorsal	Up	None	None	Child	?	Very frag.
B79	5a?	Slot	Right side	Right	3 bricks	None	10-12	?	Good
B98	5a	Slot	Dorsal	Up	1 brick	None	40-45	F	Poor
B104	5a	?	Dorsal	Up	3 bricks	None	c. 12	?	Poor

[1] Slot = plain vertical shaft; Niche = slot with offset niche to north or south
[2] All bodies, whether dorsal or on sides, were extended with heads to west
[3] Up = looking straight up; Right = head turned to right; Left = head turned to left
[4] 2 bricks = bricks at sides of head only; 3 bricks = bricks at sides and over the top of head

TABLE 9. COMPREHENSIVE REGISTER OF MEINARTI BURIALS (CONT.)

Grouped by subphase or phase

Burial no.	Phase	Shaft type[1]	Body position[2]	Head position[3]	Head cover[4]	Body cover	Age	Sex	Condition
B134	5a?	?	Right side	Right	None?	None?	2-6	?	Very frag.
B138	5a	?	Right side	Right	None	None	c. 1	?	Poor
B139	5a	Niche	Dorsal	Up	3 bricks	Bricks all along	20-21	F	Fair
B232	5a	Slot	Dorsal	Right	3 bricks	None	c. 25	M	Poor
T2	5b	Slot	Dorsal	Up	3 bricks	None	Young ad.	F?	Good
B58	5b?	?	Dorsal	Up	None	None	4-6	?	Very frag.
B148	5ab	?	Dorsal	Up	3 bricks	None	2+	?	Fair
T4	5c	Slot	Dorsal	Right	3 bricks	None	45-60	M	Very bad
B1	5/6	?	Dorsal	Up	None?	None	29-30	M?	Very frag.
B2	5/6	?	Dorsal	Up	None?	None	Young ad.	F?	Fragmentary
B3	5/6	?	Dorsal	Up	3 bricks	Bricks all along	25-30	F?	Good
B4	5/6	?	Dorsal	Left	3 bricks	None	Adult	?	Very frag.
B5	5/6	?	Dorsal	Up	3 bricks	Bricks all along	c. 30	F	Fragmentary
B6	5/6	Slot	Dorsal	Up	3 bricks	None	27-30	M	Good
B7	5/6	?	Dorsal	Up	3 bricks	Bricks all along?	10	?	Poor
B9	5/6	?	Dorsal	Up	3 bricks	Bricks all along	27-30	M	Fragmentary
B10	5/6	?	Dorsal	Up	3 bricks	Bricks all along	25-27	?	Very frag.
B11	5/6	?	Dorsal	Up	3 bricks	None	Adult	?	Very frag.
B12	5/6	?	Dorsal	Up	3 bricks	Bricks all along	7 months	?	Poor
B13	5/6	?	Dorsal	Up	3 bricks	Bricks all along	2-6	?	Poor
B15	5/6	?	Dorsal	Up	3 bricks	Bricks all along	39-40	F	Very frag.
B16	5/6	?	?	?	?	?	Young ad.	?	Very dist.
B17	5/6	?	?	?	?	Bricks	Child	?	Very dist.
B18	5/6	?	Dorsal	Up	3 bricks	None	2-6	?	Fair
B20	5/6	?	?	?	?	Bricks	Young ad.	?	Very dist.
B22	5/6	?	Dorsal	Up	3 bricks	None	30-34	M	Fair
B25	5/6	?	?	?	3 bricks	?	Adult	M	Skull only
B28	5/6	?	Dorsal	Up	3 bricks	Bricks all along	30-35	M	Good
B29	5/6	?	Dorsal	Up	3 bricks	Bricks all along	6-8	?	Fair
B30	5/6	?	Dorsal	Up	3 bricks	None	35-40	F	(not rec.)
B31	5/6	Slot	Dorsal	Up	3 bricks	None	25-27	F	Good
B32	5/6	?	Dorsal	Up	3 bricks	None	27-30	M	Fair
B33	5/6	?	?	?	?	?	c. 45	?	Very dist.
B34	5/6	?	Dorsal	Up	?	?	c. 25	F	Fair
B35	5/6	?	Dorsal	Up	None?	None	6-8	?	Good
B36	5/6	?	Dorsal	Up	3 bricks	None	8-10	?	Fair
B37	5/6	?	Left side	Left	3 bricks	None	c. 2	?	Fair
B38	5/6	?	?	?	?	?	Adult	?	Very frag.
B39	5/6	?	Dorsal	Up	?	?	c. 7	?	Very frag.
B40	5/6	?	Dorsal	Up	None	None	18-20	?	Poor
B41	5/6	?	Dorsal	Right	None	None	2-6	?	Fair
B42	5/6	?	Dorsal	Up	3 bricks	None	25-30?	M?	Fair
B43	5/6	?	Dorsal	Left	3 bricks	None	c. 1	?	Good
B44	5/6	?	Dorsal	Up	3 bricks	Bricks all along	Sub-adult	?	Good
B45	5/6	?	Dorsal	Up	3 bricks	None	2-6	?	Fair
B46	5/6	?	Dorsal	Up	3 bricks	None	20-24	F	Fair
B47	5/6	Slot	Dorsal	Up	3 bricks	None	20-24	F	Good
B48	5/6	Slot	Dorsal	Up	3 bricks	Bricks all along	2-6	?	Good
B49	5/6	Slot	Dorsal	Up	3 bricks	Bricks all round	c. 20	?	Good
B50	5/6	?	Dorsal	Up	3 bricks	None	20-24	?	Fair
B51	5/6	?	Dorsal	Left	3 bricks	None	c. 10	?	Fair
B52	5/6	?	?	?	3 bricks	None	10-14	?	Very dist.
B54	5/6	Slot	Dorsal	Up	3 bricks	None	c. 5	?	Good
B55	5/6	Slot	Dorsal	Up	3 bricks	None	Sub-adult	?	Fair
B56	5/6	Slot	Dorsal	Right	3 bricks	None	6-8	?	Poor

[1] Slot = plain vertical shaft; Niche = slot with offset niche to north or south
[2] All bodies, whether dorsal or on sides, were extended with heads to west
[3] Up = looking straight up; Right = head turned to right; Left = head turned to left
[4] 2 bricks = bricks at sides of head only; 3 bricks = bricks at sides and over the top of head

TABLE 9. COMPREHENSIVE REGISTER OF MEINARTI BURIALS (CONT.)

Grouped by subphase or phase

Burial no.	Phase	Shaft type[1]	Body position[2]	Head position[3]	Head cover[4]	Body cover	Age	Sex	Condition
B57	5/6	Slot	Dorsal	Up	None	None	Sub-adult	?	Poor
B60	5/6	Slot	Dorsal	Up	?	?	*c.* 25	?	Poor
B53	(same as T45, q.v.)								
B19	(burial not found)								
B21	(burial not found)								
B23	(burial not found)								
B24	(burial not found)								
B27	(burial not found)								

[1] Slot = plain vertical shaft; Niche = slot with offset niche to north or south
[2] All bodies, whether dorsal or on sides, were extended with heads to west
[3] Up = looking straight up; Right = head turned to right; Left = head turned to left
[4] 2 bricks = bricks at sides of head only; 3 bricks = bricks at sides and over the top of head

in nine cases toward the left (north). Again this was a departure from the practice at Kulubnarti, where heads were far more often turned toward the left (Adams 1998b, 28). The practice of turning the head of the deceased also seems to have been more common at Phase 4 than it was later.

Placement of arms and hands did not follow any uniform usage. In the largest number of cases the hands rested on the pubis (Plates 9e, 14a, 14b), but in many instances the arms and hands were at the sides (Plates 9c, 14c). In at least two cases the left arm only was flexed, and in one case both arms were crossed over the breast.

Grave goods

It is very probable that most or all of the Meinarti burials were originally shrouded, as was found to be the case at Kulubnarti (Adams *et al.* 1999, 23, 37) and Qasr Ibrim (author's unpublished field notes). Due to the frequent flooding of the cemetery, however, no shrouds were preserved. Otherwise, grave goods were found only in the cases of a few infant and adolescent burials. One had a bronze earring and a glass pendant, and two had each one iron anklet. One of the latter had also a necklace of cowrie shell beads. Obviously, these were not funerary offerings in the usual sense; they were merely small items of personal jewelry that were not removed at the time of burial.

As previously noted, there were external votive lamps on many of the tombs, and one such lamp was found within the vaulted chamber of Tomb 8. Registered finds from the cemetery are enumerated in Table 16.

Resumé of chronological development

Subphases 4a and 4b (= Levels 9 and 8; Figure 17)
As previously noted, tombs and burials from these two subphases could be differentiated only in a very few cases. The two subphases together witnessed the most extensive horizontal development of the Meinarti Cemetery, when it numbered at least 63 tomb burials and 83 burials without superstructures. An additional 11 burials without

superstructures might also belong to these subphases. The cemetery at its maximum development extended north for about 5m from the church walls, east for about 15m, and south for about 30m (cf. Figure 17). Tombs were most densely clustered in the immediate vicinity of the church on the north and east, where they stood practically shoulder-to-shoulder, while they were slightly more dispersed in the southerly part of the cemetery. However, there was a sizable area immediately adjoining the south church wall where all of the superstructures as well as many of the burials had been destroyed by subsequent digging.

The cemetery surface on which tomb superstructures were built had from the beginning a considerable slope from west to east, and a lesser slope from north to south; that is, away from the church walls (cf. Figure 3). Since all the tombs and burials attributable to Subphase 4a were close to the church walls, it seems evident that the cemetery over time grew outward from that original nucleus. The surface upon which the superstructures were built was compacted and easy to follow archaeologically; it was the same surface that extended between the houses of Subphases 4a and 4b. As elsewhere, it was extensively littered with sherds and other refuse, which further aided in the dating of the surface and its associated tombs.

Infant burials were especially numerous in Subphases 4a and 4b. They were often interred directly alongside the superstructures of adult burials, possibly reflecting a family connection. Infants seem often to have been put into rather small holes, with the result that the knees had to be partially flexed, and the backs sometimes bent or twisted.

The major tombs

It is notable that all of the largest and most elaborate of the surviving superstructures from Subphases 4a and 4b were on the north or northwest side of the church, and close to the walls. This may be misleading, however, because there is some evidence that a number of tombs close to the church wall on the south side were deliberately razed at Subphase 4c.

Tomb T11, close to the north church wall, was probably the oldest tomb superstructure at Meinarti. It is one of

TABLE 10. DISTRIBUTION OF BURIALS BY
AGE, SEX, AND PERIOD

Subphases	Burials under tombs	Burials without tombs	Totals
Subphases 4a-b			
Adults			
Males	15	10	25
Females	20	21	41
Sex uncertain	9	10	19
Adolescents	4	5	9
Infants	13	35	48
Age undetermined	2	2	4
Foetus in pot		2	2
Total Subphases 4a-b	63	85	148
Subphases 4a-c			
Adults			
Males		1	1
Females		6	6
Infants		2	2
Age undetermined		2	2
Total Subphases 4a-c		11	11
Subphase 4c			
Adults			
Male	30	9	39
Female	13	16	29
Sex uncertain		4	4
Adolescents		6	6
Infants	1	25	26
Foetus in pot		1	1
Total Subphase 4c	44	61	105
Subphase 5a			
Adults			
Males		2	2
Females		2	2
Adolescents		2	2
Infants		7	7
Total Subphase 5a		13	13
Subphase 5b			
Adolescent		1	1
Total Subphase 5b		1	1
Phases 5/6			
Adults			
Male	4	11	15
Female	3	12	15
Sex uncertain		10	10
Adolescents		9	9
Infants		24	24
Total Phases 5/6	7	66	73
Total all phases	114	237	351

only two that can be securely dated to Subphase 4a, because it was built earlier than the retaining wall at the east side of the church, which was added at Subphase 4b. It was a tomb of Type 1B: a hollow square of brick masonry originally surmounted by a dome. It was not however a chamber tomb; there were no lateral entrances to the interior of the square, and the associated burial was beneath rather than within it. The burial was probably but

not certainly of a female, of mature age.

The superstructure was originally covered with a thick, smooth grey plaster, which exhibited traces of a good many randomly scratched graffiti, mostly having geometric patterns. At the west side, about 50cm above the ground, there was an impression 36cm wide and 7cm deep, where a tombstone had originally been inset. This might possibly have been the original locus of a tombstone, dated 1037 (Khartoum no. 14), which was collected by an earlier visitor to Meinarti (see Monneret de Villard 1935, 119-20) At the base of the walls, at least on the north and west sides, the structure was adjoined by a pavement 40cm wide, of bricks set on edge. It was the only occurrence of such a pavement in the cemetery.

Sometime after its construction, the Tomb T11 superstructure was adjoined on its eastern side by the terminus of the brick retaining wall that was built along the north and east sides of the church. The superstructure itself thus became in effect a part of the retaining wall. At a much later date, when the exterior was probably deeply sanded up, the top of the dome was broken in, and the interior was filled with a great quantity of refuse. Later still – most probably at Subphase 5a – Tomb T3 was directly overbuilt, and its burial was cut down into the interior of the buried Tomb T11 superstructure.

Tomb T12, also on the north side of the church and slightly to the east of Tomb 11, was the other tomb that could be dated securely to Subphase 4a. It was a cross-topped mastaba of Type 2B, but differed from other tombs of this type in that the western pylon was considerably taller than usual, to allow for the installation of a tombstone at the west end. The stone (registered as 6-K-3/832 and shown in Plates 13a and 17a) was 48cm high and 31cm wide, and bore a Coptic inscription of 16 lines, with a date equivalent to A.D. 1045. The tomb was covered with pink plaster. The burial was that of a female, aged 34 according to the tombstone inscription.

Tomb T18, close to the northwest corner of the church, was the largest of the Meinarti *qubba* tombs (Plates 10b and 10c). It was built directly adjoining the northwest corner of the church retaining wall built at Subphase 4b, in such a way that the retaining wall also formed a part of the western wall of the superstructure (see Figure 10). Like Tomb T11, Tomb T18 was a hollow square of masonry surmounted by a dome (Type 1B), of which however only a small part survived. As in the case of Tomb T11 there were no lateral openings to the chamber, and the disarticulated adult bones found within it had evidently been dropped in as refuse at a much later date, after the top had been broken in. The superstructure was covered with pink plaster, but there was no place where a tombstone could have been set. The interment, in a shaft beneath the tomb, was that of a female of 30+ years, with a foetus or newborn infant placed between the thighs. Probably therefore it was a woman who had died in childbirth.

Tomb T19 was another very large *qubba* tomb of Type 1B, built directly adjoining the east wall of the church at its northern end. The superstructure was a "split-level" affair in that it partly overlapped the terrace adjoining the west side of the church. That is, the western two-thirds of the superstructure was built directly on top of the terrace, and the vertical part of the walls was relatively low, while the eastern third was built on lower ground below the terrace, and the vertical portion of the walls was about 1m higher than in the western portion. A cross-section is shown in Figure 18. The superstructure was rather poorly preserved, with only a very small part of the dome surviving, and most of the north wall missing. Apparently the church wall itself had formed the western wall of the tomb. The structure was covered with thick grey plaster, but obviously it could have had no tombstone or lamp box, since its west side abutted directly against the church. The burial shaft was cut down into the fill of the terrace, and partly through the terrace retaining wall. The burial, that of an adult female, was very badly preserved.

perfectly preserved, except that at Subphase 4c, when just the top projected above the accumulated sand, it was subjected to considerable wear from persons approaching the church. At Subphase 5b, when it was deeply buried, the burial from Tomb T2 was partly cut into the top (visible especially in Plates 9f and 12e).

Other tombs

Virtually all of the different superstructure types shown in Figure 16 occurred at Subphases 4a and 4b, in considerable numbers. Altogether, 68 superstructures could be dated to these two subphases.

Tomb T33. The body was found immediately under the superstructure, rather than in an excavated shaft.

Tomb T68. A very unusual structure, to which a separate

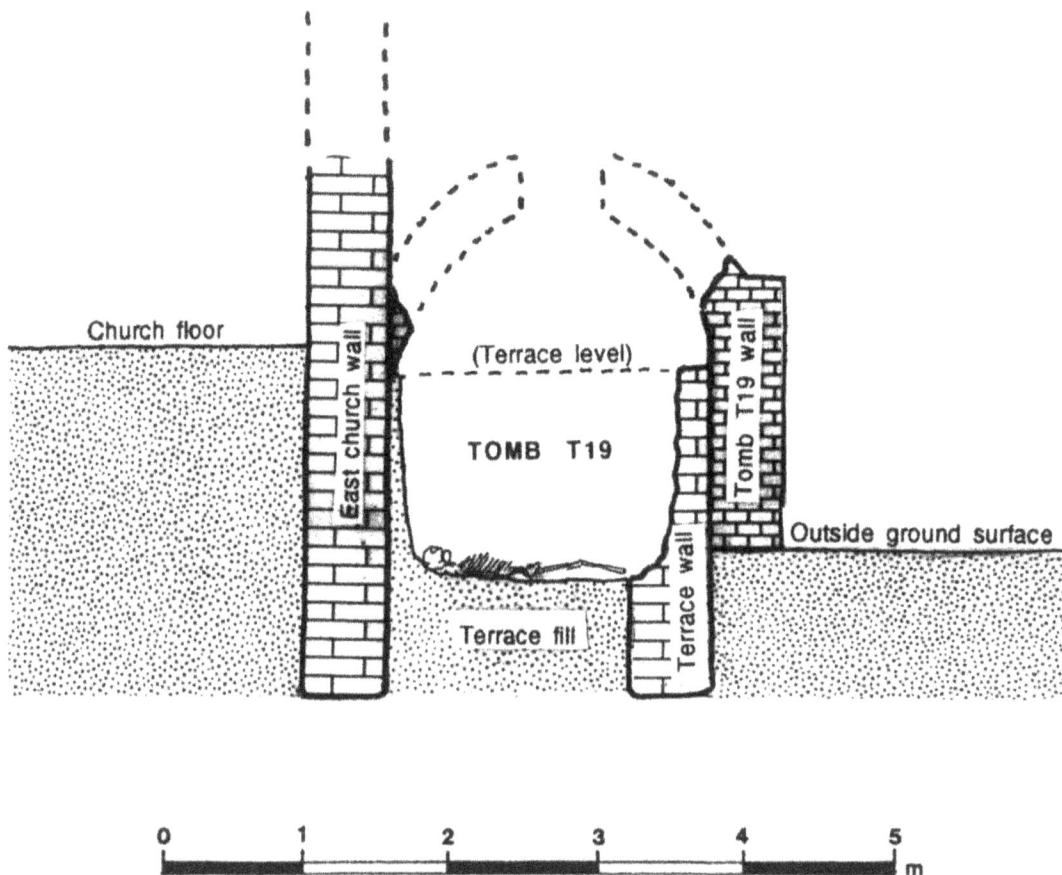

Figure 18. Reconstructed cross-section of Tomb T19, which was constructed so that the superstructure "straddled" the platform adjoining the eastern church wall, while the burial itself was intruded into the platform. Bricks are not shown to actual scale.

Tomb T120 was a cruciform tomb of Type 8A, built directly adjoining the north wall of the church, below its central window. It was a solid mass of brick masonry in the form of a nearly equal-armed cross, although the eastern and western arms were slightly longer than the north and south arms (Plates 9f, 12e, and 12f). All around the top of the structure, the edges were stepped down in three small steps. The tomb had apparently been whitewashed, though this was not absolutely certain. There was no tombstone or lamp box. The burial was that of a female, aged 45 or older. The superstructure was almost

type number was not assigned (Plate 13b). It appeared to be a plain rectangular mastaba (Type 4A), but instead of being formed of solid brick masonry, only the sides were formed by thin mud bricks, while the whole interior was filled with sand. The top was presumably also covered with mud or mud bricks, but it was not preserved.

Burials without superstructures

Burial B116. This burial, of a female, appears to have been crowded into a grave pit that was much too small. The knees were sharply flexed upward, and the arms were also flexed upward, with the hands above the head. There was no brick covering of the head.

Burial B230 was that of a young female, aged 22-25, who probably died in childbirth, since she was buried in dorsal position with a foetus between the knees. The arms were folded on the breast rather than in the more conventional position at the sides.

Subphase 4c (= Level 7; Figure 19)

Before the end of this subphase, sand had accumulated to a depth of just about 1m over the whole surface area of the cemetery. As a result the older mastaba tombs were entirely buried, while the tops of *qubba* tombs still projected for a considerable distance above the surface. It seems that these were still respected to the extent that their projecting tops were not disturbed at Subphase 4c. Despite the sanding over of the earlier tombs, the cemetery presented very nearly the same appearance as at Subphases 4a and 4b, because the newly built superstructures were of the same types as their predecessors. Most of the best preserved cross-topped tombs were found at this level, in two fairly orderly rows near the south end of the cemetery (Plates 8e and 8f). Burials were just as densely clustered, especially close to the church walls, as before, but the most southerly end of the cemetery was apparently no longer used (cf. Figure 19). The southernmost identifiable tombs from Subphase 4c were only 20m south of the church wall, while the cemetery at Subphase 4b had extended another 10m to the south.

The cemetery at Subphase 4c numbered at least 44 burials under tombs and 60 without superstructures, but an additional 11 burials without superstructures might also date from Subphase 4c. These figures are somewhat less than the totals for Subphases 4a and 4b. Taken together with the diminished areal extent of the cemetery, they might possibly indicate a decline in the village population, given that the time spans of Subphases 4ab and of Subphase 4c were about the same (cf. Table 1).

There were a number of new interments on the north side of the church, but space here was limited because the tops of the Subphase 4ab *qubbas* still projected above ground level. The same limitation did not apply on the south side, where the earlier tomb superstructures were completely buried. Consequently, the great majority of newly built superstructures, including all of the largest ones, were on the south side of the church. However, in the area immediately adjoining the south side, and more particularly toward its eastern end, there were no preserved superstructures. Instead, the Subphase 4c surface was occupied by a jumbled mass of brick which probably represents dismantled tomb superstructures, both from this subphase and from the earlier ones. A number of bodies (Burials B74 to B82), found in two orderly rows at a depth of about 1m below this material, are believed to be those of individuals who were originally covered by the destroyed superstructures. The reason for this destruction is not clear, since the area was never subsequently overbuilt.

The major tombs

It is a surprising fact that all of the burials in, or under, the large *qubba* tombs of this subphase were those of young adults in their 20s.

Tombs T5, T6, and T7 formed a contiguous row in a north-south line, with Tomb T5, at the north, being close to but not adjoining the south church wall. All three were tombs of Type 1X; that is, their lower parts were square enclosures of brick, but not enough survived of the upper parts to tell whether or not they had been domed. All three were chamber tombs in which burials were placed on a hard pavement within the superstructure walls. Their spaciousness suggests that these tombs were meant as family vaults (i.e. for repeated use), but in fact each contained only a single body, which in each case had subsequently been disturbed. The disturbance was probably the work of robbers, who may have mistaken these for pre-Christian tombs because of their shape.

The tops of all three tombs had been deliberately leveled, to what was then the ground level, at Subphase 5a, perhaps to facilitate entrance to the south side of the church. Tomb T8 was subsequently built in such a way that it partly overlay the western ends of Tombs T6 and T7.

Tomb T6 was covered with thick grey plaster, while Tombs T5 and T7 had a thin whitewash over pale pink plaster. None of the three had had a tombstone. The contiguous relationship of the three tombs suggests that they all belonged to members of the same family.

Tomb T6, the middle member of the three, was obviously built first, and was enclosed by 40-cm walls on all four sides. On a hard-packed mud pavement within the superstructure was the disturbed body of a young male, aged about 20. Tomb T5, adjoining the north side of Tomb T6, had 40-cm walls on the north and west, but the south wall, directly adjoining Tomb T6, was only a 20-cm wall. The east wall was not preserved. On the floor within the tomb walls was the disturbed body of a young female of about 20. This however may have been a later intrusion, for another interment, that of a male of about 25, was found in a pit beneath the tomb. Tomb T7 was built adjoining the south side of Tomb T6, and had no north wall of its own; it simply used the south wall of Tomb T6. The walls on the other three sides were 40-cm walls. On the floor within was the disturbed body of a young adult, apparently male.

Tomb T87, of Type 1B, was the only *qubba* tomb at Meinarti that was fully preserved; it was also the only one that stood at a considerable distance from the church walls, on the south side (Plate 10a). The vertical lower walls, to a height of 80cm, formed a brick masonry rectangle measuring 2.4m east-west by 1.7m north-south. In the centers of all four sides were arched openings, 30cm wide and 35cm high, set at heights 20 to 30cm above the ground level. Within the interior, at a level flush with the bases of the openings, was a flat pavement of brick with a + embossed in brick in the center. The vertical lower walls were surmounted by a conical dome 80cm high, open at the top. The diameter at the base was 1.7m; that is, corresponding to the north-south dimension of the tomb. The cone had a consistent taper, to a diameter of 80cm at the top. The whole structure was covered with hard pink plaster, but it had neither tombstone nor lamp box. The underlying burial, in a conventional shaft, was that of a young male, aged 22 to 24.

Tombs T14 and T15 were the only two stepped mastaba tombs (Type 3) in the entire Meinarti cemetery. They were built exactly side by side (Plate 12a) and very possibly at the same time; at any rate they were surely for individuals of the same family. Both had mud plaster, and Tomb T15, at least, had a lamp box. In the case of Tomb T14 the western end was too destroyed to determine if a lamp box was present. Both tombs covered the bodies of adult males of middle age.

Tomb T119 was the only tomb of Type 8B; that is, it was made in the shape of a cross having a very wide (80cm) central member and two much narrower (40cm) transepts (Plate 12e). One transept was at the conventional place near the middle, and the other at the west end. The tomb was built immediately beside the other cruciform tomb, Tomb T120, but at Subphase 4c rather than Subphase 4b. The top of the tomb had been completely leveled off at Subphase 5a, so that there was no surviving adornment of the upper surface. The tomb had apparently only mud plaster rendering, and had no lamp box. The underlying burial was that of a female, aged between 39 and 44.

Other tombs

Most of the Meinarti tomb types were once again represented at Subphase 4c, in proportions similar to those at Subphases 4a-b. As before, infant burials were numerous, but at this subphase only one had a superstructure.

Tomb T21. The burial in this tomb, that of a female in her late 30s, had a disarticulated skull directly on top of the bricks that covered the face of the burial. There were also a few loose vertebrae. Probably these were the bones of an earlier burial accidentally disturbed when the shaft for T21 was dug.

Tomb T25. In this very wide superstructure, two bodies (B146 and B147) appear to have been actually built into the superstructure itself. The bodies, which lay closely side by side, exactly fitted the dimensions of the superstructure, and they were totally encased in the mud of the structure (see Plate 13c). These circumstances tended to rule out the possibility that the burials were accidental intrusions from a later date. The bodies were those of a male in his late 20s, and a female in her late 30s.

Tomb T61. In this tomb the body was found immediately under the superstructure, rather than in an excavated shaft.

Burials without superstructures.

Burial B105. This individual, although he looks very relaxed in the photo (Plate 14d), was actually buried in a very awkward position, in a grave that was obviously much too small. Probably this was a hasty interment. The body was that of a male, aged 22-24.

Burials B219-B229. At the eastern extremity of the cemetery, directly east of the church, there was a concentration of eleven burials stacked so close together that at least some of them must have been buried in a common grave (Plates 14e and 14f). They had all been laid out in the traditional dorsally extended position, yet their close proximity in other respects points to hasty interment. With two exceptions, the identifiable bodies were all those of

females, mostly aged about 30. The exceptions were a male and a female, each aged between 45 and 50. These were the lowest-lying burials anywhere in the Meinarti cemetery, and had been under water so long and so often that it was impossible to tell if the bodies had had brick coverings over the heads or bodies. Some had been disturbed by the roots of a dom palm growing nearby. Because there were no preserved superstructures and no other burials close by, it was also impossible to assign these burials definitely to any subphase. Because of their distance from the church, however, it is very tentatively suggested here that they may have belonged to Subphase 4c.

Phases 5 and 6 (= Levels 3-6; Figure 20)

Throughout most of the cemetery area, the ground surfaces from the later Christian period had been destroyed by subsequent deflation, and consequently no tomb superstructures were preserved. The only exceptions were at the western, or upper, ends of the cemetery, close to the church walls. Here, Tombs T3, T8, and T9 could be dated specifically to Subphase 5a, Tomb T2 to Subphase 5b, and Tomb T4 (within the church itself) either to Subphase 5c or to Phase 6. There were, in addition, 13 burials without superstructures that could be dated, on stratigraphic grounds, to Subphase 5a, and one to Subphase 5b. All other burials, totaling 73 altogether, could only be assigned to Phases 5 or 6, without specification of a subphase.

The cemetery at Phase 5 appears to have very considerably contracted, on the south side. The most southerly preserved burials were at a distance of only 13m from the church walls (cf. Figure 20). It is possible however that more southerly graves had been destroyed in their entirety by flood erosion, since this was the low end of the cemetery. To the east and north of the church, burials occupied pretty much the same space as before.

The major tombs

Tomb T3, on the north side of the church, could be dated on stratigraphic grounds to Subphase 5a. It was apparently a tomb of Type 1X: a solid square of brick masonry which may have been surmounted by a dome. However, only about the western third of the structure was preserved, and only to a height of about 40cm, above which it had been deliberately leveled at Subphase 5b. The more easterly portions had been entirely destroyed by flood action. The tomb was covered in dark, golden pink plaster with a thin overlay of whitewash. Plaster of this same color was used in Building II-III at Subphase 5a, but never at any other subphase. A recess in the west side of the superstructure, 32cm wide and situated 25cm above the ground, showed where a tombstone had once been affixed. Directly below it at ground level was a covered lamp box, which was partly destroyed when Tomb T2 was built alongside at Subphase 5b. The burial from Tomb T3 was intruded down into the buried top of Tomb T11; it was that of a young adult, probably female.

Tomb T8 was located on the south side of the church, and directly in line with the south doorway. It was the only tomb of Type 1C at Meinarti. Like Tomb T3 it could be

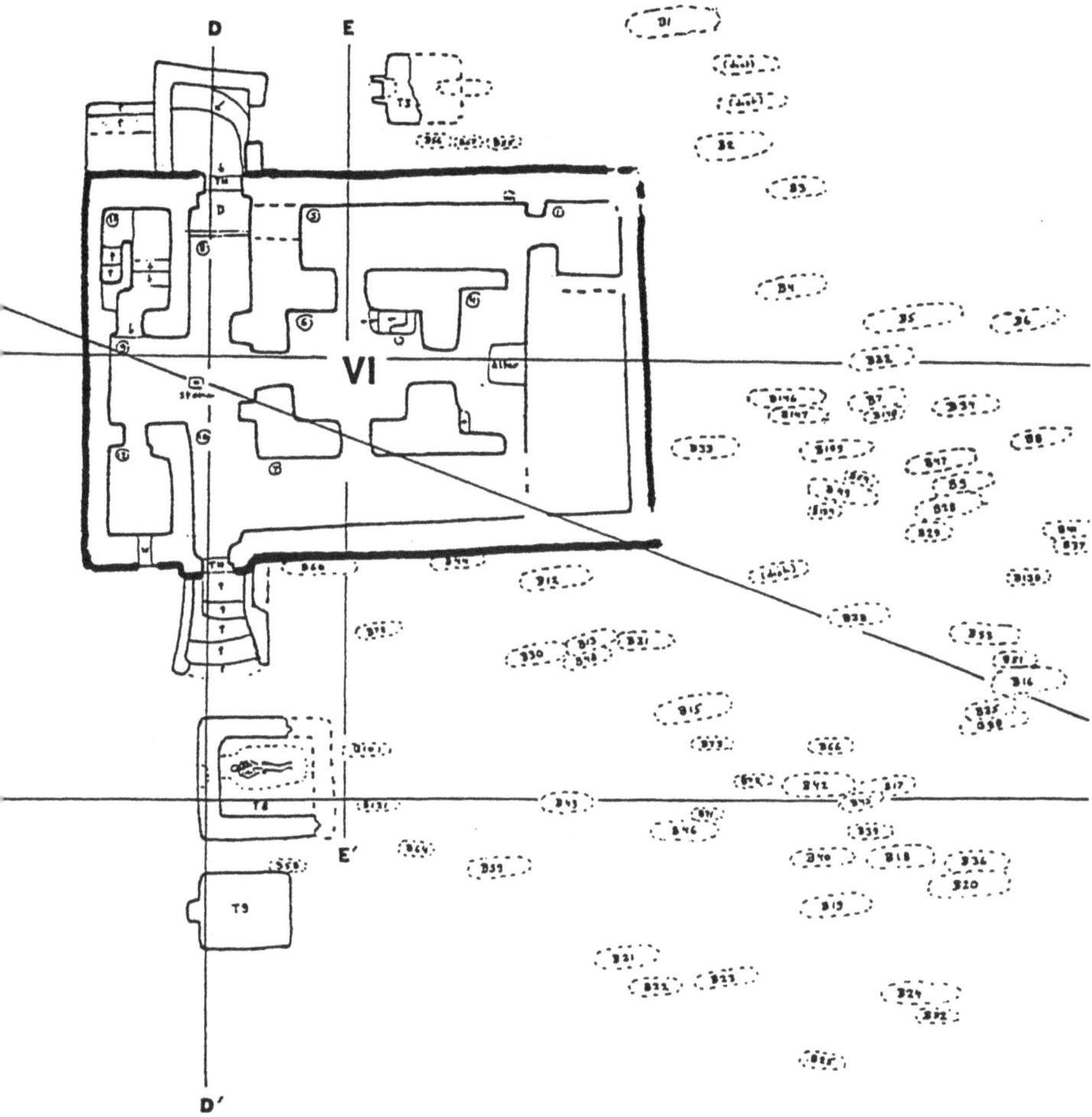

D   E

T3

VI

Altar

stone

T5

T6

D1

(A31)

(A32)

B2

B3

B4

B35   B36

B22

B46   B7   B39

B47   B9

B33   B109   B51   B5   B53   B28

B41   B44   B29   B54   B57

B105   B130

E'   B12   (A30)   B23

B11   B13

B30   B13   B21   B71

B8   B16

B15   B25   B52

B73   B66

B50   B42   B17

B10   B43   B52   B48

B46   B44   B33

T8   B31   B40   B18   B34

B64   B20

B58   B33   B19

T9

B21

B22   B23   B24   B72

D'   E'   B27

6-K-3
MEINARTI
LATE CHRISTIAN PHASE 5a
(= Level 6)
c. 1200 A.D.

0   1   2   3   4   5   6   7   8   9   10
                                    Meters

Figure 20. Plan of the cemetery at Subphase 5a.

dated specifically to Subphase 5a on stratigraphic grounds, as well as by the distinctive color of its plaster. The above-ground portion was a hollow square of masonry, having a flat interior floor of mud. It may or may not have supported a dome, for the uppermost parts of the walls were not preserved, and the east wall as well as a small part of the north wall were missing entirely. The structure, like that of Tomb T3, was covered with dark golden pink plaster with a thin whitewash overlay. A tombstone about 38cm wide had been set into the west side at a distance of 50cm above the base; it had already been prised out when the staircase to the south church door was overbuilt at Subphase 5c. There was no lamp box.

The floor in Tomb T8 was directly underlain by a brick vaulted chamber about 1m high, running the full length of the tomb from east to west (Plate 10d). The spaces between the incurving sides of the vault and the vertical side walls of the chamber were filled in with bricks laid vertically, many of which had obviously been robbed from the superstructures of the underlying Tombs T5-T7. The vault had been cut away at the east end by robbers or *maroq* diggers, but the western half was fully preserved. It was entered from the west end through an arched opening 45cm wide and 55cm high, which when found was firmly blocked with dry-laid brick .

The vault of Tomb T8 contained three bodies laid more or less on top of each other. The two lowermost bodies (T8:2 and T8:3), lying directly on the floor, were those of an adult male of uncertain age, and a female, aged 30 to 35 (Plate 14c). The upper body, T8:1, was in the center of the vault, partly overlying both T8:2 and T8:3 (Plate 14b). It was that of a male, aged 27-30. Against the south wall of the burial chamber was a fairly large dish lamp, possibly of Ware R21, which showed evidence of burning on more than one occasion (visible at the upper left in Plate 14b).

Tomb T8, like all Meinarti tombs, eventually became deeply buried in sand. When, at Subphase 5b, the staircase leading down to the south church doorway was extended upward, its uppermost steps were built directly adjoining the west wall of the tomb, which served as a kind of stair retaining wall (cf. Figure 13). At Subphase 5c however the steps were extended upward still further, and directly over the top of Tomb T8. It is probable that the uppermost part of the tomb (perhaps a dome) was demolished at that time, to allow building of the steps.

Tomb T9 was located just to the south of Tomb T8 and in a direct line with it. It was built on the same ground surface as Tomb T8, and can also be dated securely to Subphase 5a. The remains, which were preserved to a maximum height of about 45cm, appeared to be those of a tomb of Type 1A: a solid, square mass of brick masonry that was presumably surmounted by a dome. The tomb had the same dark pink plaster, overlaid with whitewash, as had Tomb 8, and had an intact lamp box at the west end. The presence or absence of a tombstone could not be determined, as the top had apparently been deliberately leveled at Subphase 5b. The underlying burial was that of a male, aged 27 to 30.

Tomb T2, located on the north side of the church just west of the north doorway, was the only tomb specifically datable to Subphase 5b. It was built very close to the west side of Tomb T3, but at a level about 40cm higher, and its construction resulted in the partial destruction of the lamp box on Tomb T3. Tomb T2 was a *qubba* tomb of Type 1A, comprising a solid mass of brick masonry surmounted by a hollow dome, of which a small remnant survived. The height of the solid masonry portion was a little over 1m. The tomb was covered with golden pink plaster, somewhat lighter in color than the plaster on Tombs T3 and T8. The underlying burial was that of a young adult, probably but not certainly female.

At some time after its construction, but apparently still within Subphase 5b, the southwest corner of the superstructure was hacked away, apparently to facilitate entry to the north doorway of the church. At a still later date, the retaining wall outside the church doorway was extended eastward so that it partly intruded over the top of Tomb T2.

Tomb T4 was the only tomb ever built within the Meinarti Church. It was most probably built at Subphase 5c, during the last years when the church was still functioning a such. It was built in the south aisle, adjoining the south side of the southeast nave pilaster, and would almost completely have blocked the aisle. Only the western end of the superstructure survived, but it appears to have been a rather large brick mastaba, about 1.2m wide and perhaps 2m long. A lamp box adjoined the west end. The structure survived only to a height of 25cm above the floor, so that the original form of the top could not be determined. The tomb had dark pink plaster covered by whitewash, as did the adjoining nave pilaster and a part of the nearby church floor. The underlying burial was that of a male, aged 45 to 50.

Other late burials

As Table 9 shows, there were 66 burials without superstructures that were attributed on stratigraphic grounds either to Phase 5 or to Phase 6. The surviving features (body covering, body position, etc.) differed in no way from those of earlier burials, except that fewer of the individuals were lying on their sides.

Although the Meinarti Church almost certainly went out of use at Phase 6, there is no reason to suppose that use of the cemetery did not continue until the final abandonment of the village. There was certainly no cemetery adjoining the west bank church at Abdel Qadir, where I have surmised that the Meinarti folk worshipped during Phase 6.

The skeletal evidence

Despite the poor preservation of many of the Meinarti burials, the Colorado anthropologists who examined the skeletons were able to record at least some information from all but six of them. They have described their methodology thus:

> Insofar as possible, the basic measurements and observations on the skeletal material were made in the field due to the problems involved in shipment of so

large a sample. Approximately 500 measurements and observations were made on each complete skeleton: the skulls were photographed and samples of bone-sections and hair and tissue where available. A collection was also made of skeletal pathologies, and an extensive dentition sample was obtained.

(Armelagos *et al.* 1965, 26)

All of the information presented in the following paragraphs is derived from the studies of the Colorado anthropologists, either published or in the form of personal communications to the present author.

The Meinarti material was not analyzed separately from other Christian Nubian burials, except with regard to demographics and mortality. In their studies of craniology, dentition, and pathology, the Colorado anthropologists combined the Meinarti burials with those from other cemeteries to form a single study population. The features described in the next paragraphs are not therefore based on the study of Meinarti skeletons alone.

Somatic characteristics

During much of the twentieth century, interpretations of Nubian cultural history were beclouded by a false issue of race. Elliot Smith, Wood Jones, and Douglas Derry, the anatomists who examined the finds from the First Archaeological Survey of Nubia (1907-1911), thought that they could identify racial differences between each of the successive Nubian cultural groups, from A-Group to X-Group (cf. especially Elliot Smith and Jones 1910). On that basis it became fashionable to attribute each of the cultural

of its own. It remained the dominant paradigm for the interpretation of culture change in Nubia at least down to the time of the High Dam Campaign (cf. Emery 1965).[3]

In the 1960s I began to suggest that the multiple-migration theory could not be sustained on the basis of cultural evidence; that is, there was far more evidence of continuity than of change between each culture period and the next (cf. Adams 1966a, 156-62; Adams 1967). However, the theory of racial change was most conclusively laid to rest by the work of the Colorado anthropologists, using a far more complete and sophisticated set of analytical tools than had been available to earlier students. In their analyses of material from eight Meroitic, X-Group, and Christian cemeteries, including Meinarti, they were able to show that there were no significant differences among the three populations, in terms of either cranial or dental characteristics.

Craniology

The studies of Elliot Smith, Jones, and Batrawi were based exclusively on the comparative study of skulls, for no other skeletal material was collected by the early anthropologists. Although other features of skeletal morphology have since been subjected to comparative study, it remains true that cranial features provide the best indications of biological relationships among populations. The Meinarti skulls, as well as those from other Lower Nubian cemeteries, were intensively analyzed by the Colorado anthropologists; their statistical findings are summarized in Table 11 (adapted from Adams *et al.* 1999, 75).

TABLE 11. SUMMARY STATISTICS OF MEROITIC, X-GROUP, AND CHRISTIAN CRANIAL REMAINS, IN MILLIMETERS

	Meroitic		X-Group		Christian	
Measurement	Avg.	S.D.*	Avg.	S.D.*	Avg.	S.D.*
Cranial length	178	6.9	179	6.7	179.2	9.2
Cranial width	131	5.2	132	5.1	129.8	7.4
Basion/bregma height	127	6.3	130	6.1	126.9	8.4
Auricular height	107	6.6	107	6.6	107.1	7.1
Endobasion/prosthion height	93.3	5.6	94.9	6.1	92.1	7.8
Bizygomatic diameter	119	8.6	120	7.3	118.7	10.6
Nasion/prosthion height	61.2	6.6	65.1	5.5	59.2	7.7
Palatal length	45.4	4.2	49.9	5.2	36.8	3.8
Mandibular length	84.3	7.9	84.1	5.8	79.4	8.9
Mandibular thickness	14.5	1.7	14.9	4.3	14.1	1.9
Bigonial width	91.9	11.3	88.8	8.6	86.6	10.1

* Standard deviation

changes in Nubia to the migration of a new group, somewhat distinct racially from its predecessor (see Adams 1977, 91-5 for discussion). Although Ahmed Batrawi was able to show a generation later that the anatomical basis for this theory was erroneous (see Batrawi 1935), the multiple-migration theory by that time had acquired a life

The implications of these figures are clear. At least in terms of their cephalic characteristics, the medieval Nubians looked just like their Meroitic and X-Group predecessors, and also just like their modern-day descendants.

Dentition

Since the time of Smith, Jones, and Batrawi, a major advance in the study of biological relationships has come about through the development of dental anthropology. It has been found that features of dental morphology are

³ Actually, multiple-migration theories were the dominant paradigm for the interpretation of prehistory just about everywhere in the Old World, in the 19th and early 20th centuries. See Adams *et al.* 1978 and Adams 1978.

nearly as variable from one human population to another as are those of cranial morphology, and they also are genetically transmitted. As a subject for study, teeth have one major advantage over bones: they are much better preserved under conditions of burial, and this was conspicuously true in the case of the Meinarti burials.

Dental characteristics of the Meinarti population were most fully analyzed by David L. Greene (Greene 1967; Greene 1982). His findings fully confirmed those of the craniologists: in teeth as well as in bones, there was no significant difference between the Meroitic, X-Group, and Christian populations in Lower Nubia (cf. especially Greene 1967, 57).

Pathology

The poor condition of most of the Meinarti burials did not provide a satisfactory basis for the study of several kinds of skeletal pathology. The main exception was in the case of osteoporosis (cortical bone loss from the long bones), which was studied by cutting sections, 8-9cm long, from the left femur (upper leg bone), and taking measurements of the cortical thickness (Dewey n.d., 14-16). The results, as in nearly all human populations, were markedly different in the case of males and females. Males retained and indeed somewhat increased the thickness of cortical bone from birth until the fifth decade, when it began to show a gradual but continual decline. Females on the other hand began to lose cortical bone immediately at puberty, and continued to do so throughout the remainder of their lives. This finding is in contrast to the norm among modern populations, in which females do not begin to show cortical loss until the fourth decade (Dewey n.d., 44).

Demography and mortality

Preliminary cautions. Everywhere in the archaeological world, the interpretation or mortuary evidence presents certain problems. First of all, there are never enough burials to account for more than a fraction of the population – and where are the others? At Meinarti, for example, the total of 356 recovered burials is probably just about equal to the population of the village over one generation, yet the burials are believed to have been interred over a period of more than four centuries. Consequently the cemetery, as always, must be treated as no more than a sample of the total population.

But – how representative a sample? There is always a possibility that the sexes are not equally represented. Younger males are much more likely to die (and be buried) away from home than are females, and therefore to be missing from the cemetery. This is particularly true in the case of warlike peoples. Fortunately the medieval Nubians do not fit that category, but there is still a probability that some males died while away on trading activities, or on pilgrimage. There is also a possibility that certain age cohorts may be underrepresented; especially foetuses and neonates, which may be the subject of special interment practices. All these cautions must be borne in mind in considering the demographic and mortality figures presented below.

Demography. Among Meinarti burials whose sex could be identified, females outnumbered males in a proportion of about 7 to 6. However, the proportions were quite different at different phases or subphases, and also in different age cohorts, as can be seen in Table 12.

The above figures must however be treated with some reserve, since they are based on less than half the total population of Meinarti burials. In the remaining cases either the sex, or the age, or both could not be determined. The seeming disproportion of males at Subphase 4c, for example, is probably not a true indication of the population at that time; it largely disappears if the Subphase 4abc burials are added in.

If life expectancy figures are calculated for those individuals whose sex could be determined, the figures in Table 13 are obtained.

The relatively high life expectancy (*c.* 30 years) suggested by these figures is of course not a reliable figure, since individuals below the age of 15 (i.e. those whose sex could not be determined) were necessarily omitted from the calculations. The actual life expectancy for all individuals at Meinarti, calculated without reference to sex, was about 19.7 years (see below). On the other hand, the near uniformity of life expectancy for males and for females, and its continuity almost unchanged from Subphase 4a until the end of Subphase 5b, appears to be a reliable finding, and a surprising one.[4] In most peasant populations, female mortality is considerably higher than that of males during the child-bearing years, but becomes lower in the post-menopausal years. The diminished life expectancy seen in the late Meinarti burials (Phases 5/6) is probably a legitimate reflection of deteriorating social and political conditions in those times.

Mortality. When sexual identity is disregarded, the mortality figures become much more reliable, since they can be calculated for a little over 75% of the Meinarti burials. Table 14 shows the age at death of individuals respectively at Subphases 4ab, Subphase 4c, Phases 5/6, and for the total Meinarti population, divided into 10-year age cohorts. The figures are percentages of individuals in that particular subphase or phase (figures from Armelagos n.d., 9-11).

Average life expectancy at birth, calculated for 269 individuals whose age could be reasonably estimated, was 19.7 years.

The mortality figures from Meinarti are typical for peasant and tribal populations in some respects, but not in others. Very high infant mortality is characteristic of all such populations; indeed, the figures from Meinarti are actually somewhat lower than expected (Armelagos n.d., 9), and lower than the figures from the two Early Christian cemeteries at Kulubnarti. At Meinarti, almost 60% of the population lived beyond the age of 20, while in the two Kulubnarti cemeteries the figures for those who lived beyond 20 were respectively 27% and 51% (Adams *et al.* 1999, 10, 47). The low mortality rate for individuals in the second decade of life is a particular surprise, since females typically bear at least one or two children during their teens. The Meinarti figures are not paralleled by the

---

[4] The anomalous figure for males in Subphase 4abc is explained by the fact that only a single burial is represented.

TABLE 12. DISTRIBUTION OF BURIALS BY SEX AND AGE COHORT

Sex	Age cohorts					Totals
	10-19	20-29	30-39	40-49	50+	
Subphases 4ab						
Males	1	9	5	5		30
Females	7	11	10	5	2	35
Subphase 4c						
Males	1	20	5	5	1	32
Females	2	12	5	5		24
Subphases 4abc						
Males				1		1
Females		3	2	1		6
Subphases 5ab						
Males		5			1	6
Females		1	3	1		5
Phases 5/6						
Males		5	2			7
Females		5	3			8
Totals						
Males	1	39	12	11	2	65
Females	10	32	23	12	2	78
Both sexes	**11**	**71**	**35**	**23**	**4**	**144**

TABLE 13. AVERAGE LIFE EXPECTANCY FOR MALES AND FEMALES, CALCULATED FOR THE MAJOR CHRONOLOGICAL GROUPINGS

Sex	Subphases or phases					Total population
	Subphase 4ab	Subphase 4c	Subphase 4abc	Subphase 5ab	Phases 5/6	
Males	32.0	30.3	45.0	30.0	27.8	31.2
Females	30.7	30.4	31.7	35.0	28.7	30.7
Both sexes	31.1	30.3	33.5	32.2	28.3	30.7

TABLE 14. PERCENTAGE OF INDIVIDUALS AT AGE OF DEATH, IN EACH 10-YEAR AGE COHORT

Age cohort	Subphases 4ab	Subphase 4c	Phases 5/6	Total population
0-10 years	37.9%	27.8%	38.4%	34.2%
11-20 years	6.9%	4.8%	10.9%	6.9%
21-30 years	27.5%	39.2%	36.0%	33.1%
31-40 years	14.6%	15.9%	11.5%	14.5%
41-50 years	9.7%	12.3%	3.2%	9.3%
51+ years	1.0%	0%	0%	0.4%

findings from other Lower Nubian cemeteries, which typically showed a mortality rate of between 12% and 20% for individuals in their teens (Armelagos n.d., 45-60).

When the figures for infant and adolescent mortality are broken down into smaller increments, a particularly surprising pattern emerges. These figures were calculated only for Subphases 4ab and 4c, the only two groups that had any significant number of pre-adult burials. The results are shown in Table 15; the figures again are percentages of the total population at that subphase (figures from Armelagos n.d., 32).

TABLE 15. PRE-ADULT MORTALITY RATES FOR
SUBPHASES 4AB AND 4C

Age cohort	Subphases 4ab	Subphase 4c
Foetus	0.0%	0.0%
0-6 months	0.0%	0.0%
7-12 months	3.4%	4.8%
13-24 months	5.5%	5.7%
25 months - 6 years	22.1%	11.5%
7-10 years	6.9%	5.8%
11-15 years	2.8%	3.8%
16-20 years	4.1%	9.0%

These figures may not be totally reliable, since there is always a possibility that neonates were underrepresented in the cemetery. It seems clear nevertheless that the most vulnerable years for Meinarti infants were not those immediately after birth, but those between the ages of two and six years. This finding, though not seemingly logical, is paralleled by the findings of Hamed Ammar in his study of the modern Egyptian village of Silwa. The author found that children in the earliest years of life received a high degree of maternal care and protection, but were conspicuously and even deliberately neglected after about the age of two.

"They are less clean in body and clothes, and it is not an unusual sight to find nasal mucus on the children's faces. Mothers justify this neglect on the grounds that the child at this stage, where he is usually out with other children and thus exposed to the public, should not appear attractive for fear of the evil eye" (Ammar 1966, 111).

As a result, the highest mortality rate for children, at Silwa as at Meinarti, was between the ages of two and five (*ibid.*, 112).

Finds from the cemetery

Registered finds from the cemetery consist mostly of votive lamps, recovered from the lamp boxes at the west end of the tombs. There are also a few small items of jewelry found on the bodies, and a few objects found within the windblown fill around the graves. All the finds are listed in Table 16. Figures in parentheses, in the succeeding paragraphs of discussion, are registration numbers. For the Sudan National Museum accession numbers see the Appendix.

Votive lamps
Votive lamps were used, in cemeteries and elsewhere,

throughout the Christian period. However, the preferred vessel form underwent an interesting series of changes (see Adams 1998b, 24-5). The overwhelming preference of the Early Christians was for an oval-shaped bottle-lamp (Forms P1-P2), with embossed floral or religious designs, made usually of the pink Aswan Ware R4.[5] In Classic Christian times these gave way to locally made lamps, having a shape something like a candle-holder (Forms P17-P20), in the Classic Christian Wares R5, W6, and W10. Some examples are shown in Plate 15b. These in turn were displaced by simple, open bowls, at first of the Aswan Wares W12 and U6 (Form P28, shown in Plate 15a), and finally of local hand-made Wares H5 and H8 (Forms P24-26).[6] However, broken base fragments from large bowls and vases were also extensively reused as lamps in the Late Christian period.

A part of that evolutionary process is reflected in the finds from the Meinarti cemetery, as shown in Table 16. A few of the tombs from Subphases 4a and 4b still had lamps of Classic Christian ware; some plain bowls and some of "candle-holder" type. However, the overwhelming majority had open bowls of Aswan Ware W12, as did all the tombs of Subphase 4c.[7] This is a rather coarse and evidently mass-produced ware, with a slip color that shades from buff to dull pink. Most of the lamps are otherwise undecorated, but three have simple designs in black with red filling, in the late Aswan Style A.IV (see Adams 1986, 376, design elements M and N). The special appeal of these vessels must have been their inexpensiveness, to judge from the enormous numbers of them that have been found throughout Nubia (cf. *Meinarti II*, 86). A selection of the Ware W12 lamps is shown in Plate 15a.

The few lamps found loose in the upper fill of the cemetery are presumed to have been displaced from the late tombs of Phases 5 and 6. Among them there is only one example of the Ware W12 lamp form; all the others are broken fragments of Nubian-made vases or footed bowls. The lamp (662) found in the vaulted chamber of Tomb T8 had originally been a footed bowl of Form D23, but its edges had been broken off and then ground down all the way around to give it a rather flat shape (Form D30). This vessel can be seen in Plate 14b.

The lamp (342) found in the lamp box of the very late Tomb T4, shown in Plate 15f, no. 3, calls for special remark. It is made from a very hard stoneware, and has a purplish surface color. The exterior has molded decoration, having something like the appearance of grape clusters.[8] Neither the fabric nor the surface treatment are closely similar to any of the familiar Nubian or Egyptian wares, and the vessel might have come from somewhere further abroad. The fragment had been used as a lamp, but originally it was almost certainly a "naphtha grenade" – a missile designed to be filled with flaming naphtha

[5] For illustrations see especially Griffith 1927, 79-80.

[6] For discussion and illustrations of the different lamp forms see Adams 1986, 103 and 150-54; also Adams 1998b, 24-5.

[7] For discussion of the form see Adams 1986, 103; for illustration see *ibid.*, 153. For discussion of the ware see *ibid.*, 558-9.

[8] For a very similar specimen from Egypt, collected by Denon at the beginning of the 19th century, see Denon 1988, vol. v, pl. 76, no. 8. See also no. 16 in the same plate.

TABLE 16. REGISTERED FINDS FROM THE MEINARTI CEMETERY

Votive lamps

Reg. no.	Ware[1]	Form desig.[2]	Form	Portion	Colors	Style[3]	Sub-phase	Tomb no.
713	W12	P28	Bowl lamp	Complete	Pale pink	II	4a	?
714	W12	P28	Bowl lamp	Complete	Buff	II	4a	?
726	W9	C21	Bowl	Portion	R/W	V	4ab	T126
334	W6	C22	Bowl	Complete	Yellow	II	4ab	T18
557	W5	C22	Bowl	Nearly complete	R/W	N.IVB	4ab	T91
335	W10	C23	Bowl	Complete	Cream	II	4ab	T28
704	W12?	D19	Footed bowl	Nearly complete	Cream	II	4ab	T125
360	R5	P18	Lamp	Nearly complete	Red	I	4ab	T60
555	W6	P20	Lamp	Portion	Buff	II	4ab	T102
354	W12	P28	Bowl lamp	Complete	Cream	II	4ab	T21
356	W12	P28	Bowl lamp	Complete	Buff	II	4ab	T53
357	W12	P28	Bowl lamp	Complete	Cream	II	4ab	T23
358	W12	P28	Bowl lamp	Portion	R+B/W	A.IV	4ab	T33
362	W12	P28	Bowl lamp	Complete	Buff	II	4ab	T50
363	W12	P28	Bowl lamp	Complete	R/Buff	V	4ab	T64
375	W12	P28	Bowl lamp	Complete (R)	Pink	II	4ab	T39
548	W12	P28	Bowl lamp	Complete	Pink	II	4ab	T86
564	W12	P28	Bowl lamp	Complete	Buff	II	4ab	T56
565	W12	P28	Bowl lamp	Complete	Buff	II	4ab	T48
585	W12	P28	Bowl lamp	Complete	Buff	II	4ab	T58
693	W12	P30	Cup lamp	Complete	Pink	II	4ab	T47
355	W12	P28	Bowl lamp	Complete	Cream	II	4c	T21
549	W12	P28	Bowl lamp	Complete	Buff	II	4c	T104
552	W12	P28	Bowl lamp	Complete	R+B/W	A.IV	4c	T103
553	W12	P28	Bowl lamp	Complete	R+B/W	A.IV	4c	T83
662	R21?	D24	Footed bowl	Complete	Orange	I?	5a	T8
342	?	P36	Small bottle	Portion	Purple	X	5/6	T4
364	R17	C23	Bowl	Fragment	B+W/R	N.VIB	?	Float
365	R11	C23	Bowl	Portion	Br/R	N.VIB	?	Float
351	R17	C93	Bowl	Portion (R)	B/R	N.VIB	?	Float
536	W12	P28	Bowl lamp	Complete	Buff	II	?	Float

[1] For wares see Adams 1986, 405-597
[2] For vessel forms see Adams 1986, 89-192
[3] For decorative styles see Adams 1986, 213-392

Personal jewelry

Reg. no.	Material	Object	Condition	Burial no.	Plate
577	Bronze	Earring	Complete	B36	
676	Bronze	Earring	Complete	B58	
823	Bronze	Finger ring	Complete	T96	
576	Carnelian + bronze	Pendant	Complete	B36	16b
822	Glass	Beads	c. 180 beads	T96	
824	Iron	Bracelet	Complete (R)	T10	
574	Iron	Anklet	4 fragments	B37	16d, 1
575	Iron	Anklet	2 fragments	B41	16d, 2
709	Gold + silver	Medallion	Nearly complete	T6 shaft	16e

(Greek fire), and hurled into enemy towns or camps in order to set them afire.[9] The use of naphtha fire in a siege of Meinarti in 1366 is specifically mentioned in Maqrizi's *Suluk* (see Vantini 1975, 701), but the specimen discussed here may date from an earlier siege.

[9] For discussion on this point see Adams 1996, 144 and nn. 32-34.

Personal jewelry

A few small items of personal jewelry had been left on

TABLE 16. REGISTERED FINDS FROM THE MEINARTI CEMETERY (CONT.)

Miscellaneous finds in the fill

Reg. no.	Material	Object	Condition	Sub-phase	Plate
348	Pottery (W23)	Vase (F20)	Portion (R)	?	15e, 1
349	Pottery (W15?)	Vase (F23)	Nearly complete	?	15e, 4
359	Ceramic	Basin	Mostly comp. (R)	?	15a
350	Sandstone	Tombstone	Fragment	?	17b, 6
832	Sandstone	Tombstone	Complete	4a	17a
678	Bronze	Bell	Complete (R)	4c	16c, 2
347	Bronze	Rivet	Complete	?	
821	Iron	Unidentified object	Portion?	4b	
371	Wool fabric	2 scraps	Scraps	?	

the bodies, mostly of young children. Burials B36 and B58 each had a simple bronze[10] earring, made from a loop of wire, in the right ear (577 and 676). B36 also had at the neck a finely made pendant bead of carnelian, pierced by a bronze suspension loop (576, shown in Plate 16b). The infant burials B37 and B41 each had a simple iron anklet, made from a loop of thin iron rod, around the left ankle (574 and 575, shown in Plate 16d, nos. 1 and 2). The adult burial in Tomb T10 had a similarly made iron bracelet on the right wrist (824, shown in Plate 16d, no. 3).

The adult burial in Tomb T96 was the only one that bore any substantial adornment. The body, of undetermined sex, had a simple bronze ring (823) on one finger, and one or more strings of beads, mostly of glass, around the neck (822). There are about 180 beads altogether, of which most are of an opaque, dark brown glass of a poor quality. They occur in a considerable variety of sizes and shapes, some quite irregular. There are also about 40 small beads of pale green glass, and 10 small beads of white faience.

The object (709) shown in Plate 16e was found in the fill about half way down in the grave shaft of Tomb T6, where most probably it was lost by accident as the grave was being filled. It is a small medallion of gold and silver, 36mm in diameter. The same repoussé design, of a bearded holy figure holding a staff, appears on both faces, one in thin sheet gold (shown in the photo) and the other in thin sheet silver. The clasping around the edges, which is partly broken away, is of fairly thick silver. It is considerably corroded, but no trace of decoration can be observed on it. There is also no surviving evidence of any attachment for suspension.

When the medallion was taken apart for restoration at the Centre de Recherches de l'Histoire de Sidérurgie, in Jarville, the interior was found to contain traces of bone and of organic matter.[11] Apparently therefore this was a reliquary.

Miscellaneous finds in the cemetery fill

Pottery vases. The rather elegant little decorated vase (348) shown in Plate 15e, no. 1, and the larger vase (349)

shown in Plate 15e, no. 4, were found loose in the fill of the cemetery. The larger specimen had clearly been used as a lamp.

Ceramic basin (359). The large basin of Ware U10, shown in Plate 16a seems to have been discarded in the cemetery, where it was perhaps used for scooping sand. It had been broken in antiquity, and then drilled with mending holes along the sides of the crack.

Tombstone fragment (350). The fragment shown in Plate 17b, no. 6, from the lower right corner of a Christian tombstone, was "adrift" in the high fill of the cemetery. It will be more fully discussed in the next section.

Bronze tinkler bell (678). The object shown at right in Plate 16c, no. 2, is a small, spherical tinkler of cast bronze, 16mm in diameter. It has a tiny ingot of lead for a clapper. There is a single wavy line of decoration on the body of the bell.

Other items of refuse that accidentally found their way into the cemetery fill include a bronze rivet (347), an iron knob of uncertain use (821), and two small scraps of dark wool cloth (371).

Tombstones

Our excavations yielded one complete and five fragmentary Christian tombstones, and two complete and four fragmentary Islamic tombstones. An additional three stones were collected by earlier visitors to the island.[12] These latter have been published previously, but without translation (see Table 17 for references). It seems desirable to publish the translations here, along with translations of our own finds, in order to complete the documentation of life and death at Meinarti.[13]

---

[10] The term "bronze" will here be used to designate any alloy of copper, other than brass.

[11] Reported in a letter in the author's possession.

[12] How these stone came to be on the surface when they were collected in the 1920s is something of a mystery. The dates indicate that they must surely have come originally from Subphase 4a tombs, yet these at the time of our excavations were buried under more than 2m of sand.

[13] An additional five stones, collected in earlier years, were attributed to Meinarti by Monneret de Villard (1935, 220-21), but the evidence for this attribution was not given. Łajtar and van der Vliet (1998, 36, n. 8) consider that the attribution is doubtful.

TABLE 17. LIST OF TOMBSTONES FOUND AT MEINARTI

Access. or reg. no.	Portion	Language	Date	Found at phase	Published references
			Christian tombstones		
Kht 14*	Complete	Coptic; last 3 lines Greek	1037	Surface	Monneret de Villard 1935, 219-20
6-K-3/832	Complete	Coptic; 1st and last lines Greek	1046	4a	Adams 1965, 172; Łajtar & van der Vliet 1998, 38-9
6-K-3/527	Fragment	Coptic	?	4b	*Meinarti II*, 99 and pl. 35c
Kht 16*	Complete	Greek	1080	Surface	Crowfoot 1927, 230-1; Monneret de Villard 1935, 218
Kht 3726	Complete	Greek	1161	Surface	Monneret de Villard 1935, 218-19; Barns 1954, 26-7
6-K-3/350	Fragment	Greek	?	?	*Meinarti II*, 99 and pl. 35d
6-K-3/423	Fragment	?	?	5a	*Meinarti II*, pl. 35e, no. 2
6-K-3/138	Fragment	?	?	5c	*Meinarti III*, pl. 35e, no. 4
6-K-3/261	Fragment	?	?	?	*Meinarti II*, 99 and pl. 35e, no. 6
			Islamic tombstones		
6-K-3/147	Complete	Arabic	1061	5b	Sherif 1964, 249; *Meinarti III*, pl. 20d, no. 1
6-K-3/625	Complete	Arabic	1063	5a	*Meinarti III*, 80 and pl. 20d, no. 2
6-K-3/486	Half	Arabic	?	4c	Meinarti II, 100 and pl. 35f
6-K-3/146	Fragment	Arabic	?	5b	Sherif 1964, 249-50; *Meinarti III*, pl. 20e, no. 1
6-K-3/302	Portion	Arabic	?	5b	Sherif 1964, 250; *Meinarti III*, pl. 20e, no. 3
6-K-3/27	Fragment	Arabic	?	5	*Meinarti III*, pl. 20c, no. 6

* Old registration number

Although most of the stones were found in Phase 5 deposits, it is interesting to note that all of them that can be dated, both Christian and Islamic, belong to Phase 4. This reinforces the supposition that the use of superstructures (and hence of tombstones) became much less common in Late Christian times (see Adams 1998b, 36).

Christian tombstones

The Christian tombstones from Meinarti are of unusual interest, partly because three are in Coptic – not the usual language found in Nubian tombstones, except at major ecclesiastical centers (see Adams 1998b, 25) – and partly because of the content of the texts themselves.

Coptic texts

Epitaph of Iesousyko (6-K-3/832). The stela shown in Plate 17a is the only complete Christian tombstone found *in situ* at Meinarti. It was affixed to the superstructure of Tomb T12, at Level 9 (Subphase 4a), as shown in Plate 12a. Like nearly all Nubian tombstones it is made of local sandstone, and measures 49cm high by 32cm wide. As can be seen, it is well carved, with the inscription framed within a triumphal arch, and topped by a half-rosette or conch. Of the framing design Professors Łajtar and van der Vliet have written that "... Among stelae from Christian Nubia, where unembellished plaques highlighting a plainly incised text are more or less standard, it stands out by its nicely sculptured and painted decoration, which clearly continues late antique patterns. Its text is framed by an *aedicula* consisting of two columns which support an arched canopy containing a conch."[14] Not clearly visible in the photo are traces of red painted decoration on the enclosing arch and columns, and around the conch. The painting on the arch

consists of tangent red circles, and there are also wing-like projections outward from the arch at each of the upper corners.

The epitaph is that of a woman, Iesousyko, who died on January 9 in the year 1046, at the age of 34.[15] The inscription begins and ends with Greek invocations, while the remainder of the text is in Coptic, and adheres generally to a familiar formula found on Coptic tombstones:[16]

Jesus Christ, light of life. Through the providence of God, the creator of all, He who said to Adam, the first man: "Adam, you are earth, and to the earth you shall once more return," - thus went to rest Iesousyko, owner of (the Church of Saint) Philotheos..., (on) Tybi, day fourteen, (year) since Diocletian, 762. May God, the good one, who loves man, grant her rest in the kingdom of heavens, and place her in the bosom of Abraham and Isaac and Jacob, in the paradise of delight, in order to hear that blessed voice, that which will say: "Come, o blessed ones...!" The lifetime which she spent on earth: 34 (years). Rest (her) soul.[17]

Epitaph of Michaeliko (Khartoum no. 14). Closely similar is the text of a tombstone collected by J. W. Crowfoot near the beginning of the 20th century (Khartoum

[14] Łajtar and van der Vliet 1998, 38. The authors go on to cite a number of similarly embellished tombstones from other Lower Nubian sites (*ibid*, 38-9).

[15] The actual date given is 14 Tybi in the year 762, according to the usual Coptic formula in which dates are calculated from the reign of Diocletian (beginning in A.D. 284) rather than from the birth of Jesus.

[16] The bulk of the text is a quotation from Genesis 3:19.

[17] Translation kindly furnished by Professor Jacques van der Vliet (pers. comm.).

Museum, old no. 14), and published by Monneret de Villard (1935, 219-20). The stone is described as "rectangular slab of grey sandstone, 47 x 36 x 4.5cms.; complete and rather well preserved, but for chips from the outer margins and the embossed border; some small surface damage, rarely affecting the text. Outer edges carelessly finished."[18]

The epitaph is again that of a woman, Michaeliko, who died on December 11, 1037, at the age of 75.[19] It begins and ends with Greek invocations, which are slightly longer than those in the Iesousyko text. The intervening Coptic inscription is also slightly longer, and includes a plea that God will cause the archangel Michael to watch over the bones of the deceased. Michaeliko is identified as the daughter of the priest Iohannou, and as the owner of the Church of Saint Michael in Argin. The following translation was kindly furnished by Professor van der Vliet:[20]

> (Greek) + Jesus Christ, light of life. Alpha - Omega.
>
> (Coptic) Through the providence of God, the creator of all, he who said to Adam, the first man: "Adam, you are earth and to earth you shall once more return," – thus went to rest the blessed Michaeliko, daughter of Iohannou the priest, she who owns (the Church of Saint) Michael at Argine, on day 15 of the month Khoiak, Anno Martyrum 754. May then God, the good one, who loves man, grant her rest in the kingdom of heavens, and may He place her in the bosom of Abraham and Isaac and Jacob, in the paradise of delight, and may He cause the archangel Michael to watch over her bones, and may He make her worthy to hear the blessed voice which shall say: "come, blessed one of my Father, and inherit the kingdom which has been prepared for you since the foundation of the world, and may He make her inherit with all his saints. Amen. The lifetime which she spent on earth: 75 years.
>
> (Greek) Grant rest, Christ our God, to the soul of your servant Michaeliko, in the kingdom of heavens!

Epitaph of Petronia (6-K-3/527). An additional fragmentary stone found by us, and shown in Plate 17b, no. 3, appears to bear a text identical to that of Michaeliko. The inscription is on dark purple sandstone, within a wide, embossed border which is considerably damaged. The surviving text is from the upper left-hand corner of the original stone, and retains parts of 15 lines of Coptic text. There is, once again, a plea that the archangel Michael may watch over the bones of the deceased, a woman named Petronia. Her age and the date of her death are not preserved.[21] The fragment was found in the fill of Building V, at Level 8 (Subphase 4b); a depression in the back side showed that it had been used as a door pivot stone prior to its final discard. The following translation has been reconstructed by Professor van der Vliet:[22]

> + Through [the providence of God, the] creator [of all, He who said] to Adam, [the first man: "Adam, you

are] earth [and to the earth you shall once more return," – thus] then went to rest [the blessed] Petron[ia....., on day.....of the] month M[echir, year.... May] then God [the good one, who loves] man, grant [her] rest [in the kingdom of]heavens, and may He place her [in the bosom of Abraham] and Isaac and Jacob, [in the paradise of] delight, and [may He cause the archangel] Michael to watch [over her bones, and may He make her] worthy to hear the blessed [voice, that which will say: 'come, blessed ones to my Father, and inherit the kingdom which has been prepared for you since the foundation of the world"]

The translator comments that "This third lady's stela from Meinarti bears a text which, as far as preserved, is identical to that of the Meinarti stela of Michaeliko of A.D. 1037. It even includes the rare prayer 'may He (= God) cause the archangel Michael to watch over her bones.' Hence, this fragment can be confidently dated to the same period (roughly 10th-11th century). The proper name Petronia was a current one, both in Egypt and in Nubia."[23]

The special interest of the three above described stones lies not only in their Coptic language and in the fact that all were prepared for women, but above all in the fact that two of the three deceased are named as the "owners" (εχων) of churches, one of which was located at a considerable distance from Meinarti.[24] The implications of this declaration are far from clear, and have been a subject of debate. Łajtar and van der Vliet have written that "Although the precise juridical and economic implications of their ownership remain obscure, we may suppose our ladies of Meinarti to have been the wealthy patrons of ecclesiastical establishments. They may have either founded these establishments themselves or acquired them by inheritance" (Łajtar and van der Vliet 1998, 42-3).

Greek texts

No complete Greek tombstones were found by us, but two were recovered by earlier visitors to the island. Both are now in the National Museum in Khartoum.

Epitaph of the son of Mashshouda Eisminna (Khartoum no. 16). This stone, formerly in the Wadi Halfa Museum, was taken to Khartoum some time before 1927. It was published originally by J. W. Crowfoot (1927, 230-31) and later by Monneret de Villard (1935, 218). Crowfoot writes that ". . . the lettering . . . is extremely bad and full of mistakes which it is hardly worth enumerating: the lapicide cannot have had more than the barest smattering of Greek, if that" (Crowfoot 1927, 231). The text is surrounded by a rather narrow raised border, rounded in profile but without embellishment. The epitaph follows closely the traditional formula of the *Euchologion mega*.[25] and has been translated as follows by Professor G. M. Browne (personal communication):

> God of spirits and of all flesh, who destroyed Death and trampled down Hades and gave life to the world:

[18] Personal communication from Professor Jacques van der Vliet.
[19] The date actually given in the text is 15 Khoiak in the year 754.
[20] Personal communication
[21] Information again furnished by Professor van der Vliet.
[22] Personal communicaton

[23] *Ibid.*
[24] For more extended discussion see also Lajtar and van der Vliet 1998.
[25] For discussion see especially Lajtar 1996.

give rest to his spirit in the bosom of Abraham, Isaac and Jacob in the place of light, the place of refreshment, whence have fled Pain, Grief, and Lamentation. Forgive and remit every sin committed by him in word, deed or thought, since you are good and philanthropic, because there is no man who will live and not sin. For you alone are outside of sin, and your justice is justice forever, Lord; your word is truth. For you are the repose of your servant, the son of Mashhouda Eisminna, and the resurrection, and to you we give glory. In the name of the Father, the Son and the Holy Spirit, Amen. The years and days of his life were 60 [years] and 10 [days]. From the martyrs 800 years, Pachon 7th, 13th lunar day. Give rest to the Choiakishshi(1), God our Helper!

The date of death, year of the martyrs 800, is equivalent to A.D. 1083.

Epitaph of Goasse, son of Sentikol (Khartoum no. 3726). It is not known who found this stone, which was in the Wadi Halfa Museum until transferred to Khartoum in 1941. The text, without translation, has been published by Monneret de Villard (1935, 219), and Barns (1954, 26). The inscription is on a rectangle of grey sandstone, measuring 50 x 26cm, and is surrounded by a wide, raised border. The border is unembellished except that, at the top, the first line of the text (the invocation to the Trinity) is inscribed on it rather than within the recessed area. Small traces of red paint are preserved within the cut letters. The epitaph again follows the formula of the *Euchologion mega*. The following translation was kindly furnished by Professor Adam Łajtar:[26]

> In the name of the Father and the Son and the Holy Spirit, amen. God of spirits and of all flesh, You who have defeated death and trodden down Hell and given life to the world, give rest to Your servant Goasse, son of Sentikol, in the bosom of Abraham and Isaak and Jacob, in a shining place, in a place of verdure, in a place of refreshment, from which pain and grief and lamentation have fled away. Pardon every sin committed by him in word, or in deed, or in thought, since You are Good and love mankind, because there is no man who will live and will not sin. For You alone are outside sin, Your justice is justice for ever, and Your word is truth. You are the rest of Your servant Goasse, son of Sentiko(1), and to You we sing glory, to the Father, the Son and the Holy Spirit, amen. The years of his life [were] 95. [He died in the year] from the martyrs 878, in the month of Thoth [day] 18, lunar day 8. Rest the Eparch of Nobadia and Choikishsil, o God, my help.

The translator comments that ". . . the Goasse epitaph shows striking similarity to the epitaph of a woman Eikkir found at Sakiya 43, Ashkeit, near Wadi Halfa. To my mind the persons who composed the epitaphs both used the same model for the prayer for the dead. The epitaph for Eikkir should be dated between AD 1084 and 1184."[27]

The year of death given for Goasse is equivalent to A.D. 1161.

Epitaph of Sourea (6-K-3/350). The tombstone fragment shown in Plate 17b, no. 6, is from the lower right corner of the original stone. It is made of white sandstone, with traces of red paint surviving on the raised border. The text, in Greek, mentions someone named Sourea, "give him rest."[28] This fragment was found in the windblown fill within the cemetery.

Unidentifiable fragments

6-K-3/261. The fragment shown in Plate 17b, no. 2, is probably the upper right corner of a tombstone, though it could conceivably be the lower left. The text is so worn away that nothing can be deciphered. As the photo shows, it also had been used as a door pivot stone – a very common fate for broken tombstones in Nubia.

6-K-3/138. This very battered fragment, shown in Plate 17b, no. 4, is the upper right corner of the original stone. The letters A Γ H C are preserved at the end of the first line, and A T O N at the end of the second. This is the only example of a stela in which there is no border around the inscription.

6-K-3/423. This is the upper left corner of the original stone. It seems to have had some kind of decorative design along the border, but nothing can be made of the inscription.

Islamic tombstones
No Islamic tombstones were collected at Meinarti by earlier visitors, but we found two whole and four fragmentary examples, all in secondary contexts.

Epitaph of Fattimah (6-K-3/147). The complete tombstone shown at left in Plate 17c was found in two pieces, lying face-up on the floor of Building VII, at Level 5 (Subphase 5b). However, the date (453 A.H. = A.D. 1061) shows clearly that it originated during the time of Subphase 4b. The stela is rather heavy and thick in comparison to Christian tombstones, measuring 52 x 34 x 10cm. Although the inscription itself is very well cut, the top and bottom edges of the stone are rather roughly finished. The inscription is framed by incised lines, but is not inset within a raised border. There is a decorative frieze at the top, with a six-pointed star at the center, and the text concludes at the bottom with two five-pointed stars.

The text was translated as follows by the late Sayyed Negm el-Din Sherif (1964, 249 and pl. LIII):

> In the name of Allah, the Compassionate, the Merciful.
> O God, you have created her, and you have caused her to live, and you have caused her to die, and of her you know better all that is secret and all that is manifest. To intercede we have come to You; forgive her, then, her sins and have mercy upon her. O God, of her recompense dispossess us not, and after her, into error guide us not. O God, bless Mohammed the Prophet and his family; and show mercy to Your slave-

---

[26] Personal communication.
[27] *Ibid.*

[28] Information furnished by Professor G. M. Browne, personal communication.

girl, who is in need of Your mercy, Fattimah daughter of Ibrahiem son of Ishaq son of Iesa . . . . died on Sunday, first day of Bauna, year three and fifty and four hundred. May God's mercy be shown to whoever reads it and invokes mercy upon her.

The date given for Fattimah's death is interesting for its combination of a Coptic month (Bauna) with a Hegira year.

Epitaph of Rahimah (6-K-3/625). The stone at right in Plate 17d is the memorial of Rahimah, obviously a sister of Fattimah, who died two years after her sister. It had been built into the foundation wall of Church VI, when the church was rebuilt at Subphase 5a. The text is surrounded by a narrow, raised border, and, as in the Fattimah stone, there is a decorative six-pointed star at the top. The hands in this inscription and in the Fattimah inscription are so similar as to suggest that they were both executed by the same lapicide, although the shapes of the stones are rather different.

The text was translated as follows by Mr. R. H. Pinder-Wilson of the British Museum:[29]

In the name of God the Compassionate, the Merciful. Blessed be He in whose hand is the Kingdom and Over all things is He potent: who hath created death and life to prove which of you will be most righteous in deed, and He is the Mighty and the Forgiving!

Oh God! Bless Muhammad the Prophet and His Family and Thy handmaid who is in need of thy mercy. Rahimah

daughter of Ibrahim son of Ishaq son of Isa, who died on Tuesday, the 27th Dhu'l Qa'da

In the year five and fifty and four hundred. May God have mercy on him who reads this and invokes on her behalf, mercy.

According to the translator, lines 2-5 are a passage from the Quran, Sura 67 ("Sovereignty"), verses 1 and 2. It is interesting to note that the date of death given in this text employs a Muslim rather than a Coptic month.

Epitaph of Fatima (6-K-3/486). Plate 17e shows the top half of an Islamic tombstone which was found lying face up on a room floor in Building V, at Level 7. This, like no. 147, is a very heavy stone; the surviving dimensions are 34 x 25 x 14cm. It is made of local sandstone, somewhat roughly shaped; the inscription is surrounded by a raised border without decoration. The text is rather crudely carved in angular characters. Parts of the inscription are indistinct, having been either worn or weathered away. The surviving portion of text was read as follows by Professor G. M. Browne:[30]

In the name of God, the Compassionate, the Merciful.

Say: God is One, God is Eternal, He Begot not, nor was He begotten, and none Is equal to Him. O God, bless Mohammed the Prophet and his pure family, and show mercy on Your slave girl, who is in need of Your mercy, Fâtima daughter of . . . .

Epitaph of an unnamed person (6-K-3/146). The fragment shown in Plate 17f, no. 2, is the upper left corner of an Islamic tombstone. The text is surrounded by a wide but undecorated border. The inscription had been deliberately defaced by pecking, but it was not fully destroyed. The textual formula could be fairly confidently recognized, because it is identical to that in the epitaph of Fatima (6-K-3/486), described above. It was translated as follows by Negm el-Din Sherif (1964, 249-50):

[In the Name] of Allah, the Compassionate, the Merciful

[Say: 'He is Allah,] the One, the Eternal God. None [He begot, and He was] not [begotten. And none is Equal to Him. O God,] bless [Mohammed the Prophet and His family,] and have mercy upon . . . .

The text of lines 2-4 is from Sura 112 ("Unity") of the Quran.

Epitaph of an unnamed person (6-K-3/302). This fragment, shown in Plate 17f, no. 3, is from the middle portion of a thick but rather small tombstone, having a width of 25cm and a thickness of 11cm. It had been reused as a door pivot stone, as can be seen in the photo. The lettering in the inscription shows considerable resemblance to that in the Fattimah and Rahimah epitaphs, described above. This text also was published earlier by Negm el-Din Sherif (1964, 250), whose translation follows:

[In the Name of] Allah [the Compassionate, the Merciful.]

Allah and His angels [bless] the Prophet. Bless Him, then, you who are believers, and [salute Him with a worthy salutation.] O God, bless [Mohammed] the Prophet [and his family], [and] show mercy to Your slave . . . . .

The text of lines 2-4 is from Sura 33 ("Confederate Tribes") of the Quran, Verse 56.

Fragment (6-K-3/27). The small fragment shown in Plate 17b, no. 5, was found on the surface of the site. It is from the upper left corner of a tombstone, with an inscription that appears to be Arabic, although it is very indistinct.

The finding of Islamic tombstones at Meinarti obviously raises a problem: first because we have no other evidence of a resident Islamic community on the island, and second because none of the 356 graves excavated by us could be identified, by its orientation, as an Islamic grave.[31] It is possible however that there was a separate Muslim cemetery somewhere on the northern part of the island, which we did not investigate. It is also remotely possible that the tombstones were carried in from somewhere on the west bank, to be used for secondary purposes, as some other slabs apparently were. However, the fact that one complete specimen (147) had not been put to any secondary use suggests that the stones were found locally.

Although they were all found in secondary contexts (as were all but one of the Christian tombstones), only one of the Islamic stones (146) showed any evidence of defacement. The others had been displaced, but not otherwise

[29] Personal communication dated 19 July 1966.
[30] Personal communication of 7 June 1999.

[31] An Islamic grave at Meinarti should be oriented more or less north and south, allowing the deceased to face eastward, toward Mecca.

treated with any more disrespect than were Christian stele. They were relics of a time (the Fatimid Dynasty) when Nubian Christians and Muslims co-existed peacefully.

Summary and comparisons of the cemetery

The Meinarti cemetery was located at the eastern side of the community, east, north and south of the church. It was first established at the beginning of Phase 4, at the time when Church VI was built. Before that time, it is not known where the earlier inhabitants of the island were buried. Once established, the cemetery continued in use at least through Phase 5, and probably through Phase 6 as well. However, the total of 356 graves found and excavated by us cannot represent more than a fraction of the total population of Meinarti during the four or more centuries of the cemetery's use.

During its first century of use, the cemetery seems to have grown gradually outward from the immediate vicinity of the church walls, reaching its maximum horizontal extent at the end of Subphase 4b, around A.D. 1100. Thereafter it grew almost entirely upward, as new graves were dug into the windblown sand overlying the earlier ones. The result was a degree of stratification not found in any other cemetery, with the latest graves at a level over 4m above the earliest ones.

In a 1998 article, I distinguished between what I called a Lower Nubian and a Middle Nubian mortuary complex (Adams 1998b, 33-5). Meinarti however was one of a small group of cemeteries, all in the Wadi Halfa area, which exhibited a combination of Lower Nubian above-ground traits and Middle Nubian below-ground traits (*ibid.*, 35). Lower Nubian characteristics were the extensive use of mastaba superstructures, the occasional use of *qubbas,* the prevalence of lamp boxes, and the occasional use of tombstones. Middle Nubian characteristics were the occasional use of side-niche grave shafts, the common occurrence of burials lying on their sides, the practice of turning the head of the deceased toward the north, and the use of a three-brick covering over the head. However, at Meinarti and other cemeteries in the Halfa area, burials on their sides were more often on the right than on the left side, whereas in cemeteries further south they were far more often on the left.

In the character and variety of its superstructures, however, Meinarti stands alone. Graves further north usually had either flat-topped or round-topped ("loaf-shaped") mastabas (*ibid.*, 33), while those further south had almost exclusively flat stone or brick pavements (*ibid.*, 34). Meinarti however exhibited eight different major types of superstructures, and at least seven variants of the cross-topped mastaba, a type not found elsewhere. Stepped mastabas and "pillow" mastabas were also unique to this cemetery. It seems that at Meinarti, more than at any other site, the building of grave superstructures became a distinct field of artistic expression.

Whether this means that there was anything special about Meinarti in other respects it is impossible to say, for here as elsewhere it is difficult to make connections between mortuary practices and other aspects of culture and society. For example, many of the most imposing superstructures in the cemetery were those covering the graves of women and of young men, yet those persons are unlikely to have occupied the highest positions of status or of power in Meinarti society. In medieval as in modern times, funerary monuments seem to have been chiefly a measure of who was willing to spend how much – a fact particularly well illustrated by the tombs in Westminster Abbey.

At the conclusion of my 1998 survey I suggested a number of general conclusions, three of which are specifically relevant to the Meinarti cemetery:

1. There were well marked regional and local traditions in a number of burial practices, and particularly in the design of superstructures.

2. There was no very consistent association between particular types of superstructures and particular types of grave shafts, body coverings, or burial positions. Apparently, a good deal of free choice was allowed, as is common in burial practice almost everywhere in the world.

3. The size and ostentation of graves might have been an index of the wealth of families, but it was not a marker of status in any more formal sense. Some of the most elaborate graves were those of females and of juveniles (Adams 1998b, 36).

APPENDIX
COMPREHENSIVE REGISTER OF FINDS DISCUSSED IN THIS VOLUME

With Sudan National Museum (SNM) accession numbers

Reg. no.	Item	SNM
27	Tombstone	18106
138	Tombstone	18102
146	Tombstone	18099
147	Tombstone	18110
261	Tombstone	18108
302	Tombstone	18109
334	Bowl	15397
335	Bowl	15381
336	Lamp	15204
337	Lamp	15531
338	Lamp	15533
339	Lamp	15639
340	Bowl	15624
341	Lamp	17613
342	Naphtha grenade	15667
344	Lintel decoration	17402
347	Rivet	17574
348	Vase	15266
349	Vase	15295
350	Tombstone	18103
351	Bowl	15201
353	Pendant cross	17665
354	Lamp	15666
355	Lamp	15621
356	Lamp	15670
357	Lamp	15640
358	Lamp	15669
359	Basin	15772
360	Lamp	15377
362	Lamp	15643
363	Lamp	15631
364	Bowl	15239
365	Bowl	15196
371	Fabric	18121
375	Lamp	15644
423	Tombstone	18107
486	Tombstone	18104
527	Tombstone	18105
536	Lamp	15675
538	Lamp	15557
548	Lamp	15708
549	Lamp	15708
549	Lamp	15554
552	Lamp	15673
553	Lamp	15674
555	Lamp	15328
557	Bowl	15330
564	Lamp	15658
565	Lamp	15655
574	Anklet	17753
575	Anklet	17755
576	Pendant bead	17517
577	Earring	17672
585	Lamp	15715
588	Lamp	15324
589	Lamp	15563

Reg. no.	Item	SNM
625	Tombstone	18100
662	Footed bowl	15305
668	Bowl	15304
670	Cup	15300
676	Earring	17675
677	Bronze waster	17662
678	Bell	17666
679	Kohl stick?	17695
686	Lamp	17698
687	Lamp	15714
693	Lamp	15680
704	Miniature footed bowl	15692
709	Medallion	18146
710	Lamp	15549
713	Lamp	15657
714	Lamp	15679
726	Bowl	15346
737	Key	17788
739	Cylindrical plug	17523
798	Candelabrum?	17743
805	Spoon	17664
809	Sculptured slab	17401
811	Bowl	15333
812	Bowl	15576
813	Lamp	15325
814	Lamp	15314
815	Lamp	15315
821	Unidentified object	17791
822	Beads	18147
823	Ring	17796
824	Bracelet	17747
826	Lamp	15313
827	Footed bowl	15445
828	Bowl	15399
829	Bowl	15409
830	Lamp	15319
832	Tombstone	18098
854	Incense stand	15417
856	Amphora	15476
858	Bronze scrap	17715
1046	Amphora	15475
1107	Amphora	15483
1310	Footed bowl	16151
1339	Footed bowl	16232
1357	Vase	16288
1365	Footed bowl	16280
1366	Vase	16284
1484	Lamps	17832

MEINARTI V

The History of Meinarti: an Interpretive Overview

A Cautionary Introduction

There is a school of thought among field archaeologists, prevalent in earlier times and still not entirely extinct, which holds that it's for us to generate the data, and for our successors of later generations to interpret it. In theory this represents the quintessence of Baconian empiricism and Comtean Positivism; positions with which I'm not wholly unsympathetic (see Adams and Adams 1991; Adams 1998a, 399-424). But it is a doctrine which, among archaeologists, is far more often honored in the breach than in the observance, and for good reason. Most of us are apt to feel that, after the toils and tribulations of excavation (which, let's face it, is not much fun a lot of the time), we have earned the right to find some meaning in what we have done and found. Otherwise, what have we been but mere collectors, like the *dilettanti* of an earlier age?

Interpretive possibilities

Yet the meanings are seldom self-proclaiming; they must come, in one way or another, from outside the data itself. The question is not really "should we go beyond the data," but "how far should we go," and "in what direction?" Taking the second of these issues first, it is evident that archaeological data can be viewed from many perspectives.[1] The "comparative method," espoused by early evolutionists, held that we should interpret prehistoric or vanished societies in terms of our understanding of historically or ethnographically recorded societies at the same level of complexity (see Adams 1998a, 29-38). The diffusionist school, which flourished as a rival to the evolutionist, interpreted all cultural traits as having been borrowed from somewhere else, and sought to trace them to their sources. The "direct-historical" method, first advocated by name in the 1940s though certainly practiced earlier, advocated working backward from the present, interpreting earlier societies on the basis of what we know about their living descendants (see Steward 1942). The "conjunctive method" advocated by Walter Taylor (especially 1948) was an archaeological version of Functionalism, insisting that archaeological finds should be interpreted in terms of the function that they performed in the maintenance of the social or economic order. The "emic" method, borrowed from the "New Ethnologists," held that we should try always to see the world through the eyes of those we study, and should therefore make a special effort to recognize and decode symbolic systems (see especially Goodenough 1970). The "logico-deductive" approach of the self-proclaimed "New Archaeologists" demanded that archaeological findings be interpreted in terms of general propositions of causality, which they rather grandiloquently called "covering laws" (see especially Watson, LeBlanc and Redman 1971). Now we have also Post-modernists who insist that there is no empirically knowable reality; we can only characterize the world, past or present, as we see it from a very personal perspective.

The trouble with all the different approaches to inter-

[1] For extended discussion see Ehrich 1950.

pretation is not that they lack validity, but that they are not as exclusively or as invariably useful as their most ardent advocates have insisted. When all is said and done, all the grand theories and powerful methods of social science are true or useful in some contexts and false or useless in others, and that holds in archaeology as everywhere else. One can only discover their applicability in particular cases by "trying them on." Accordingly I have always employed, and will continue to employ here, a combination of the different approaches in my attempt to reconstruct the history and the culture of Meinarti. Critical readers will probably have noticed that this thread of eclecticism runs through all of my previous work on Nubia (see especially Adams 1977, 665-80).

The personal factor

While I have no sympathy with the post-modernists, whose approach seems to be mainly a license to talk about themselves, it is certain that the personal factor in the interpretation of archaeological data cannot be wholly ignored – in my case or any other. At this point it is relevant to recall that my earliest training was in ethnology (or social anthropology, as Britishers would have called it), and in the intellectual climate of the mid-twentieth century. We considered in those days that the primary unit of our study was the community, and indeed my first major anthropological work was a community study (Adams 1963). It is a perspective that I have carried over into all my subsequent research, both ethnological and archaeological, and it has affected both my excavation strategy and my interpretation of the results. It explains why I prefer habitation sites to other kinds of sites, why in their excavation I try to open up the largest contiguous area possible, and why I try when I can to investigate all the different expressions of community life: the habitations, the working areas, the places of worship, and the places of burial.

A site to me is not a succession of strata or an agglomeration of structures or a source of artifacts; it is first and foremost the discarded shell of a once-living community. My effort is to expose it in those terms during excavation, and to present it in those terms in the subsequent published report – to put the people back into the picture. Meinarti as I approached it, and as I present it here, is thus another community study. I have sometimes referred to this approach as "archaeo-ethnology."

How far we should go beyond the data in search of understanding is another and more problematical issue. One might be tempted to say, "as far as necessary to make it meaningful," and some archaeologists have surely gone to extraordinary lengths, positing impossibly long migrations, incredible coincidences between events thousands of kilometers apart, or even interplanetary visitors. But interpretation that achieves meaningfulness at the expense of believability will clearly appeal only to a small core of determinedly mystical-minded aficionados. Better to accept that we can only go so far, leaving a good deal of our data unexplainable in terms of what we currently know.

For those who are willing to go beyond the data at all, it becomes a matter of deciding on the limits of probability. Here again, for better and worse, the personal factor comes into play: probability is partly in the eye of the beholder. It is affected by the liveliness of one's imagination, but also by a personal inclination toward caution or incaution. Personally, I do not have a lively imagination, but I like to speculate all the same. At least intellectually, I have always inclined toward incaution. Readers of the previous Meinarti volumes will recognize that in the excavation of this site I pretty much "threw caution to the winds," because I had no other choice in view of its immediately impending destruction (see especially *Meinarti I*, Introduction). I cannot offer the same excuse in interpreting the history and culture of the site, but I nevertheless intend in the next pages to "throw caution to the winds" here also; not because I have no choice but simply because it is in my nature to do so.

I will try in these pages to paint a picture of the life and death of the Meinarti community as I think it is suggested by the archaeological and historical evidence, viewed through a combination of the comparative, diffusionist, direct historical, and emic approaches. Since this is a humanistic and not a scientific endeavor, I will here omit the "probablys" and "possiblys" required by scientific caution, and which readers will find abundantly in the previous volumes. In these pages I simply invite readers to decide for themselves how believable is the picture that I offer. I will narrate the story in most cases without citing the evidence or the reasoning on which my interpretations are based, for those also will be found in the preceding volumes. My only concession to scholarship will be the insertion of a few citations at points where they seem especially called for.

Archaeologists very rarely have the luxury of digging a complete site, not did I at Meinarti. They nevertheless nearly always treat what they actually found as a representative sample of the whole, even though this is not epistemologically a sound assumption. Notwithstanding the dangers, I will follow that conventional practice here. That is, my interpretations are based on the assumption that what I found in the southern half of the mound was representative of what was not found – in the houses and artifacts of the unexcavated northern half, as well as in the buildings that were carried away by erosive forces before I got there.

For the sake of simplicity I will refer to the successive episodes of occupation at Meinarti as Meroitic, Ballaña, Early Christian, Classic Christian, Late Christian, and Terminal Christian, even though these did not coincide exactly with the more general phases in Nubian history which I have elsewhere designated by those same terms, on the basis of ceramic evidence (see especially Adams 1964, 241-7).

The Meroitic settlement (Phase 1)

c. A.D. 200-425

Throughout most of its long history the Empire of Kush claimed, and intermittently exercised, sovereignty over the whole of the Nile Valley extending from the junction of the Niles to the First Cataract. This was critical for economic and strategic purposes, since the Nile was the vital lifeline that connected Kush with its trading partners to the north. Yet during the Napatan and the earlier part of the Meroitic era there was little actual settlement in the most northerly part of the empire, comprising Lower Nubia and the *Batn el-Hajjar*. The agrarian possibilities were very limited, and pastoralism impossible, in this region where the Nile does not regularly overflow its banks, and where there are no adjoining grasslands. Trading expeditions nevertheless passed regularly northbound and southbound through the region, and that trade had to be both regulated and protected. Kushite sovereignty was therefore proclaimed, and a measure of control exercised, through a garrison at Qasr Ibrim – the only place where unmistakable evidence of Napatan occupation has been found.

Sometime around the beginning of the common era, settlers began returning in considerable numbers to Lower Nubia, where they established what in time became a continuous string of farming villages. Their resettlement was facilitated by the introduction of the *saqia* (ox-driven waterwheel), making it possible for the first time to irrigate large areas of floodplain that were not often reached by natural overflow. The new settlers acknowledged Kushite sovereignty, and used the Meroitic language in written texts, but they were ethnic Nubian speakers (Nobadae) – former nomads who had migrated to the Nile Valley in earlier centuries, and had taken up residence in the Kushite territories between the Third and Fourth Cataracts. As so often happens when nomads settle, they had fully absorbed the culture of their sedentary neighbors, retaining only the ancestral language of earlier days.

When settlement in Lower Nubia had proceeded to a certain point, it became necessary for the rulers of Kush to establish a formal administrative regime in the northern territory, superseding the purely military control that had been exercised from Qasr Ibrim. A fairly complex hierarchy of administrative offices, unique to this part of the empire, was then created. Some of the officials were sent north from the capital at Meroe, but many were co-opted from among the prosperous families already resident in the north. Their functions were mainly economic, concerned with the regulation of trade and the collection of taxes, but there was also a kind of viceroy and a military commander (for extended discussion see Török 1979). The most important officials were resident at or near Qasr Ibrim; after death many of them were buried across the river at Karanog. Other important personages resided at Gebel Adda and at Faras. ·

As part of the new administrative regime, the Kushite authorities established an outpost on the island of Meinarti, just below the Second Cataract (Subphase 1a). This was a strategically important location, akin to the Island of Elephantine below the First Cataract. It was a place where southbound riverain cargoes had to be off-loaded from larger to smaller boats, for passage through the cataract, while northbound cargoes could be transferred from smaller to larger boats. It was a place too where southbound cargoes might have to be held over for considerable periods, during the low season, until the level of the Nile rose sufficiently to make boat passage feasible.

The station at Meinarti was thus connected primarily

with trade; its regulation and its promotion. There were from the beginning at least two major structures, both built with stout mud brick walls and vaulted ceilings. One was a labyrinthine administration building, having a monumental approach and entranceway, and the other was a kind of combination warehouse and market. The latter consisted of a small open plaza flanked by a row of small shops on either side, and the whole surrounded by a high wall. Each shop comprised a pair of connected rooms, an inner room for storage and an outer room for business, and each had low, vaulted cellars beneath the floors. Many trade transactions were actually carried on in the open plaza in front of the shops, an area that was divided up into separate trading floors at some time after the original construction (at Subphase 1aa).

There was at least one additional monumental building built at the same time as the administration building and market, but not enough survived to give any hint to its function. There was also one surviving building that may have been residential, and there were probably others that did not survive the extensive flood damage of subsequent times. There was however no identifiable religious structure on the island; Meinarti's functions were purely secular.

Not long after the establishment of the outpost, if not at the precise same time, a wine-pressing establishment was added to the Meinarti complex. It was made up of a group of three connected tanks: an upper tank for the foot-pressing of the grapes, a small settling tank into which the juice first flowed, and a much larger fermentation tank at the end of the series. It was one of 12 such installations built at the same time in Lower Nubia, as part of a brief and unsuccessful attempt at viticulture (see Adams 1966b). The operation at Meinarti, at least, was a state enterprise. It and the other presses can probably be seen as an effort to lessen Nubia's enormous dependence on imported wine (Adams 1977, 362).

Like many other Meroitic settlements in Lower Nubia and the *Batn el-Hajjar*, the buildings at Meinarti were constructed on extremely low ground, only about 1m above the level of the floodplain. This is one of several evidences that major floods were uncommon and not expected in Meroitic times. There was in any case no other choice at Meinarti, since it was a purely alluvial island, whose only high ground was a low sand drift near the southern end. It was here that the main buildings were constructed. The site was nevertheless attacked by floods many times in its early history, and these in time swept away considerable parts of the earliest settlement.

The outpost at Meinarti was not intended mainly for the conduct of local trade, for there were no other Meroitic settlements of consequence in the vicinity. The nearest concentration of population was at Argin, some 20km to the north, while to the south there were only tiny, scattered hamlets through the *Batn el-Hajjar*. Nevertheless local villagers did come to trade for the goods that were stored within the market compound. The officials who oversaw and conducted the trade surely lived on the island itself, although only one apparently residential structure survived. There was no cemetery on the island, however; the dead were buried in a cemetery at the long-deserted site of Kor, immediately opposite on the West bank.

There may also have been a population of ordinary peasant farmers on the island, though, as previously noted, no trace of their residences survived. They could have farmed either on the northern part of Meinarti Island, or on the immediately neighboring island of Majarab, which was connected to Meinarti during the time of the Low Nile.

The Empire of Kush collapsed in the early fourth century, and political power in Lower Nubia devolved into the hands of local "big men" who became the Kings of Nobadia, as the region came to be called. They may previously have been officials of the Meroitic state, and certainly they maintained some of the trappings of Kushite royal authority, although the Meroitic language and other aspects of Kushite culture and society were lost. According to Greek sources the new rulers oversaw a considerable bureaucracy having Greek titles, and to the very limited extent that they wrote, it was in Greek (Thompson 1969, 45-52; Török 1988, 47-69). These changes suggest the very close cultural and economic link that had been established between Lower Nubia and late Roman Egypt, at the same time when connections with the more southerly parts of Kush were cut off.

The Nobadian ruler and other officials, as nearly as we can determine from their titles, were concerned more with political and military control than with trade. It is possible however that the kings retained for a time some interest in controlling the commerce through the Second Cataract, and there may still have been officers in their service at Meinarti. The volume of trade however was vastly reduced, in comparison to Meroitic times, because Nobadia did not control a large area to the south of the cataract.

In the late third and early fourth centuries (Subphase 1b), several other factors combined to damage the fabric and to reduce the importance of the Meinarti establishment. Wine production was given up, and the disused pressing and fermentation basins became a refuse dump. The administration building was largely destroyed by a fire, which may have been deliberately set, and it was never rebuilt. Various manufacturing activities which involved fire were subsequently carried out on its dilapidated floors. Meanwhile the warehouse and market compound was very extensively damaged by one or more floods, as were all the neighboring buildings. The entire eastern range of shops was destroyed, together with one of those on the western side, and the other western shops had to be considerably rebuilt. The ultimate misfortune however was surely the end of effective Kushite sovereignty, as a result of which Meinarti lost its status as a major state outpost although it continued for a time as a nexus of local trade transactions.

After the several episodes of physical destruction, some new and very irregularly built structures began to appear among the ruins. They had brick walls of varying thickness; many were only 20cm thick, and sometimes curving. Some of the new buildings seem to have been used for water storage, or for manufacturing activities involving a great deal of water; others were certainly residences. A small suite of rooms at the southeast corner of the old administration building, the only part of the structure not heavily damaged by fire, was converted to a residence by the building of some new interior partitions, and the opening of new doorways. Meinarti however had not yet assumed the appearance of an ordinary farming village; it was still mainly devoted to activities involving manufacturing and trade.

The early fifth century saw the beginning of a process of regeneration at Meinarti (Subphase 1c), although it was short-lived. A new range of rooms was built up at the east side of the old market compound, on top of the ruins of the previous shops, and the rooms at the west side remained in use. To the south of them were two new, stoutly-built square houses, nearly identical in size and plan. Each consisted of a large outer room, and two small inner rooms behind it. One had 60-cm walls, and was two storeys high; the other was a single-storey structure having 40-cm walls. The two houses were certainly residences, but they were very unlike other dwellings of the Ballaña period; their closest resemblance was to elite residences that had been built in some of the Meroitic settlements of earlier times. The single-storey house was adjoined by a large, walled courtyard that was used both for storage and for trade.

The two new houses were the residences of important persons, who most probably were still concerned with trading activities, and perhaps with taxation. Whether they were appointees or agents of the Nobadian kings, or whether they were independent entrepreneurs, is uncertain. Elsewhere on the site there were a few surviving remnants of thin walls, suggesting the presence of the more ordinary dwellings of peasant farmers.

But Meinarti's short-lived revitalization came to an end some time around A.D. 425, when for half a century the whole settlement was abandoned. This was not occasioned by flood damage, and must have been a consequence of deteriorating economic and political conditions in the Kingdom of Nobadia. Its rulers at the time were heavily preoccupied with military operations against Blemmyan intruders in the northern part of their kingdom, and they were also sometimes at odds with the newly established Christian authorities in Egypt, who wished to deny them access to some of their traditional pagan shrines. Trade undoubtedly suffered in consequence.

The Ballaña reoccupation (Phase 2)

c. A.D. 475-650

The late fifth and early sixth centuries witnessed the apogee of power and wealth enjoyed by the rulers of Nobadia, who had now successfully consolidated their rule and expelled their Blemmyan enemies. Meanwhile the new Nubian kingdoms of Makouria and Alwa were taking shape in the old Kushite territories to the south of them, restoring a measure of stability to a region that had been in turmoil since the fall of Kush. To the extent that those kingdoms were in economic contact with Egypt, as they evidently were, their trade had to pass through the territory of Nobadia, giving the northern rulers some opportunity to profit as middlemen. A considerable volume of trade was evidently passing to the north, because the Nobadian rulers were receiving in exchange a truly prodigious quantity and variety of imported luxury goods. But few other Nubians seem to have benefited in this exchange; for the vast majority of them the Ballaña period was a time of stability rather than of prosperity. There were a few prosperous trading middlemen – possibly Greeks or Egyptians – at Qasr Ibrim, but further to the south the profits of trade passed very largely into the hands of the rulers. Meanwhile the majority of the population scratched out a living as peasant farmers, at an economic level not very far above bare subsistence.

In many respects, Nobadia had reverted from a state to a chiefdom. Despite the large court bureaucracy there was no regular system of provincial administration, and no use of written instruments. Importantly, there was no longer a priesthood or a state religion, except for the cult surrounding the ruler. Worship of the old Egyptian and Kushite gods continued, but it came to focus more and more exclusively on the figure of Isis, and it was a personal rather than a collective matter. Salvationist cults, focusing usually on one particular savior, were sweeping throughout the Graeco-Roman world at this time, and Isis – formerly a fertility and mortuary goddess – became the special savior of the Nubians. Those who could afford the journey could make a pilgrimage to her shrine at the Temple of Philae, or at Qasr Ibrim (cf. Driskell, Adams and French 1989); there was no other place of worship within Nubia itself.

It was in these circumstances that the island of Meinarti was reoccupied, toward the end of the fifth century (Subphase 2a). The island was not chosen as a place of refuge, for there was now little to be feared from enemy activity. Apparently, it was chosen because there was abundant farmland available at Meinarti and on the adjoining island of Majarab. The settlers were not necessarily descendants of those who had left; they might even have been newly arrived immigrants from the south or the west.

The reoccupied settlement at Meinarti bore almost no resemblance to that which had preceded it, even though it stood on the same ground, and parts of the older structures were restored to use. Both of the two stout-walled houses built at Subphase 1c were reoccupied, as was a remnant of the old market compound. But these were now "swallowed up" within a maze of small family dwellings which surrounded them on all sides. The new dwellings, built exclusively with thin and often curving walls, typically consisted of from two to four rooms, though a few had as many as eight. They were densely clustered into aggregations such that they appeared to lean on one another like a house of cards, while here and there very narrow and irregular streets wound among them. The structures had light roofs of poles and matting.

Although the various residential clusters grew by accretion, with new houses built up against older ones, the process of growth was a rapid one. Within a generation the community had reached the full size that it was to retain throughout the remainder of the Ballaña period, including at least forty families. The smaller residences, with two to four rooms, were those of nuclear families; the larger ones may have housed more extended kin groups.

4

Important persons occupied the two stout-walled houses. They may not have been official functionaries, but one or another of them certainly served as the village headman – the *omda* as he would later be called. For the rest, however, the community had become simply a densely nucleated peasant farming village, similar to many others of the later Ballaña period in Lower Nubia. It was an aspect that the settlement was to wear for the next seven hundred years.

Like most peasant villages at most times in history, the Meinarti community of Ballaña times was not a prosperous one. The dwelling rooms were small and crowded, and the people had little in the way of luxury possessions. The main luxury enjoyed by all was imported wine, which was consumed in enormous quantities. Apart from the dwellers in the two elite houses, there was little social differentiation in the population. Larger houses were simply the dwellings of larger families; they were not otherwise conspicuously richer than their neighbors. The dead, as in Meroitic times, were buried on the West bank rather than on the island.

There was little change in the character of the Meinarti community throughout the sixth century (Subphase 2b). The village had already reached its full size at or near the beginning of the century, and thereafter the changes that took place involved no more than the continual rearrangement of interior doorways and partitions, as housing adapted itself to the expanding needs of some families and the contracting needs of others.

According to historians the conversion of Nubia to Christianity – meaning presumably the conversion of the rulers – occurred in the latter half of the sixth century. There were already individual Christian converts at Meinarti before that date, and many more adopted the new faith immediately afterward. A few however maintained their adherence to Isis, and other gods of antiquity. Votaries of the two cults could live side by side without conflict because religion for both was essentially a personal matter, not a communal one. There was no Isis temple to the south of Qasr Ibrim, but there was also no church at Meinarti until the latter half of the seventh century. In the meantime, the coming of the new religion wrought no change in the outward aspect of the Meinarti community. Christians and pagans alike continued to bury their dead on the West bank.

By the end of the sixth century the village houses were mostly over a hundred years old, and were showing their age. Walls were sagging not only from ordinary wear and tear, but also from the pressure of drifted sand which was becoming a problem everywhere in the community. Some houses were eventually abandoned and disappeared under the drifts; others had to be shored up with reinforced walls.

In the early seventh century there began, here and there, a gradual process of repair and reinforcement (Subphase 2c). It was not a community-wide affair, but was undertaken in individual houses as need required. Generally, it involved the replacement of earlier, thin house walls with more substantial ones, usually though not always on the same alignments as before. But neither of the two former elite houses survived as a residence. One was abandoned

and sanded over, and the other became merely a storage and working area. These developments however wrought little change in the overall appearance of the community, which remained as before a tight, irregular cluster of small family dwellings.

Egypt fell to the armies of Islam between 640 and 642, and the conquerors sought immediately to add Nubia to their domains. There was an abortive invasion in 642 and a more serious one in 652. Neither was in the end successful, but it may have been the second Arab incursion that forced a temporary evacuation of Meinarti in the middle of the seventh century. Or, it may have been a disastrous flood; the first of many that were to attack the village during the next three centuries. In any event, this episode of abandonment marked the end of Phase 2.

The Early Christian period (Phase 3)

c. *A.D. 660-1000*

Following their incorporation into the pharaonic empire, the Nubians were always regarded as a civilized people, and so regarded themselves. Indeed it became a central feature of their self-image. They proclaimed their civilized status, and their superiority over surrounding peoples, in the traditional and time-honored ways: by building imposing architectural monuments, by worshipping the "civilized" gods, and above all by their use of written instruments. In later centuries they would be accepted without hesitation by Greeks and Romans as forming a part of the *oikoumenê:* the "house of civilization" extending from Italy through Greece and the Near East to India. Arab chroniclers of the Middle Ages too always wrote of them as a civilized people, since they were "people of the book."

The Nubians at the same time were always conscious of being at the outer edge of the civilized world, a situation that involved both opportunities and dangers. On one hand it allowed them to "lord it over" and to exploit their uncivilized neighbors to the south, just as the Egyptians had once done to them. On the other hand there was always the danger of marginalization or isolation, if they failed to keep up with developments in the rest of the world.

That is essentially what happened in Ballaña times, when the Nubians clung to many of the traditions of pharaonic Egypt and pharaonic Kush, while their neighbors espoused the new and revolutionary creed of Christianity. Nubians traveling to Egypt were often derided for their continued allegiance to outmoded beliefs, and were sometimes actively proselytized. Some became converts, or at least adopted as much of the new creed as they could understand and practice, in the absence of a church.

Thus is was that the Christian missionaries who entered Nubia in the sixth century found a fertile ground for their efforts. Simply, they offered the Nubians a way of re-connecting; of renewing the bond with the rest of the civilized world that was so central to their self-perception. The Nubians became not merely converts but enthusiastic and dedicated ones, and remained so for the better part of a thousand years. The symbolic trappings of

5

an earthly king, so dominant and so politically important through the preceding millennia, gave way completely and with extraordinary rapidity to the representations of a heavenly king. In the early years of conversion the simplified creed and otherworldly orientation of the new faith were an especial comfort, compensating for the rather impoverished earthly conditions of the time.

The Arab conquest of Egypt, only a century after the conversion of the Nubians, did not create a similar desire to affiliate with the world of Islam; at least not until a millennium later. For Egypt did not undergo wholesale conversion to Islam, as it did to Christianity. Like Spain, it remained for many centuries a Christian country under Muslim rule. Within Nubia itself, the *Baqt* treaty, negotiated after the second unsuccessful Arab invasion, guaranteed the country's freedom both from further invasion and from Islamic proselytization for several centuries. This agreement was to play a pivotal role in shaping the history of Nubia for generations to come.

The settlers who returned to Meinarti in the Early Christian period (Subphase 3a) found their houses in very damaged condition. They nevertheless returned in a spirit of hopeful optimism, engendered perhaps by the successful resistance to the Arab invasion, and the negotiation of the *Baqt* treaty. In consequence, the piecemeal reinforcement or rebuilding of houses, already begun in the late Ballaña period, was very much accelerated. Before long, nearly every house in the village exhibited an irregular combination of older thin walls and newly built or repaired thick ones. The new walls were generally straighter than the old ones, but only one building – not necessarily a residence – was built entirely with straight walls.

The optimism of the returning villagers was expressed above all in the building of the first village church, at the east side of the settlement. It was constructed by local villagers working under the supervision of itinerant masons, who were active in building churches all over Lower Nubia during this time. The original church had a curiously skewed plan, like some early churches in the Faras area. There was no adjoining cemetery; the dead continued to be buried, as before, on the nearby west bank.

The mood of optimism was fairly short-lived. The formalization of peaceful relations with Egypt did not result in an increase in trade; on the contrary economic conditions declined to their lowest point in several centuries. This was due partly to chaotic conditions in Egypt, and partly to the fact that Nobadia, long an independent kingdom, became subject to the neighboring and more powerful Nubian Kingdom of Makouria, whose rulers established a monopoly over trade to the south of the Second Cataract. There was evidently little opportunity even for the accumulation of agricultural surpluses, for the houses were entirely devoid of storage facilities. In addition, Meinarti and other low-lying settlements were attacked with increasing frequency by destructive floods. Under these impoverished conditions, the society of the village remained thoroughly egalitarian. If there were any differences in landholding or other aspects of status, they were not reflected in the housing.

After about a century (at Subphase 3b), the Meinarti villagers became dissatisfied with their original church,

because of its skewed outline and its rather aberrant floor plan. With the aid of professional builders, they dismantled it nearly to ground level, and built on the same site a church of a more conventional Nubian plan. A large residence for the village priest was constructed alongside, although this remained in use only for a few generations. Afterward, the village priest resided among the rest of the villagers, and in the Early Christian period he was no better housed than they. Indeed there were probably some intervals, in these retrograde times, when there was no regularly resident priest.

Significant changes were made in the church at Subphase 3c. A tribune (stepped choir seats) was built into the apse, and the sanctuary area, at the east end of the nave, was screened off from the remainder of the nave by a *higab* wall. These changes, which were made in many other Nubian churches at the same time, signaled a basic change in the liturgy. From that time onward, a portion of every holy service was conducted behind a curtain, out of sight of the congregation, as is still true in Coptic churches today.

Although the villagers had little in the way of material wealth, they were nevertheless provided in the later eighth and the ninth centuries with a kind of central "bank," available for the use of many if not all of the residents. It was a two-room house having enormously thick walls, and entered by a single narrow doorway. Within, villagers could store their most valued items of jewelry in pottery vessels buried in the floors. The construction of this facility suggests the possibility that theft may have become a problem within the community.

In general, the story of Meinarti from the eighth to the tenth century (Subphases 3b-3d) was one of gradual but continuing deterioration. As damaging floods recurred, the villagers continued for a time to take countermeasures by thickening the standing walls. But the repairs after awhile became more and more haphazard, as the necessity of frequent rebuilding came to be accepted as inevitable. As the more outlying and lower houses were destroyed altogether, some families moved away. Those who remained had perforce to crowd into a smaller and smaller space, with the result that some of the fairly large earlier rooms were subdivided into much smaller ones. The few new houses that were constructed were built with very small rooms and with thin and insubstantial walls; they were seen from the first as expendable. Housing conditions by the tenth century were the worst at any time in the history of the community; Meinarti had assumed something like the appearance of a slum. The church alone was kept in a state of decent repair, as religion provided the chief consolation for the villagers in these impoverished times. To add to their miseries, the importation of wine had been severely restricted by order of the Abbasid caliphs.

At the end of the tenth century, the people of Meinarti gave up their losing battle against the recurring floods, and moved away altogether.

The Classic Christian period (Phase 4)

c. A.D. 1020-1172

The Classic Christian period corresponded in a general way to the time of the Fatimid Caliphate in Egypt. The new, Shiite rulers in the north were almost continually at odds with their Sunni Muslim neighbors in the east, and at the same time were cut off from access to the Turkic mercenaries who had come to form the backbone of the Islamic armies in Asia. Instead, they turned increasingly to the use of Nubian mercenaries, to maintain their rather precarious regime. Under the circumstances it was very much in their interest to maintain good relations with the Nubian kingdoms, and in time a flourishing commerce was revived between the two countries. Fatimid Egypt and Christian Nubia became a trade interaction zone unto themselves. The period of the eleventh and twelfth centuries thus saw a marked revival in the prosperity of ordinary Nubians.

Meanwhile Nobadia, though subject to the suzerainty of neighboring Makouria, emerged as a semi-autonomous domain, under the governance of a kind of viceroy called the *Eparch* of Nobadia. His duties were chiefly economic, and connected with the supervision of trade with Egypt. Above all, it was his duty to see that the provisions of the *Baqt* treaty were carried out. The economic regime over which he presided was entirely different from that of Makouria, for within it Egyptian merchants were allowed to trade freely and even to settle, while to the south of the Second Cataract all foreign trade was a monopoly of the Makourian king, and foreign traders were forbidden entry. Enriched by the new free trade, and militarily secure under the protection of the *Baqt* treaty, Meinarti and other Lower Nubian communities experienced a major revitalization.

It was about a generation after the departure of the Early Christian villagers when settlers moved back, seemingly en masse, to the island of Meinarti (Subphase 4a). They were not necessarily the same people who had left, or their descendants, for they made no effort to restore old houses or to maintain old property lines. The entire village was rebuilt from the ground up, and those portions of earlier buildings that were not sanded over were systematically dismantled. Only the church survived as a reminder of the earlier settlement. It too was entirely rebuilt, but on the same plan as before, and it incorporated such parts of the earlier building as had not been destroyed by floods.

The rebuilt village of Meinarti resembled its predecessor to the extent that it was still a peasant farming community, with houses tightly clustered into large, irregular aggregations. There were several of these, separated by winding streets and small plazas. Like the clusters of earlier times they grew larger by accretion, a process that continued through almost the whole of the Classic Christian period.

The houses however were unlike anything that had preceded. They were, on average, half again as large, and were much more regularly constructed. For reasons that are unclear, the returning settlers seem to have known that they had nothing more to fear from high floods, and their houses therefore lacked altogether the stout reinforcing walls that had been prevalent in the Early Christian period. All houses were built with thin, mostly straight walls. There was however a marked variability in the size of dwellings. Many were the residences of nuclear families, but a few housed more extended kin groups. A conspicuous innovation was the inclusion of an indoor toilet facility in nearly every house. There were in addition mastabas, ovens, and other built-in architectural features that had been lacking in earlier times.

The most outstanding feature proclaiming the new-found prosperity of the villagers was the prevalence of storage facilities for grain and for dates. These took the form of tall, mud *qusebas* and of built-in bins in the room corners, many of which were roofed over. Facilities of one kind or the other, or frequently both, were found in nearly every house; in some houses they were present in several rooms. The villagers were evidently receiving the yield from lands that they owned not only on the island, but from further afield as well.

In short, the Meinarti of Classic Christian times was an abode of what Marxists like to call "rich peasants." Not merely cultivators, they were also prosperous landowners, with holdings elsewhere than in the immediate area. Two ladies of high status were reported (according to their funerary inscriptions) to be the "owners" of churches, one of which was as far away as Argin, 20km to the north. Presumably, this meant that they received a part or all of the income from the church lands. But as usual in times of prosperity, not all families prospered equally. Social and economic divisions within the community, evidenced in the houses and in the graves, were more evident than in the two preceding periods.

Two very large houses were the homes of "leading citizens," who lived surrounded by large numbers of kin or retainers. One of them was the only two-storey dwelling at Meinarti. The occupants received especially large contributions of grain and of dates from tenants or tributaries, which they poured into large, covered bins in interior store rooms. The adjacent walls were adorned with protective religious inscriptions, usually invoking the protection of the archangels. One or another of the inhabitants of these houses served as the village *omda*.

Apart from farmers, there were also potters living on the island. However they produced only the knobbed vessels (*qadus*) needed for use on the *saqia*. Other pottery vessels were received in trade, partly from Nubian sources but also in very large quantities from Aswan. Other trade goods received in abundance were textiles, objects of bronze, and glass beads.

At the time of resettlement the Meinarti church was almost wholly rebuilt, but it retained exactly the plan of its predecessor. For the first time, however, the villagers now began burying their dead in its immediate vicinity, instead of on the west bank. The cemetery gradually grew outward, to the east and especially to the south, until in time it extended along most of the east side of the community. A few graves were also added immediately to the north of the church. Evidences of social or economic disparity could be seen in the cemetery as well as in the houses, for about a third of the graves were covered by brick superstructures, of varying size and ornateness, while the remainder were unmarked at the surface. This was not a differentiation based on age or sex, for many of the tombs were those of young people, and some of the most elaborate were those of women.

A few of the most affluent individuals had carved sandstone funerary stelae, for which the village priest had to be paid. The fact that some inscriptions were in Coptic suggests an Egyptian presence at Meinarti, for the Coptic language was never used by indigenous Nubians (for discussion see Adams 1977, 485). Other tombstone inscriptions were in Greek, which remained to the end the liturgical language of the Nubian church. These funerary texts were evidently dictated by locally trained Nubian priests, whose command of the language was often quite limited.

The half dozen Arabic tombstones found at Meinarti are evidence of religious as well as socio-economic divisions within the community. Apparently there were Arab, probably Egyptian merchants resident with their families on the island, and they were able to find scribes who could execute funerary inscriptions in good, classical Arabic. Their houses were no different from those of the Christian inhabitants, but their dead were not buried in the same cemetery as were the Christians. All of the tombstones, both Christian and Muslim, were carved in the single century between 1063 and 1161, an interval which represents the apogee of medieval Nubian prosperity.

The village continued to grow through most of the eleventh and twelfth centuries, as new houses were built up against the existing ones (Subphases 4b and 4c). In time they encroached upon the former area of streets and plazas, until the village came to consist of two huge housing agglomerations, plus a few detached, outlying houses. There was, as always, a frequent rearrangement of interior doorways and partitions, to accommodate the growing needs of some families, and the declining needs of others. The newly built structures were not all residences; some were small retail shops. There were no separate storage structures; storage as before was in *qusebas* and bins within the residences.

Meinarti was never threatened by a major flood during the Classic Christian period, except along the outer margins of the settlement. On the other hand drifting sand, blowing off the broad sandbar at the northern end of the island, was an ever growing problem. It was not the coarse yellow sand of the west bank, but a much finer riverain sand which carried very readily on the wind, and accumulated with extraordinary rapidity. As it piled up against the outside of northern and western house walls, it became necessary for the inhabitants to raise the interior floor levels to offset the pressure. The raising of floors eventually necessitated in turn the raising of roof levels. The church, standing by itself near the eastern side of the village, was especially vulnerable to the drifting sand, and it became necessary to raise the threshold levels, as well as interior floor levels, several times. In the cemetery, drifting sand covered the tomb superstructures of earlier times, and new graves were then dug directly into them from above. The cemetery grew upward rather than outward throughout its later centuries.

One of the most extensively damaged buildings at Meinarti was the two-storey house of the *omda*, at the northern end of the village. Its floor levels and its roof level were eventually raised by over a meter. In the end (at Subphase 4c) it was replaced altogether by a more stoutly constructed house, with 40-cm walls, built directly alongside. It was the first of a number of "unit houses" that were to become the dominant form of residence in the Late Christian period. But the village was still enjoying a high level of stability and prosperity when, in the year 1172, it was abruptly abandoned in the face of a new and wholly unexpected menace from the north. Before leaving, however, the villagers took time to seal up many of their house doors with brick, against the intrusion of sand during their absence. That done, they took refuge among the islands of the Second Cataract and the *Batn el-Hajjar*, as their successors were to do several more times in the centuries to come.

The Late Christian period (Phase 5)

c. A.D. 1200-1365

In 1172, Salah ed-Din ibn Ayyub (otherwise Saladin) deposed the last of the Fatimid Caliphs and proclaimed himself ruler of Egypt, at the same time returning the country to the Sunni Muslim fold. Fearing a possible reprisal from the Nubian allies of his deposed predecessor, the new ruler despatched a pre-emptive expedition into Nubia—the first military incursion into that country since the signing of the *Baqt* accord five hundred years earlier. The invaders moved in force as far as Qasr Ibrim, where they drove out the inhabitants, killed or captured many, and extensively damaged the town and its churches. They then established a temporary headquarters in the captured town, from which they launched raiding parties into the surrounding districts, and as far south as the Second Cataract. It was the presence of this marauding force that had precipitated the abandonment of Meinarti, at the end of Phase 4.

A single incursion was enough to serve the purposes of the Ayyubids, and after a few months the intruders withdrew. They never again attacked Nubia, for Salah ed-Din and his rather weak successors were very largely preoccupied with military threats on their eastern flank, both from Crusader armies and from rival Muslim states. Trade relations with the Nubian kingdoms were soon reestablished, though never again with the same intimacy as in the Fatimid era. Nevertheless, the Nubians continued for another century to enjoy a considerable level of economic prosperity as well as of peace. The volume of back-and-forth trade between Nobadia and Makouria also considerably increased, as evidenced by the quantities of southern-made pottery found at Meinarti and other northern sites.

For most Nubians, the damage done by the Ayyubid raiders was more psychological than physical. Not many of their houses were attacked, but they could sense nevertheless that the 500-year *Pax Nubica* was at an end; they could never again rely entirely on a treaty for protection against their northern neighbors. The long-neglected fortress walls at Qasr Ibrim were hastily rebuilt, people moved into defensible localities like the old pharaonic fortress of Serra and the more remote islands of the Second Cataract, and a new and more defensible form of house architecture was adopted. The *Eparch* of Nobadia, whose earlier duties had been primarily economic, now assumed a military role as well, for it was he who had to manage the defense of Nubia's northern frontier. Meinarti came to play a crucial role in his strategic plans, although he continued to reside mainly at Qasr Ibrim.

After the abandonment of 1172, it was at least a generation before Meinarti was reoccupied (Subphase 5a). In the interval, the roof timbers had been removed from the abandoned houses, for use elsewhere, and the buildings were deeply filled with drifted sand. When settlers returned, some use could still be made of a few rooms, whose walls stood a meter or more above the sand level, and the *omda's* house with its stout walls was still inhabitable. The church was once again restored to use, although with extensive modifications. They were partly reinforcing measures against the pressure of drifted sand, but the basic interior plan was also altered, to bring it into conformity with the newly prevailing style in Late Christian church architecture.

Elsewhere the village was the scene of wholesale new building, and along entirely new lines. There was now a conspicuous architectural division between the northern and southern halves of the community, which was to persist through the whole of the Late Christian period. In the northern half, a few surviving rooms from Classic Christian times were briefly returned to use (at Subphase 5a), but they were soon dismantled and overbuilt. In their place there appeared, one after another, a group of stout-walled family dwellings, generally similar to the *omda's* house that had been built earlier. They were roughly equal in size and shape to the dwellings of the Classic Christian period, and had the same interior arrangement of rooms, including a toilet at the back of the house. However, they were much more sturdily constructed, with walls either 40 or 60cm thick, and no house shared a party wall with any other.

The number of these dwellings never exceeded eight or ten; it was not nearly as great as was the number of Classic Christian dwellings during Phase 4. The inhabitants as before were farming families, but they were not the large absentee landholders of earlier times. Their holdings were confined to the island and its immediate vicinity. The physical separation of their houses suggests a growing spirit of individualism, and a departure from the strongly communal orientation of the earlier villagers.

Meanwhile the *Eparch* took possession of the southern half of the village; not for regular residency but for intermittent use as trade or military conditions required. At his direction there was constructed a group of large, open courtyards, for the receipt and temporary housing of goods, possibly including slaves. The central courtyard was also arranged as a reception hall where visiting traders or tributaries could be met.

These arrangements however lasted only for about a generation. As the *Eparch* began to visit Meinarti with increased frequency, and with an enlarged retinue, the interior space of the original open courtyards was subdivided into a large number of rooms, most of which were roofed over (Subphase 5b). At the center was the *Eparch's* reception room, decorated with inscriptions; around it on three sides were storage and working rooms, and on the fourth side a large open kitchen. This inner cluster was surrounded in turn by small residential rooms. There was however only one toilet, close to the *Eparch's* inner quarters, to serve the entire cluster of more than 90 rooms. The whole complex, including the toilet chamber, was decorated throughout with salmon-pink plaster on the walls.

When the Mamluks seized power in Egypt, in 1250, the *Pax Nubica* was permanently at an end. Egypt's new rulers were military adventurists, and they very soon began exercising their muscle in Nubia, as they did also in the Levant. There were several Mamluk invasions during the later thirteenth and fourteenth centuries, resulting in increasing political instability as well as military insecurity. On a number of these occasions the *Eparch* retreated from Qasr Ibrim to his base at Meinarti, where he could organize a defense based in the Second Cataract area.

In 1286, in the face of one such incursion, the Makourian king at Dongola decided against armed defense. Instead, he gave orders to the *Eparch* that the whole of Lower Nubia should be evacuated. The villagers at Meinarti dutifully obeyed, but before leaving they took time to bury some of their most treasured possessions under the house floors, and sometimes to fill up and then seal off whole rooms. A couple of families allowed their homes to be used for the burial of goods belonging to a group of neighboring families. That done, they retreated to temporary refuge among the islands of the Second Cataract.

The invaders however made straight for Dongola, and did not pause to plunder Meinarti. As a result, the villagers found their houses little damaged when they moved back a few years later (Subphase 5c). During the ensuing century the eparchal complex in the southern half of the village continued to function as before. There was some rearrangement of partitions and doors, and the whole cluster of rooms was now whitewashed. In addition, the complex was newly provided with a stout watchtower, at its southern end. Primitive murals, unique among Nubian wall decoration, were painted in the interior chamber which served as the *Eparch's* reception hall. However, many of the valuables buried by the inhabitants before their departure were never dug up; they remained under the house floors until found by the archaeologist.

Meanwhile, the unit houses in the northern half of the village were systematically strengthened. Walls were thickened, the original pole and mat roofs were removed and replaced with brick vaults, and some houses were equipped with inner strong-rooms, accessible only from above.

After their incursion of 1286 the Mamluk sultans claimed suzerainty over Lower Nubia, which they called the Province of al-Maris. However, they never exercised it in any effective way; they merely used it as an excuse to intervene in Nubian affairs, in support of this or that claimant to the Makourian throne. In fact, the most northerly portion of Lower Nubia had fallen into the hands of a "barbarian warband," the Beni Kanz, who were under the control of neither the Mamluks nor the Nubian rulers. For a time most of their depredations were directed against southern Egypt, and they thus served as a kind of buffer between the Nubians and the Egyptian rulers. Behind that shield, the *Eparch* of Nobadia and his retinue continued to perform their functions, and Makouria retained its independence.

Arab nomad groups, some expelled from Egypt by Mamluk pressure, allied themselves from time to time with the Beni Kanz, and carried out depredations both in Egypt and in Nubia. In the later fourteenth century one such group, the Beni Ikrima, drove out the inhabitants and established themselves at Meinarti, which they used as a base while marauding in the surrounding districts. They made use of the unit houses as pens for their livestock, while residing within the rooms of the eparchal complex, or in tents nearby. As they were professing Muslims, they systematically defaced the murals both in the church and in the eparchal complex. They in turn were driven out by a Mamluk force in 1365, but meanwhile they had brought the Late Christian occupation and the eparchal establishment at Meinarti to an end. The island was not reoccupied until the beginning of the fifteenth century.

The Terminal Christian and post-Christian
occupation (Phase 6)
c. A.D. 1400-1600

In the later middle ages a spirit of military adventurism was prevalent throughout the lands of the Mediterranean basin, both Christian and Muslim. It was especially pervasive in the Levant, where Crusaders had brought with them the European model of warlordism, along with new techniques and new weapons of siege warfare. Their example was soon enough copied by the local emirs, and eventually, above all, by the Mamluks. Throughout the Near East, the castle replaced the mosque and the church, as the dominant architectural expression of a secularizing and a warlike age.

At the same time another kind of warlordism was taking shape along the Middle Nile, in the former territories of Makouria and Alwa. Those long-peaceful Christian kingdoms were overrun and destroyed by migrating Arab nomads from Egypt and from the Arabian Peninsula. Different tribal groups carved out a whole series of petty, warrior kingdoms up and down the length of the river, and settled down to rule over and to exploit the Nubian farming populations. Their sheikhs founded what were meant to be hereditary monarchies, and took for themselves the title *mek* (from the Arabic *melek,* king). Their advent signaled the end not only of the Christian kingdoms but of the organized practice of Christianity, since all of the rulers were nominal Muslims. No more priests were trained or were sent from Egypt, although individual Nubians clung to as much of their faith as they could remember for generations longer.

For a while Lower Nubia was spared a similar fate. In the north it was protected, if inadvertently, by the Beni Kanz, whose depredations were directed largely against Egypt rather than against their Nubian neighbors. To the south, east, and west it was protected by the surrounding deserts, whose total lack of pastoral resources offered no inducement to nomad settlers. Within this protected enclave, a splinter kingdom called Dotawo, more or less a relic of the old Nobadia, survived until the end of the fifteenth century. The King of Dotawo, the *Eparch* of Nobadia, and the Bishop of Ibrim all continued to hold office within its restricted domain, which included Meinarti.

Although confronted by warrior states to the north and to the south, Dotawo itself was not a warring kingdom. It survived only because nobody wanted its territory, not because of an active defense. However, its people were not wholly unaffected by the military spirit of the time, and they could not afford to neglect defensive measures altogether. Here and there, especially through the *Batn el-Hajjar,* local big men began building castle-like two-storey houses and assuming a measure of independent control of the surrounding districts. Although Egypt had been a potential enemy for centuries, the castle-builders were more concerned about attacks by the Arab warlords to the south than about attacks from the north.

At the beginning of the fifteenth century (at Subphase 6a), the *Eparch* of Nobadia built one such castle-house at Meinarti, on top of the sanded-up remains of the earlier eparchal complex. He was still enough of a professing Christian so that the walls of his new house were adorned with Christian inscriptions, but he made no effort to restore the church, whose paintings had been systematically defaced by the Beni Ikrima during their interval of occupation. Instead, he commissioned the building of a tiny church on the nearby west bank, and it was here that the last Christian parishioners of Meinarti worshipped. Their numbers evidently increased over time, for additional aisles were added to each side of the original church.

Close to the castle-house, the *Eparch* built himself a new audience chamber. The presence of a good many late-period graves shows that there were other fifteenth-century residents at Meinarti beside the *Eparch,* but the community was probably not as large as in any earlier period. The number of residents could not be estimated, since no trace of their houses survived.

The Kingdom of Dotawo disappeared near the end of the fifteenth century, under circumstances that remain unclear. Thereafter, there was no central government in Lower Nubia until the Ottomans took possession over half a century later. Meanwhile, such authority as survived was in the hands of the local castle-dwellers, especially in the *Batn el-Hajjar.*

After the disappearance of the eparchate another family took possession of the Meinarti castle-house (Subphase 6b). They exercised such authority as there was in the immediately surrounding district. Their descendants were still in possession when the Ottomans took control of Lower Nubia in 1558, and they probably stayed on for a generation or two after that. Their circumstances however were very impoverished, for Ottoman tax policy brought economic ruin throughout the region (cf. Burckhardt 1819, 137-8).

It was probably Ottoman tax collectors who demanded that the dwellers in the Meinarti castle-house, and in other castle-houses throughout the region, should open up the secret chambers and storage compartments of their homes, so that no valuables could be concealed. For that purpose new doorways were hacked through the outside walls, giving access to ground-floor rooms that were formerly entered only from above. Ragged holes were also hacked through the vaulted ceilings, into the storage compartments above. These were the last architectural modifications ever made at Meinarti, for around the end of the sixteenth century the last of the inhabitants departed. Residence on the island no longer offered any advantages, either economic, strategic, or protective.

But the ultimate blame for the ruin of Nubia lies not with the Ottomans but with the European maritime powers, who from the fifteenth century onward opened up seaborne trade with the West African coasts. Export of African luxury products – gold, ivory, ebony, dark-skinned slaves, and a variety of other exotica – had always been the economic mainstay not only of the Nilotic civilizations, but of most other African civilizations. For more than two millennia the Nubians had enjoyed a near monopoly on that trade, while the Nile valley offered the only safe passage across the Sahara. The opening of Red Sea trade by the Greeks, and later of trans-Saharan caravan trade by the Arabs, cut into the Nubian monopoly, but the Nile still remained the least hazardous and most dependable route for trade with the north. Once the European powers had established their trading factories on the West African coasts, however, they were able to tap into wholly new resource areas, at a time when the catchment areas of the upper Nile were becoming depleted. Even more importantly, they had a sea-level trade route which bypassed all of the middlemen who for millennia had taken their rake-off from the export trade. The route was not wholly free from sea pirates, but at least it was safe from land pirates.

In the aftermath, Nubia reverted to an economic condition hardly more advanced than that of A-Group times. It was graphically, and movingly, depicted by J. L. Burckhardt at the beginning of the nineteenth century:

> The habitations of the Nubians are built either of mud or of loose stones; those of stone . . . stand generally on the declivity of the hills, and consist of two separate round buildings, one of which is occupied by the males, and the other by the females of the family. The mud dwellings are generally so low, that one can hardly stand upright in them: the roof is covered by Dhourra stalks, which last till they are eaten up by the cattle, when palm leaves are laid across. The utensils of a Nubian's house consist of about half a dozen coarse earthen jars, from one to two feet in diameter and about five feet in height, in which the provisions of the family are kept;[2] a few earthen plates; a handmill;[3] a hatchet; and a few round sticks, over which the loom is laid.
>
> South of Derr, and principally at Sukkot and in Mahass, grown up people go quite naked, with the exception of the sexual parts, which the men conceal in a small sack

(Burckhardt 1819, 140-41)

> Those Nubians who have resided in Egypt, and can speak Arabic, are for the most part good Mussulmen, and repeat their prayers daily: but in general the only prayer known to the others is the exclamation of Allahu Akbar.

(*ibid.*, 148)

No one, contemplating the archaeological finds from Meinarti, can fail to recognize what a catastrophic decline had taken place during the centuries after the site was abandoned. Fortunately it was not the end of the story, for in the twentieth century the Nubians made a major economic and cultural recovery, as they had also done many times in the past.

---

[2] Here Burckhardt is evidently describing the *quseba*.

[3] Presumably the *rahaya*, or quern.

BIBLIOGRAPHY

Adams, W. Y. 1963. *Shonto: a Study of the Role of the Trader in a Modern Navaho Community*. Smithsonian Institution, Bureau of American Ethnology, Bulletin 188. Washington.

Adams, W. Y. 1964. 'Sudan Antiquities Service Excavations in Nubia: Fourth Season, 1962-63', *Kush* 12, 216-50.

Adams, W. Y. 1965. 'Architectural Evolution of the Nubian Church, 500-1400 A.D', *Journal of the American Research Center in Egypt* 4, 87-139.

Adams, W. Y. 1966a. 'Post-Pharaonic Nubia in the Light of Archaeology. III', *Journal of Egyptian Archaeology* 52, 147-62.

Adams, W. Y. 1966b. 'The Vintage of Nubia', *Kush* 14, 262-83.

Adams, W. Y. 1967. 'Continuity and Change in Nubian Cultural History', *Sudan Notes and Records* 48, 1-32.

Adams, W. Y. 1977. *Nubia: Corridor to Africa*. Princeton and London.

Adams, W. Y. 1978. 'On Migration and Diffusion as Rival Paradigms', in Duke *et al.* 1978, 1-5.

Adams, W. Y. 1986. *Ceramic Industries of Medieval Nubia,* (2 vols.) Memoirs of the UNESCO Archaeological Survey of Sudanese Nubia, no. 1. Lexington.

Adams, W. Y. 1987. 'Islamic Archaeology in Nubia: an Introductory Survey', in Hägg 1987, 327-61.

Adams, W. Y. 1994a. 'Castle-Houses of Late Medieval Nubia', *Archéologie du Nil Moyen* 6, 11-46.

Adams, W. Y. 1994b. *Kulubnarti I: the Architectural Remains*. Lexington.

Adams, W. Y. 1996. *Qasr Ibrim: the Late Medieval Period*. Egypt Exploration Society, Excavation Memoir 59. London.

Adams, W. Y. 1998a. *The Philosophical Roots of Anthropology*. Stanford.

Adams, W. Y. 1998b. 'Toward a Comparative Study of Christian Nubian Burial Practice', *Archéologie du Nil Moyen* 8, 13-41.

Adams, W. Y. 1999. 'The Murals of Meinarti', *Nubica et Aethiopica IV/V*, 3-14.

Adams, W. Y. 2000. *Meinarti I*. Sudan Archaeological Research Society, Publication no. 5, London.

Adams, W. Y. 2001. *Meinarti II*. Sudan Archaeological Research Society, Publication no. 6, London.

Adams, W. Y. 2002. *Meinarti III*. Sudan Archaeological Research Society, Publication no. 9, London.

Adams, W. Y. and E. W. Adams 1991. *Archaeological Typology and Practical Reality*. Cambridge.

Adams, W. Y. and N. K. Adams 1998. *Kulubnarti II: the Artifactual Remains*. Sudan Archaeological Research Society Publication no. 2, London.

Adams, W. Y. and H.-Å. Nordström 1963. 'The Archaeological Survey on the West Bank of the Nile: Third Season, 1961-62', *Kush* 11, 10-46.

Adams, W. Y., D. P. Van Gerven and R. S. Levy 1978. 'The Retreat from Migrationism', *Annual Review of Anthropology* 7, 483-532.

Adams, W. Y., N. K. Adams, D. P. Van Gerven and D. L. Greene 1999. *Kulubnarti III: the Cemeteries*. Sudan Archaeological Research Society Publication no. 4, London.

Ammar, H. 1966. *Growing Up in an Egyptian Village*. New York.

Armelagos, G. J. n.d. 'Vital Statistics' MS in the author's possession.

Armelagos, G. J., G. H. Ewing, D. L. Greene, and K. K. Greene 1965. 'Report of the Physical Anthropology Section of the University of Colorado Nubian Expedition', *Kush* 13, 24-27.

Atiya, A. S. (ed.) 1991. *The Coptic Encyclopedia* (8 vols.). New York.

Barns, J. W. B. 1954. 'Christian Monuments from Nubia,' *Kush* 2, 26-32.

Batrawi, A. M. 1935. *Report on the Human Remans*. Cairo.

Bonnet, C. (ed.) 1992. *Études Nubiennes I*. Geneva.

Burckhardt, J. L. 1819. *Travels in Nubia*. London.

Castiglione, L. *et al.* 1975. *Abdallah Nirqi 1964*. Budapest.

Clarke, S. 1912. *Christian Antiquities in the Nile Valley*. Oxford.

Crowfoot, J. W. 1927. 'Five Greek Inscriptions from Nubia', *Journal of Egyptian Archaeology* 13, 226-31.

Denon, V. 1988. *Description de l'Égypte*. 1988 reimpression. Paris.

Dewey, J. R. n.d. *Metric Assessment of Osteoporotic Bone Loss in Meroitic, X-Group, and Christian Archaeological Populations from Sudanese Nubia*. Unpublished M. A. thesis, Department of Anthropology, University of Utah.

Dinkler, E. (ed.) 1970. *Kunst und Geschichte Nubiens in Christlicher Zeit*. Recklinghausen.

Donadoni, S. 1970. 'Les Fouilles à l'Église de Sonqi Tino', in Dinkler 1970, 209-18.

Driskell, B. N., N. K. Adams and P. G. French 1989. 'A Newly Discovered Temple at Qasr Ibrim Preliminary Report', *Archéologie du Nil Moyen* 3, 11-54.

du Bourguet, P. 1991. 'Menas the Miracle Maker, Saint,' in Atiya 1991, vol. 2, 534.

Duke, P. G., J. Ebert, G. Langemann and A. P. Buchner (eds) 1978. *Diffusion and Migration: their Roles in Cultural Development*. Proceesings of the Tenth Annual Chacmool Conference, Calgary, Alberta.

Ehrich, R. W. 1950. 'Some Reflections on Archaeological Interpretation', *American Anthropologist* 52, 468-82.

Elliot Smith, G. and F. W. Jones 1910. *Report on the Human Remains*. The Archaeological Survey of Nubia, Report for 1907-1908, vol. 2. Cairo.

Emery, W. B. 1965. *Egypt in Nubia*. London.

Gardberg, C. J. 1970. *Late Nubian Sites*. Scandinavian Joint Expedition to Sudanese Nubia, vol. 7. Stockholm.

Goodenough, W. 1970. *Description and Comparison in Cultural Anthropology*. Chicago.

Greene, D. L. 1967. *Dentition of Meroitic, X-Group, and Christian Populations from Wadi Halfa, Sudan*. University of Utah Anthropological Papers, 85. Salt Lake City.

Greene, D. L. 1982. 'Discrete Dental Variations and Biological Distances in Nubian Populations', *American Journal of Physical Anthropology* 58, 75-9.

Griffith, F. Ll. 1926. 'Oxford Excavations in Nubia XLIII-XLVIII', *University of Liverpool Annals of Archaeology and Anthropology* 13, 49-93.

Griffith, F. Ll. 1927. 'Oxford Excavations in Nubia XLIX-LV', *University of Liverpool Annals of Archaeology and Anthropology* 14, 57-113.

Griffith, F. Ll. 1928. 'Oxford Excavations in Nubia LVI-LXI', *University of Liverpool Annals of Archaeology and Anthropology* 15, 63-88.

Hägg, T. (ed.) 1987. *Nubian Culture Past and Present*. Kungl. Vitterhets Historie och Antikvitets Akademien, Konferenser 17. Stockholm.

Hasan, Y. F. 1967. *The Arabs and the Sudan*. Edinburgh.

Łajtar, A. 1996. 'Varia Nubica IV: Das älteste nubische Epitaph mit dem Gebet vom sogennanten Typus Euchologion Mega?', *Zeitschrift für Papyrologie und Epigraphik* 113, 101-8.

Łajtar, A. and J. Van der Vliet 1998. 'Rich Ladies of Meinarti and Their Churches', *Journal of Juristic Papyrology* 28, 35-53.

Martens-Czarnecka, M. 1992. 'Late Christian Painting in Nubia', in Bonnet 1992, 307-16.

Martens-Czarnecka, M. 'New Mural Paintings from Old Dongola', *Cahier de Recherches de l'Institut de Papyrologie et d'Égyptologie de Lille* 17/2, 211-25.

Martens-Czarnecka, M. 1998. 'Mural Paintings from Old Dongola', *Gdansk Archaeological Museum African Reports* 1, 95-113.

Michałowski, K. 1961. *Faras, Fouilles Pononaises 1961*. Warsaw.

Michałowski, K. 1970. 'Open Problems in Nubian Art and Culture in the Light of the Discoveries at Faras', in Dinkler 1970, 11-28.

Michałowski, K. and G. Gerster 1967. *Faras, die Kathedrale aus dem Wüstensand*. Zurich and Cologne.

Mileham, G. S. 1910. *Churches in Lower Nubia*. University of Pennsylvania Museum, Eckley B. Coxe Junior Expedition to Nubia, vol. 1. Philadelphia.

Mills, A. J. and H.-Å. Nordström 1966. 'The Archaeological Survey from Gemai to Dal. Preliminary Report for the Season 1964-65', *Kush* 14, 1-15.

Monneret de Villard, U. 1935. *La Nubia Medioevale I-II* (2 vols.). Cairo.

Monneret de Villard, U. 1957. *La Nubia Medioevale III-IV* (2 vols.). Cairo.

Presedo Velo, F. J. 1963. *Antigüedades Cristianas de la Isla de Kasar-Ico*. Comité Español de la UNESCO para Nubia, Memórias de la Misión Arqueológica, 1. Madrid.

Sherif, N. M. 1964. 'The Arabic Inscriptions from Meinarti', *Kush* 12, 249-50.

Shinnie, P. L. and M. Shinnie 1978. *Debeira West*. Warminster.

Steward, J. H. 1942. 'The Direct Historical Approach to Archaeology', *American Antiquity* 7, 337-43.

Taylor, W. W. 1948. *A Study of Archaeology*. American Anthropological Association, Memoir 69. Menasha.

Thompson, L. A. 1969. 'Eastern Africa and the Graeco-Roman World', in Thompson and Ferguson 1969, 26-61.

Thompson, L. A. and J. Ferguson (eds) 1969. *Africa in Classical Antiquity*. Ibadan.

Török, L. 1979. *Economic Offices and Officials in Meroitic Nubia (a Study in Territorial Administration in the Late Meroitic Kingdom)*. Studia Aegyptiaca 5. Budapest.

Török, L. 1988. *Late Antique Nubia*. Antaeus Communicationes ex Instituto Archaeologico Academiae Scientiarum Hungaricae 16/1987. Budapest.

Trigger, B. G. 1967. *The Late Nubian Settlement at Arminna West*. Publications of the Pennsylvania-Yale Expedition to Egypt, 2. Philadelphia.

Van Moorsel, P. J. Jacquet and H. D. Schneider, 1975. *The Central Church of Abdallah Nirqi*. Leiden.

Vantini, G. 1975. *Oriental Sources Concerning Nubia*. Heidelberg and Warsaw.

Vercoutter, J. 1955. 'Kor est-il Iken?', *Kush* 3, 4-19.

Watson, P. J., S. A. LeBlanc and C. R. Redman 1971. *Explanation in Archaeology, an Explicitly Scientific Approach*. New York.

Welsby, D. A. 2002. *The Medieval Kingdoms of Nubia. Pagans, Christians and Muslims along the Middle Nile*. London.

العصر المسيحي الكلاسيكي (الطور ٤)، حوالى ١٠٢٠-١١٧٢م

مع بداية العصر المسيحي الكلاسيكي تمت إعادة بناء قرية مينارتي و كنيستها بالكامل، و من الراجح أن إعادة البناء كانت قد سبقتها فترة إضمحلال قصيرة هجر فيها السكان الموقع. لم يتم استخدام أي من المباني القديمة. و ظلت مينارتي قرية زراعية، كما أن شوارعها ظلت ضيقة و متعرجة، و دورها ملتصقة و لكن ازدادت مساحتها عن سابقتها. و من الجلي أن ذلك العصر كان غنياً من حيث الإنتاج الزراعي، حيث عثر على صوامع الغلال خارج الدور. و باستثناء مبنيين ضخمين، من الراجح أن أحدهم كان مقر إقامة عمد القرية. و استمر الموقع في التوسع و النمو حيث وصل إلى أقصى اتساع له في القرن الثاني عشر. و في بداية القرن الحادي تمت إعادة بناء القرية الكنيسة، و إلى جوارها الجبانة، التي امتدت إلى الشرق و الجنوب من الكنيسة.

و في سنة ١١٧٢ هجر السكان مواقعهم بالجزيرة، تفادياً للغزو المدمر الذي شنته الجيوش المصرية تحت إمرة شمس الدولة، و هو التأريخ الذي سجل لنهاية العصر المسيحي الكلاسيكي.

(الطور ٥)، ١٢٠٠-١٣٦٥م العصر المسيحي المتأخر

دام نزوح السكان عن مينارتي عقب الغزو الذي شنه شمس الدولة ما يقرب من جيل كامل. شهد الموقع بعد ذلك التاريخ حركة نشطة استهدفت إعادة الإعمار، حيث كانت الرمال قد غطت الدور القديمة. و تغيرت الخارطة القديمة للمساكن و أضيف إليها السقوف المقببة، و الجدران السميكة. و بينما احتل ذلك النوع من الدور القسم الشمالي من القرية، عثر على مبنى مكون ٩٠ حجرة أقيمت حول حجرة مركزية على جدرانها لوحات رديئة الصنع. تم ملاط الحجرات الأخرى بالجص الوردي اللون. و من الراجح أن المجمع كان مقراً مؤقتاً لرئيس أساقفة نوباطيا. في أواخر القرن الرابع عشر جاءت نهاية العصر المسيحي على يد قبائل بني عكرمة العربية البدوية حيث فرضت سيطرتها على مينارتي و أخرجوا أهلها منها.

العصر المسيحي الأخير و ما بعده (الطور ٦)، حوالى ١٤٠٠-١٦٠٠م

أرخ العام ١٤٠٠م إلى بداية العصر الأخير الذي شهده الموقع الأثري بمينارتي، حيث تم إعماره من جديد على أيدي المماليك الذين بسطوا سلطانهم و أخرجوا قبائل بني عكرمة منه. و ظلت الجزيرة مقراً مؤقتاً لرئيس أساقفة نوباطيا، و لكن تم استبدال المجمع القديم بمسكن حصين من طابقين، شاع طرازه بعد ذلك فعم كل منطقة النوبة. و على مقربة منه عثر على قاعة للمداولات. و باستثناء ذلك لم يعثر إلا على مخلفات القليل من مباني ذلك العصر. و من الراجح أن السبب في ذلك يعود إلى النشاط التخريبي و النهب الذي تعرض له الموقع خلال القرون التي عقبت نزوح الأهالى عنه. جاءت نهاية المملكة المسيحية النوبية المستقلة قبيل العام ١٥٠٠، كما تبع ذلك نهاية أبرشية نوباطيا. و ظل المنزل الحصين بمينارتي مستخدماً، ربما بطريقة عشوائية، لمدة قرن آخر. و من الراجح أن الهجرة الأخيرة عن جزيرة مينارتى في حوالى سنة ١٦٠٠م، تمت بأمر السلطان العثماني الذي كان قد بسط سيطرته على صعيد مصر.

موضعين كان بهما شاهدي قبر. أيضاً عثر على شاهد قبر كامل و خمسة أخرى مفتتة بردیم الموقع. استخدم النص القبطي بثلاثة من شواهد القبور و الإغريقي بأربعة أخرى. حملت شواهد القبور الآمارات العامة المتعارف عليها، و باستثناء شاهدين لإمرأتين عرفتا بمالكة الكنيسة.

عثر على أربعة شواهد قبور إسلامية مفتتة، و اثنان مكتملان لأختين هما، فاطمة المتوفية في سنة ٤٥٣ هـ، و رحيمة المتوفية في ٤٥٥ هـ.

مينارتي

المجلد الخامس

تاريخ مينارتي: دراسة تفسيرية

في هذا القسم سأقوم بتقديم ملخص عن تاريخ المجموعة السكانية لمينارتي، و ذلك من خلال الرؤية التي تكونت لدي بوصفي خبيراً بالعلوم الإنسانية. يشتمل الملخص على الكثير من وجهات النظر الخاصة بالمؤلف، و التي ربما لا يتفق البعض حول تأويلها.

الموقع السكني لعصر مروي (الطور ١) حوالى سنة ٢٠٠-٤٢٥ م

تم إنشاء الموقع السكني المروي بمينارتي ضمن مشروع لإعادة بسط سيطرة الإدارة الكوشية على صعيد مصر في أواخر العصر المروي. وقع الإختيار على جزيرة مينارتي نسبة لموقعها الإستراتيجي أسفل الشلال الثاني لتكون مركزاً إدارياً و تجارياً. من الأبنية التي ما زالت بالموقع مبنى ضخم ربما كان مركزاً إدارياً، و سوق و مخازن و و عصارة نبيذ. و لم يعثر على مساكن العامة باستثناء بعض الإشارات التي تدل على آثارهم. و في اثناء الوجود المروي بمينارتي غمرت الفيضانات الموقع مما أحدث ضرراً كبيراً، و لم يمكث المرويون بالموقع بعد سنة ٤٢٥ م.

عصر بلانة (الطور ٢)، حوالى سنة ٤٢٥-٦٥٠ م

في أواخر القرن الخامس الميلادي فرضت ثقافة بلانة سيطرتها على مينارتي. و على الرغم من بعض المباني المروية أعيد استخدامها، إلا أن التركيبة السكانية اختلفت عن سابقتها المروية. فصارت مينارتي قرية نوبية نموذجية تعمل بالزراعة، و كانت القرية مكتظة بالسكان و كانت الدور فقيرة و ملتصقة تفصل بينها شوارع ضيقة و ملتوية. و باستثناء مبنيين ضخمين، من الراجح أنهما كانا لمسؤولين في الإدارة أو أحد الأعيان.

العصر المسيحي القديم (الطور ٣)، حوالى ٦٦٠-١٠٠٠م

كان اعتناق الثقافة النوبية للديانة المسيحية في النصف الثاني من القرن السادس، ولكن لم تشهد مينارتي قيام كنيسة بها إلا بعد مضي قرن كامل من الزمان. و خلال تلك الفترة لم يحدث الكثير من التحول، إذ ظلت مينارتي على حالها قرية زراعية بسيطة. و شهدت القرون التي أعقبت ذلك العديد من الفيضانات، و كانت صيانة الدور بعد كل فيضان تتم بصورة عشوائية و أكثر سوءاً من سابقتها. و بحلول القرن العشوائية، و يستثنى من العاشر تهدمت المساكن وصارت مينارتي أكثر شبهاً بالقرى ذلك الكنيسة التي كانت صيانتها تتم بانتظام، و قد أعيد بناؤها بالكامل عقب أحد تلك الفيضانات.

البناء الفوقي

أبرزت المدافن بمينارتي ما يقرب من دزينتين من الطرز المختلفة، و لم يعثر على أي من الجبانات النوبية الأخرى و هي تذخر بمثل هذا التنوع و الاختلاف. و باستثناء أحد تلك المدافن فإن البقية لها بناء فوقي إما من الآجر أو الطوب اللبن. و قد عثر على البناء الفوقي لتلك المدافن محفوظاً حتى منتصفه بصورة جيدة. و كانت أغلب المدافن من طراز المسطبة المتعامد أعلاها و التي امتاز بها على الأقل ٧ طرز مختلفة. و كان البناء عبارة عن مستطيل مصمت يبلغ طوله مترين و عرضه متر واحد، و بلغ ارتفاعه ٧٠ سم، تمت زخرفة أعلى البناء بنحت بارز لصليب. اشتملت أغلب المدافن على صندوق بارز لوضع المصباح على الجانب الغربي لها.

من مجموع المدافن التي تم تصنيفها يأتي في المرتبة الثانية المدافن المربعة الشكل ذات البناء المقبب، و عددها ١٢ قبراً هذا بالإضافة إلى ثلاثة أنواع أخرى، استخدم ملاط الجص الملون، كالألوان الوردية و الوردية الذهبية و الرمادية في كل واحد منها. و من الطرز الأخرى غير الشائعة المساطب المدرجة و التي بني على أعلاها ضلع طولى أيضاً المساطب التي اتخذت شكل الصليب، و المساطب بدرجتين على كل جانب، و المستطيلة البناء، و كذلك الأكوام الطينية العادية ذات الحواف المبنية من الطوب، و بناء مستطيل من الطوب. و الطرز الأخيرة من أكثرها شيوعاً في مدافن العصر المسيحي الكلاسيكي، و لم يعثر إلا على ٦ مدافن فقط بمينارتي.

المدافن

بلغ عدد الهياكل العظمية ٣٥١، و هو أقل من عدد المدافن، و ذلك نسبة للعثور على بعض المدافن خالية. وضعت الأجداث في وضع ممدد، ووضع الرأس على الطرف الغربي للمدفن، و عثر على أمثلة قليلة كانت الركبتان فيها محنيتان. كانت معظم الهياكل العظمية مسجاة على ظهورها، و كان من بينها ٣٢ هيكلاً ترقد على جانبها الأيمن، و عدد ١١ على الجانب الأيسر. و كان الرأس محمياً ببناء من ثلاث قطع من الآجر في أغلب الأحيان.

عثر على العظام في حالة رديئة من الحفظ، تسبب في ذلك وقوع الجبانة على أرض منخفضة يغمرها الفيضان. عثر على عدد قليل من مدافن العصور الأخيرة، و التي كانت تقع على أرض مرتفعة. و باستثناء ٦ من المدافن، عثر على البقية في وضعها الأصلي، تركت العظام في مكانها الأصلي. قام بدراسة العظام انثروبولوجيين من جامعة كلورادو، و من نتائج البحث الذي قاموا به أن الجبانة بمينارتي احتوت على نفس المجموعة السكانية التي تنتمي إلى الأصل النوبي و التي عثر عليها بمدافن عصور مروي، و مروي، و العصر المسيحي. و كما جرت العادة بمدافن العصر المسيحي، إذ عثر على أغلبها خالية إلا من الهياكل العظمية، و ذلك باستثناء بعض المتعلقات الشخصية و الحلي التي عثر عليها على أجداث الراشدين و الأحداث على حد سواء. و في خارج المدافن و في أبنية صندوقية الشكل عثر على عدد ٢٩ مصباحاً، كما عثر على أحد المصابيح داخل قبو المدفن.

عثر على شاهد قبر، في و ضعه الأصلي، بالبناء الفوقي لأحد المدافن، كما عثر على

سنة ١٢٠٠م تم إجراء نهائي و كبير، تسبب فيه تراكم الرمال على الجدران الخارجية للكنيسة. و كانت الرمال قد تراكمت حتى سدت النوافذ بالجدارين الشمالي و الغربي، أيضاً تم بناء جدار عرضي بين الجدار الشمالي و أحد أعمدة قاعة المصلين ليكون دعامة للجدار الخارجي حتى لا يميل إلى الداخل. و في نفس الاثناء تمت تقوية و زيادة حجم الأعمدة المركزية الأربعة بالقاعة الرئيسية. تم عمل ملاط من الجص للكنيسة، و لوحات جداريةجديدة، و في خلال القرن الرابع عشر تم تكرار نفس العمل و لكن للمرة الأخيرة.

أصابت الأجزاء العليا للكنيسة عوامل التعرية و التآكل. و من الراجح و لكن من غير المؤكد أن البناء نصف الدائري البارز كان قد ردمه، ليشكل جداراً شرقياً مستقيماً يتصل مباشرة مع المذبح. و الحال كذلك، فإن المبنى كان في الأصل مقاماً على شكل الطراز رقم ٤ من الكنائس النوبية.

و في اثناء البناء الأول للكنيسة ٦، دعت الحاجة إلى بناء مزالق خارج المداخل، و ذلك لحمايتها من الرمال الزاحفة. و في كل مرة تم فيها إجراء تعديلات على بناء الكنيسة تم عمل التحوطات اللازمة لدرء خطر الرمال الزاحفة. في البدء تم بناء جدران حاجزة حول المزالق المرتفعة أمام المداخل. و في وقت لاحق أضيف الدرج الذي يهبط حتى يتصل بالعتب، أيضاً تمت إضافة درجات صاعدة عدة مرات. في الطور الأخير من مراحل البناء تم إغلاق البوابة الشمالية، و تم بناء درج للوصول للبوابة الجنوبية بلغ عمقه ثلاثة امتار من سطح الأرض.

شهد أواخر القرن الرابع عشر الانهيار التام للكنيسة، كما فرضت القبائل البدوية سيطرتها على الموقع، فأهملت الكنيسة، و انتقل الناس لممارسة شعائرهم الدينية إلى كنيسة أصغر حجماً في قرية عبد القادر، بالضفة الغربية لنهر النيل.

الجبانة

لم يعثر على أي من المدافن التي يرجع تأريخها إلى عصر مروي، بلانة أو العصر المسيحي القديم بالموقع الأثري بمينارتي. و ربما كانت مدافن تلك العصور قد تمت مواراتها في مكان آخر بالجزيرة أو بالشاطئ الغربي، حيث تم التأريخ للمدافن التى عثر عليها في بداية المشروع إلى أوائل القرن الحادي عشر، و هو ذات التأريخ الذي أقيمت فيه الكنيسة ٦. كان موقع المدافن القديمة على مقربة من الجدار الشرقي للكنيسة، اتسعت مساحة الجبانة في اتجاه الشرق و الجنوب، و بحلول القرن الثالث عشر بلغ امتدادها ٣٠ متراً إلى ناحية الجنوب و ١٢ متراً إلى جهة الشرق. إلى الشمال أيضاً تم العثور على عدد قليل من المدافن، و منذ ذلك الزمن صار اتساع المقبرة رأسياً، بدلاً عن أفقياً، و تم حفر المدافن الجديدة على قمة المدافن القديمة التي كانت قد غطتها الرمال.

بلغ عدد المدافن التي تم التنقيب فيها بمينارتي عدد ٣٦٥ مدفناً، منها ١١٩ قبراً ذات بناء فوقي من الآجر، و كذلك الحال في معظم المدافن القديمة، و ساعدت الرمال في أن تحتفظ بعض هذه المدافن ببنائها الأصلى. و بالإضافة إلى ذلك الطراز من المدافن عثر على مدافن لأجنة موضوعة في آنية من الفخار.

عثر بها على المخلفات التي يرجع تأريخها إلى العصر المسيحي الأخير ١١٧٢–١٦٠٠ م. امتازت هذه الحقبة باشتمالها على الطورين ٥ و ٦، و التي كانت تفصل بينهما فترة زمنية قصيرة حيث سيطرت على الموقع مجموعات من البدو. شهد الموقع أيضاً فترة إنتقالية أخرى بعد نهاية العصر المسيحي، ربما استمرت حتى عام ١٦٠٠ م.

ينقسم المجلد الحالي إلى جزئين، يعالج الأول، و هو الرابع في سلسلة مينارتي مظاهر محددة للموقع كانت المجلدات السابقة قد تعرضت لها بإيجاز و هي الكنائس و الجبانة. و أما الجزء الثاني، مينارتي ٥، فهو يتعرض للسرد التاريخي للموقع، و ذلك بالاستفادة من المادة الأثرية و التاريخية في إعادة بناء الحوادث التاريخية.

مينارتي ٤: الكنيسة و الجبانة

الكنيسة

عثر بالموقع الأثري بمينارتي على ثلاث كنائس متعاقبة، و هي تقع على الجانب الشرقي للقرية. و تم بناء الكنيستين الأخيرتين على أساس الكنائس القديمة التي سبقتهما و التي تم هدمها. شكلت مادة الآجر بناء الكنائس الثلاث.

الكنيسة ٣٨، و هي أقدم الكنائس، و من الراجح أن بناءها كان في منتصف القرن السابع الميلادي، الأمر الذي لم يكن التحقق منه ممكناً. عثر على أساس الكنيسة، و الذي أبرز جانبه الشرقي ذات الملامح التي تمتاز بها الكنيسة النوبية طراز ٢أ، لم يعثر بالجانب الغربي على مخلفات جديرة بالذكر. تمتاز الكنيسة

الكنيسة ٣٦، الكنيسة الثانية، تأخر بناؤها بحوالى قرن عن سابقتها. تمتاز الكنيسة ٣٦، بأنها الكنيسة الثانية، و كان بناؤها قد تأخر بحوالى قرن عن سابقتها. و تم بناؤها على أساس الكنيسة ٣٨ مباشرة. أقيمت الجدران الجانبية للكنيسة على جدران الكنيسة القديمة مباشرة، كما أقيمت جدران جديدة لتعديل خارطة الكنيسة القديمة تمت تغطية الأرضية القديمة بملاط من الطين.

و عليه فإن الكنيسة ٣٦ تنتمي إلى طراز الكنيسة النوبية ٢أ. و هي تشتمل عل بناء نصف دائري صغير في طرفها الشرقي على جانبيه حجرتان، و على الركنين الغربين عثر على حجرتين يوازي موقعهما الوضع السابق. و في الأصل لم تكن هنالك المساطب المدرجة أو المنبر، و لكن تمت إضافتهما لاحقاً. و على غير ما جرت عليه العادة في معظم الكنائس النوبية، لم يعثر على أثر للدرج بحجرات الركن الغربي. أحيط بناء الكنيسة الخارجي بمساطب مرتفعة، لم يعرف الغرض منها على وجه التحديد.

الكنيسة ٦، تم بناؤها على ركام و مخلفات الكنيسة ٣٦، بعد أن دمرها الفيضان. و يؤرخ لهذا الحادث بأوائل القرن الحادي عشر. تبنت الكنيسة الجديدة الخارطة القديمة للكنيسة ٣٦، وذلك باستثناء الحجرات بالركن الغربي. تم تغيير مواضع الأبواب بالحجرتين، كما أقيم الدرج بحجرة الركن الشمالي الغربي. عثر على بقايا اللوحات الجدارية التي تخلفت من إعادة البناء الأولى للكنيسة.و كان معظمها قد تمت تغطيه بالدهان أو التعديلات المعمارية التي أجريت على البناء. و في الأصل كانت الجدران الشمالية و الغربية متصلة بمساطب مرتفعة.

و في خلال القرنين اللذين تليا بناء الكنيسة جرت تعديلات طفيفة بداخلها. في حوالي

مينارتي ٤-٥

موجز باللغة العربية

كانت مينارتي عبارة عن جزيرة صغيرة غمرتها مياه بحيرة النوبة و هي تقع إلي الشمال من الشلال الثاني لنهر بالقرب من وادي حلفا. و على الجزء الجنوبي من الجزيرة شغل الموقع الأثري و هو عبارة عن ربوة (كوم) ذات طبقات أثرية يزيد ارتفاعها عن اثني عشر متراً ضمت بين طبقاتها سلسلة من المخلفات الأثرية و التي يؤرخ لها بالفترات المروية و بلانه (العصر المروي المتأخر) و مخلفات العصر المسيحي، ما بين سنة ٢٠٠ و ١٦٠٠ للميلاد.

و في عامي ١٩٦٣ و ١٩٦٤ قامت مصلحة الآثار السودانية بإرسال فريق من خبراء الآثار تحت ادارة وليام ي. أدمز للتنقيب بالموقع الأثري بجزيرة مينارتي و ذلك نسبة إلى أن الموقع صار مهدداً بالغرق الوشيك، و قد شهدت أعمال التنقيب الأثري بالموقع عدداً ضخماً من الخبراء و عمال الحفريات المدربين إذ بلغ العدد الكلي ٢٥٠ في أغلب الأوقات. و قد بدأ العمل بالتنقيب في أحد نصفي الموقع و الذي شغل مساحة تقدر بحوالى الثمانين متراً مربعاً، و تم الكشف عن طبقاته الأثرية الواحدة تلو الأخرى من أعلى قمته إلى القاعدة. و قد نتج عن ذلك الكشف عدد ١٨ طبقة احتوى عليها الموقع، و كانت كل طبقة قد تكونت في مدى زمني تراوح بين ٥٠ إلى ٢٠٠ عام. و في غضون تلك الفترة التي شهدتها أعمال التنقيب تم الكشف عن عدد ٦٠ من المباني على اختلاف اشكالها، كما تم التوثيق لأكثر من ١٥٠٠ من المخلفات و اللقى الأثرية. و بالإضافة إلى ذلك تم التنقيب بالجبانة الأثرية و التي احتوت على ما يقرب من عدد ٤٠٠ قبراً.

و هذا المجلد و هو الأخير في سلسلة من أربعة مجلدات احتوت على تقارير اللقى الأثرية بمينارتي. و كان المجلد الأول قد استهل بوصف تفصيلي لمناهج البحث و التنقيب الأثري التي تم اتباعها. كما قدم الفصلان اللذان تليا الفصل الأول من المجلد وصفاً تفصيلياً للقى و المباني الأثرية التي عثر عليها بالطورين الأكثر قدماً (و هي الطبقات الأثرية الموجودة بالمستويات الدنيا للموقع (الكوم)، و يؤرخ لهما على التوالى بعصري مروي و بلانه. و قد امتدت الفترة التي شملها البحث من سنة ٢٠٠ إلى ٦٥٠ ميلادية.

أما المجلد الثاني فقد قام بنقل الرواية التاريخية لجزيرة مينارتي عبر العصر المسيحي القديم لبلاد النوبة، من حوالى سنة ٦٥٠ إلى ١١٧٢ للميلاد. في هذا المجلد تم عرض المخلفات الأثرية التي عثر عليها بثمانية مستويات للطبقات الأثرية المتراصفة (مستويات ١٣ إلى ٧). و على الرغم من أن مينارتي ظلت قرية زراعية بسيطة توارثتها الأجيال المتعاقبة و التي انتمت إلى سلف واحد، فإن المخلفات الأثرية التي عثر عليها بالموقع قدمت الدليل على وجود طورين امتاز كل واحد منهما بأعمال البناء. و الطور الأول، و المعروف بالطور رقم ٣، و الذي يوافق العصر المسيحي القديم، و أما الثاني، الطور رقم ٤، فهو يوافق العصر المسيحي الكلاسيكي.

و يقوم المجلد الثالث بتغطية الحقبة التي اشتملت على الطبقات الأثرية ٦-١، و التي

a. The church interior from the west end.

b. The eastern end of the church. Impressions in the floor pavement show where dismantled piers once stood. The cross-wall separating eastern and western portions is in the foreground.

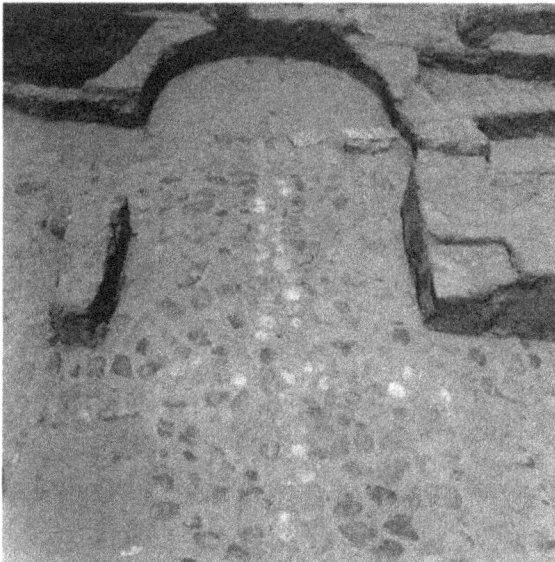

c. The "mosaic" cross design in the floor.

d. Close-up of the "mosaic" cross design in the floor.

e. The amphora cache outside the west wall.

Plate 1. Views of Church XXXVIII.

f. Amphorae from the amphora cache.

a. The church remains from the north. The built-up platform adjoining the north wall can be seen in the middle of the photo.

b. Interior of the church, looking east.

c. The eastern end of the church, looking east. The remnant of higab wall can be seen in the middle distance.

d. Dromos *entryway to the crypt adjoining the south wall. The amphora was actually found within the crypt, not where shown.*

e. The superstructure of the crypt, forming a kind of mastaba adjoining the south church wall.

f. Part of the "border ridge" paralleling the north church wall. Photo shows the eastern portion, formed of upright stones.

Plate 2. Views of Church XXXVI.

a. The western wall. The upper portions lack plaster as a result of weathering in the church's late years. The lower walls were buried under drifted sand, preserving the plaster. Note mastaba adjoining the base of the wall.

b. The church from the southwest. Note slot window in the wall near southwest corner. The structures in the foreground are tomb superstructures.

c. The church from the north. Note slot window in the wall above the door, and larger window to the east of it. The structure in the foreground is the northern church platform from Phase 3, which had actually been buried by the time of Phase 4.

d. The church from the east. The structure in the foreground is the eastern church platform from Phase 3, which had actually been buried by the time of Phase 4.

Plate 3. Exterior views of Church VI at Phase 4.

a. Interior of the church, looking east through the nave. The pulpit is at the left.

b. Interior of the church, looking west through the nave.

c. Remains of the tribune in the apse.

d. The pulpit. The upper portion was probably a later addition.

e. Worn-down remnants of the stairway in the northwest corner room, seen through the doorway.

Plate 4. Interior views of Church VI at Phase 4.

a. Steps descending to the south doorway, after final modification at Subphase 5c.

b. The southern door jambs, showing votive grooves.

c. Interior doorway between the northwest and southwest nave piers.

d. Arched doorway through the reinforcing wall built across the north aisle.

e. The pulpit.

Plate 5. Views of Church VI at Phase 5.

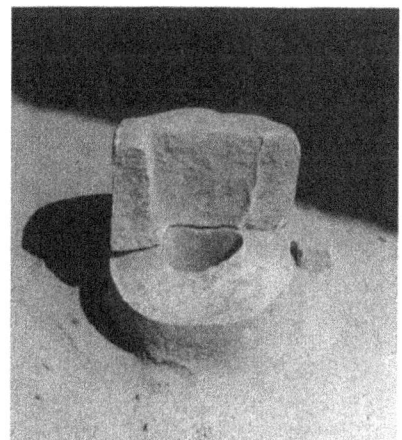

f. Hollowed sandstone column set into the western nave floor.

a. Top portion of ceramic incense stand (854), found in the fill of Church XXXVIII. Scale increments are 5cm.

b. Sections of heavy iron rod (798), one with a small bronze cup attached, found on the floor of Church XXXVI, at Subphase 3d. Scale increments are 5cm.

c. Metal objects. 1, iron key (737), found on the floor of Church VI, at Subphase 4b. 2, bronze kohl stick (679), found on the floor of Church VI, at Subphase 5a. 3, bronze pectoral cross, found in the apse fill of Church VI, at Subphase 5a. 4, bronze spoon (805), found on the apse floor in Church XXXVI, at Subphase 3d. Scale increments are 5cm.

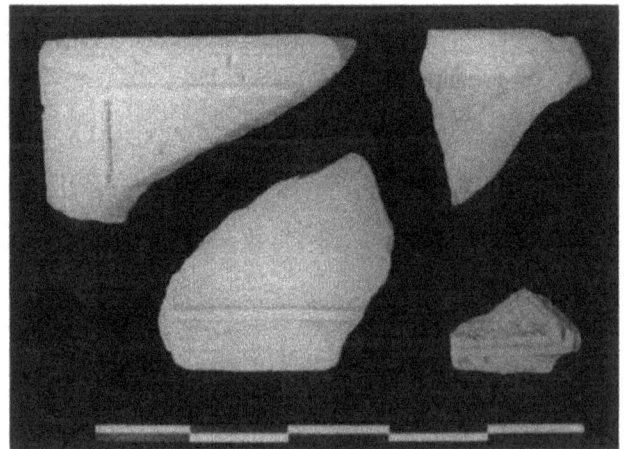

d. Fragments of sculptured sandstone slab (809), which may be an altar top. Found in the fill of Church VI, overlying the Subphase 4b floor. Scale increments are 10cm.

e. Sculptured sandstone tablet (344) originally set above an interior doorway in Church VI, at Phase 5. Scale increments are 10cm.

f. Islamic tombstone (625), which was found face-down, set into a Subphase 5a room floor. The height is 47cm.

Plate 6. Registered finds from the churches.

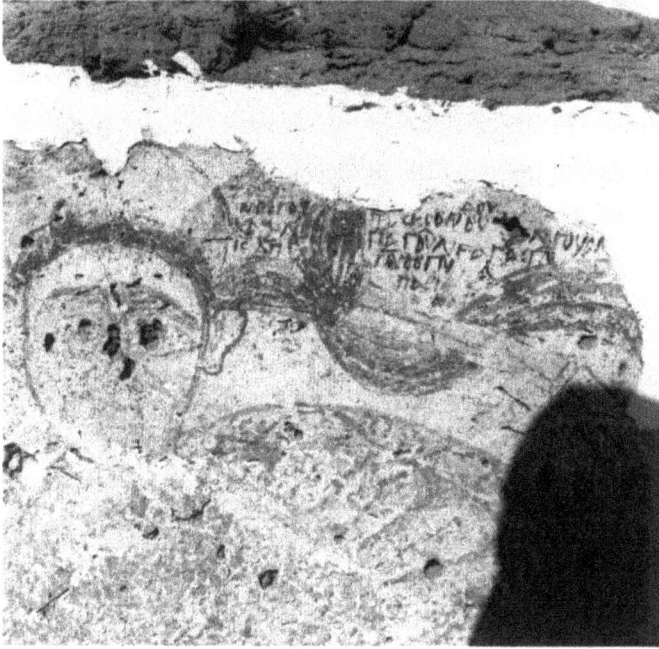

a. Inscription accompanying mural painting No. 64.

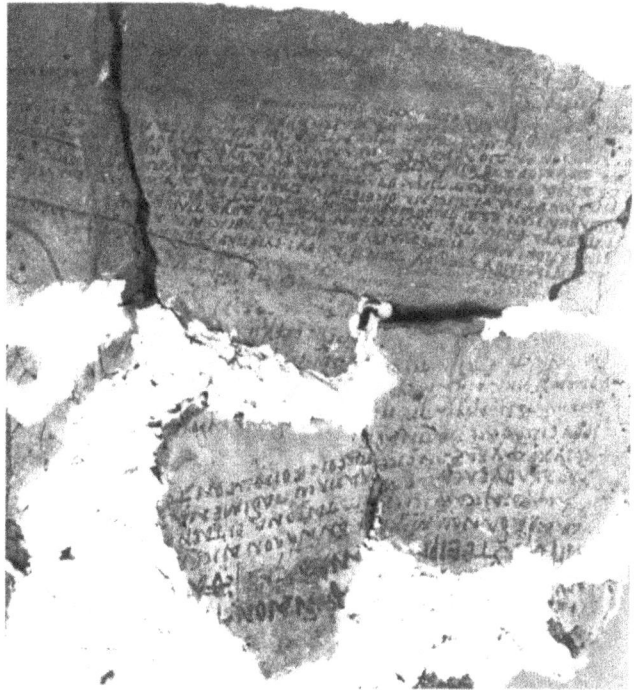

b. Inscriptions accompanying mural painting no. 72.

Plate 7. Mural inscriptions in Church VI.

a. View looking southwestward. The large building in the background is a portion of the wall of House III.

b. The northeastern tombs. Qubba tomb T87 is just visible at the far left.

c. Tombs east of the church, looking northwestward. Note the denuded tops of most of these tombs.

d. Tombs directly east of the church, looking eastward. The denuded condition of the more easterly tombs can be clearly seen.

e. The most southerly, and best preserved, tombs.

Plate 8. General views over the cemetery, at Phase 4.

f. The most southerly tombs, looking eastward. Lamp boxes are most clearly seen in this photo.

a. This photo shows how the superstructure of T16, of Subphase 4c, partly overlaps the earlier superstructure of T14, of Subphase 4ab. Note how part of the top of T16 was itself later cut away when a late burial was intruded.

b. Burial B4, cut into the top of Tomb T23 superstructure.

c. Burial B49, whose head is cut through the superstructure of Tomb T27.

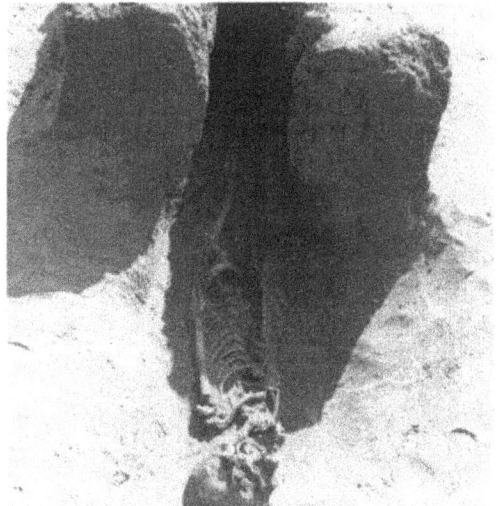

d. Burial B6, whose feet are cut through the superstructure of Tomb T39.

e. Burial B53, whose feet are cut through the superstructure of Tomb T45.

f. Phase 4 superstructures to the north of the church. At the lower right, note the slot grave of Burial T2, cut into the top of cruciform superstructure T120.

Plate 9. Examples of burial intrusions.

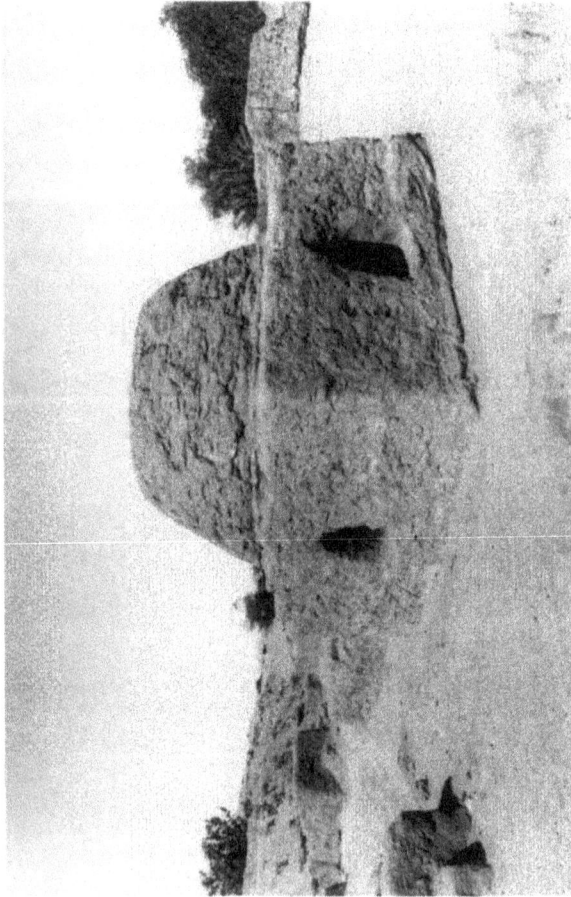

a. Subtype 1A.
Tomb T87.

b. Subtype 1B, Tomb T18, seen from the east.

c. Subtype 1B, Tomb T18, seen from the southeast,

d. The vaulted chamber of Tomb T8, Subtype 1C.

Plate 10. *Qubba* superstructures, Type 1.

a. Subtype 2A, Tomb T76 in the foreground.

b. Subtype 2C, Tomb T89 in the foreground.

*c. Subtype 2A, Tomb T104 in the foreground; Subtype 2D,
Tomb T105 behind it.*

*d. Subtype 2D, Tomb T105 in the foreground,
Subtype 2X, Tomb T106 behind it.*

e. Subtype 2F, Tomb T78 in the foreground.

Plate 11. Cross-topped mastabas, Type 2.

f. Subtype 2G, Tomb T31.

a. Stepped mastabas of Type 3. Tomb T14 at left center, with Tomb T15 at far left.

b. "Pillow" mastaba of Type 5, Tomb T83.

c. Ovoid pavement of Type 6, Tomb T108.

d. Brick pavement of Type 7C, Tomb T100.

e. Cruciform superstructures. Tomb T120, of Type 8A, in the foreground, with Tomb T119, of Type 8b, behind it.

Plate 12. Superstructure Types 3-8.

f. Cruciform superstructure of Type 8A, Tomb T120.

a. West end of Tomb T12, showing tombstone (832) in situ. Tomb T11 is in the right foreground.

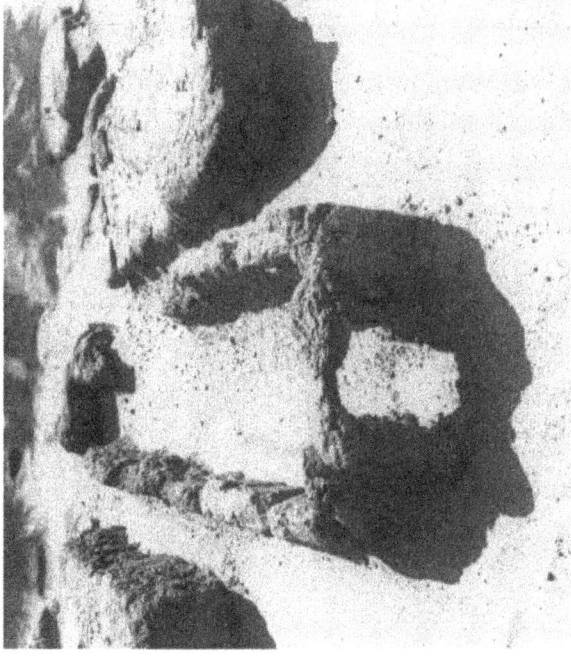

b. Unique superstructure of Tomb T68. The sides were formed of mud brick, while the interior was filled with sand. The top was missing.

c. Very wide super-structure of Tomb T9, which was probably a qubba of Type 1A.

d. Burials B146 (left) and B147, encased within the mud of Tomb T25 super-structure.

Plate 13. Miscellaneous superstructures.

a. Burial T9, showing brick cover over face. Note that this very late burial is at the same level as the Subphase 4c ground surface, on which the qubba *tomb T87 was built.*

b. The upper burial, T8:1, in the chamber of Tomb T8. Note bowl at the right side of head, used as votive lamp.

c. The lower burials, T8:2 (left) and T8:3, in the chamber of Tomb T8.

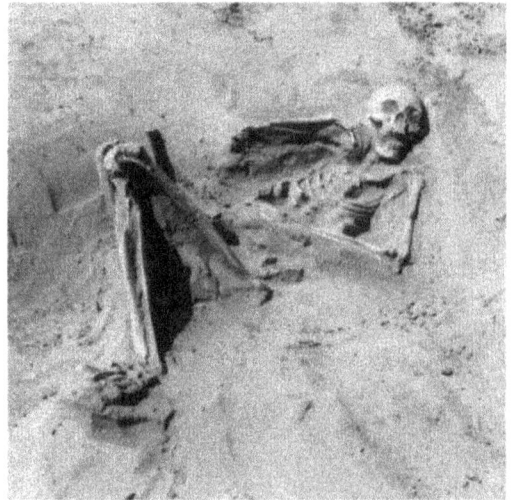

d. The "happy camper," Burial B105.

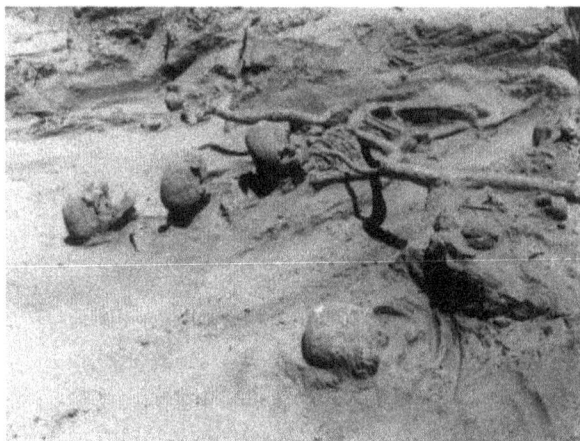

e. Stacked burials, B219-B229, at the eastern edge of the cemetery. The burials were partly disturbed by the growth of dom palm roots.

Plate 14. Burials.

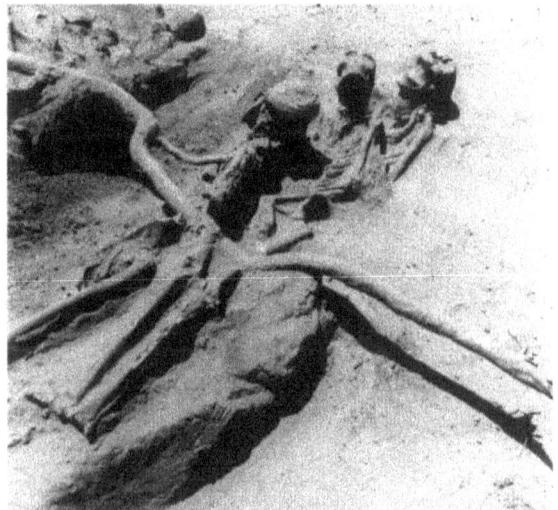

f. Stacked burials, B219-B229, at the eastern edge of the cemetery. The burials were partly disturbed by the growth of dom palm roots.

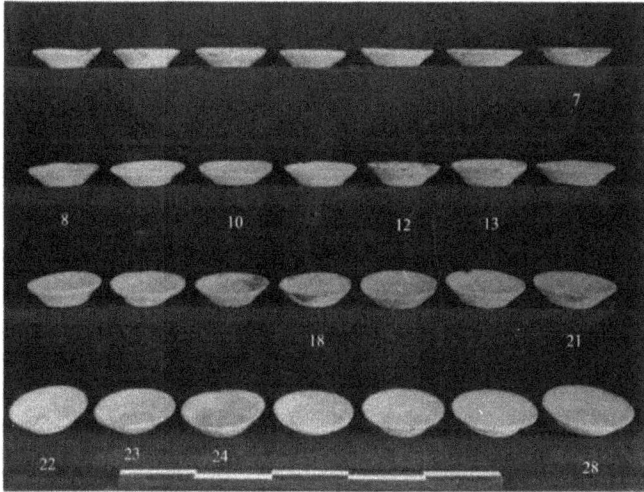

a. "Saucer lamps" of Aswan Ware W12, Form P28. **7**, (355); **8**, (354); **10**, (356); **12**, (713); **13**, (564); **18**, (549); **21**, (565); **22**, (548); **23**, (714); **24**, (585); **28**, (536). Other items are not from the cemetery. Scale increments are 10cm.

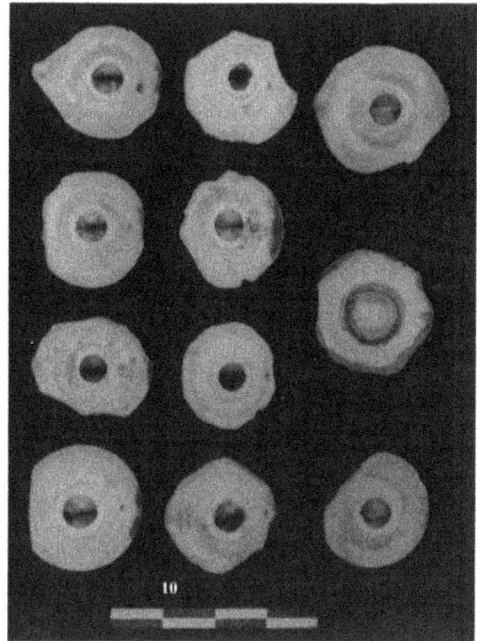

b. "Candle-holder" lamps of Classic Christian wares. **10**, lamp of Ware W6, Form P20 (555). Other items are not from the cemetery. Scale increments are 5cm.

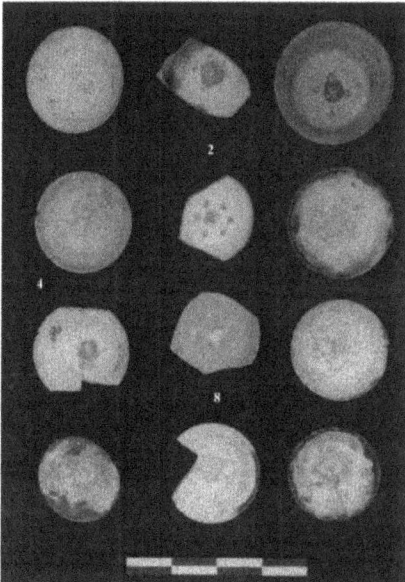

c. Small Classic Christian bowls used as lamps. **2**, Ware W10, Form C23 (335); **4**, Ware W6, Form C22 (334); **8**, Ware W5, Form C22 (557). Other items are not from the cemetery. Scale increments are 5cm.

d. Small Late Christian bowls used as lamps. **1**, Ware R11, Form C23 (365); **5**, Ware R17, Form C23 (364). Other items are not from the cemetery. Scale increments are 10cm.

e. Late Christian vases found in the cemetery fill. **1**, Ware W23, Form F20 (348); **4**, Ware W15(?), Form F23 (349). Other items are not from the cemetery. Scale increments are 10cm.

f. Naphtha grenades, used as lamps. **3**, Form P36, of an unknown stoneware (342). Other items are not from the cemetery. Scale increments are 5cm.

Plate 15. Votive lamps from the cemetery.

a. Basin of Ware U10, Form T5 (359). It had been broken and drilled
for mending in antiquity. Scale increments are 10cm.

b. Pendant bead of carnelian,
with bronze suspension loop
(576). It was found at the neck
of Burial B36. The total length,
including the suspension loop,
is 18mm.

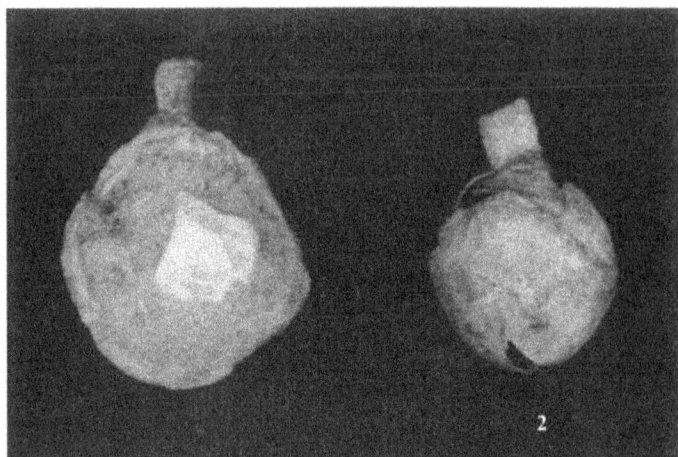

c. Bronze tinkler
bells. 2, found in the
Subphase 4c fill
(678). The diameter
is 13mm.

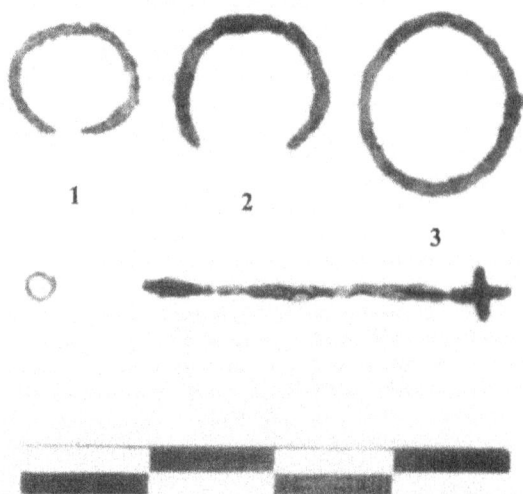

d. Small iron objects. 1, anklet found on Burial B37 (574);
2, anklet found on Burial B41 (575); 3, bracelet found on
Burial T10 (824). Other items are not from the cemetery.
Scale increments are 5cm.

e. Gold and silver reliquary medallion (709), found
in the fill of Grave T6. Photo shows the gold side.
The diameter is 36mm.

Plate 16. Miscellaneous finds from the cemetery.

a. Complete tombstone (832), Coptic epitaph of Iesousyko, found on Tomb T12. The full height is 49cm.

b. Tombstone fragments. 1, in unidentified language (423); 2, in unidentified language (261); 3, Coptic epitaph of Petronia (527); 4, in unidentified language (138); 5, in Arabic? (27); 6, Greek epitaph of Sourea (350). Scale increments are 10cm.

c. Complete tombstone (147), Arabic epitaph of Fattimah. The height of the piece is 52cm.

d. Complete tombstone (625), Arabic epitaph of Rahimah. The height of the piece is 47cm.

e. Top half of tombstone (486), Arabic epitaph of Fatima. The width of the piece is 34cm.

Plate 17. Tombstones.

f. Islamic tombstone fragments. 1, half of tombstone of Fatima (486), shown in Plate 16e; 2, fragment with very defaced Arabic text (146); 3, fragment with well drawn text (302), reused as a door pivot stone. The width of no. 1 is 34cm.